The State of the
African American Male

COURAGEOUS CONVERSATIONS SERIES

The State of the African American Male

Edited by
EBONI M. ZAMANI-GALLAHER
and VERNON C. POLITE

MICHIGAN STATE UNIVERSITY PRESS • EAST LANSING

Michigan State University Press
East Lansing, Michigan 48823-5245

Printed and bound in the United States of America.

16 15 14 13 12 11 10   1 2 3 4 5 6 7 8 9 10

LIBRARY OF CONGRESS CATALOGING-IN-PUBLICATION DATA
The state of the African American male / Eboni M. Zamani-Gallaher
and Vernon C. Polite, editors.
p. cm.— (Courageous conversations)
Includes bibliographical references.
ISBN 978-0-87013-870-6 (pbk. : alk. paper) 1. African American boys—Educa-
tion. 2. African American young men—Education. 3. African American boys—
Social conditions. 4. African American young men—Social conditions. 5.
Academic achievement—United States. 6. Educational equalization—United
States. I. Zamani-Gallaher, Eboni M., 1971– II. Polite, Vernon C.
LC2731.S73 2010
371.829'96073—dc22
2009049806

Cover design by David Drummond, Salamander Design
Book design by Charlie Sharp, Sharp Designs, Lansing, Michigan

Michigan State University Press is a member of the Green Press Initiative and is
committed to developing and encouraging ecologically responsible publishing
practices. For more information about the Green Press Initiative and the use
of recycled paper in book publishing, please visit *www.greenpressinitiative.org.*

Visit Michigan State University Press on the World Wide Web
www.msupress.msu.edu

Heartfelt thanks to my husband James, father Richard House, father-in-law James W. Gallaher Sr., cousin Trevor Eccleston, and Leroy "Poppa" Frost for being loving and dedicated family men.

» E.M.Z.G.

I dedicate this work to the next generation of African American youth in the state of Michigan and nationwide.

» V.C.P.

This text is devoted to the memory and legacy of Dr. Lenoar "Len" Foster—an exemplar in serving, promoting, and advancing the positive engagement and achievement of African American students across the educational pipeline.

A former high school principal and curriculum coordinator, Dr. Foster was active shaping the discourse on leadership in secondary schools and higher education as associate dean at Washington State University. He was a nationally known scholar on the principal leadership school reform and historically black colleges and universities. He authored "The Practice of Educational Leadership in African American Communities of Learning: Context, Scope and Meaning" and "Administrator and Teacher Recruitment and Selection Post-Brown: Issues, Challenges, and Strategies." He was the editor of ASHE Reader Series in Higher Education and of *The Black College Review: Research, Policy and Practice*, and chair of the National Task Force on Principal Preparation, National Association of Secondary School Principals (2004–2006).

» E.M.Z.G. and V.C.P.

Contents

Part 1. K–12 Educational Challenges

Foreword

DENNIS ARCHER

I am delighted that Drs. Eboni M. Zamani-Gallaher and Vernon C. Polite, at Eastern Michigan University, have produced such an important and timely volume. This work will positively influence urban educators, policymakers, and scholars who continue to struggle with a myriad of dilemmas affecting the lives of African American men and their families in our nation. This book is truly timely and essential.

We have seen encouraging signs of progress in the mentoring of young African American males in Michigan and around the nation. Regrettably, an enormous

---

In 1970, Dennis Archer embarked on a distinguished career as a lawyer and public servant. He served as president of the Wolverine Bar Association, and became the first African American president of the Michigan State Bar Association and the American Bar Association. He was also president of the National Bar Association. In 1985, he was appointed by Governor James Blanchard as an associate justice of the Michigan Supreme Court. The following year he was elected to the Michigan Supreme Court and served until 1990. When he resigned, he joined the law firm of Dickinson Wright in anticipation of running for mayor of Detroit.

Mr. Archer was elected and successfully served as mayor of Detroit from 1994 to 2001, at which time he returned to Dickinson Wright and became its chairman, a post that he continues to hold today. He was president of the American Bar Association from 2003 to 2004 and is distinguished for being the first African American president of that organization. In January 2002, Archer was elected to the Board of Directors of Compuware and Johnson Controls, Inc. In 2004, he was elected to the Board of Directors of Masco, Inc. In October 2004, Mr. Archer was appointed legal guardian for famed civil rights leader Mrs. Rosa Parks. In 2004, Michigan governor Jennifer Granholm appointed Mr. Archer to the Board of Trustees of Western Michigan University to serve an eight-year term.

agenda remains with respect to changing the economic, educational, political, and social development of young African American men. The reality is that the overwhelming number of young African American boys and young men have few contacts with positive role models in their communities. The unfortunate reality is that many African American males live in communities marred by negative peer pressures, inadequate schooling and counseling, and too few interactions with African American men who positively affect their communities. Two exceptional examples of mentoring programs are the 100 Black Men of Greater Detroit and the Alpha Esquires of Flint (Michigan).

The 100 Black Men of Greater Detroit program has received numerous state and national awards for mentoring young African American males. The program is known nationally for its strong mentoring, economic development training, community health, and community leadership training. The students mentored receive exposure to higher education opportunities, economic development, responsible fatherhood, as well as matters of health and wellness.

Similarly, the Alpha Esquires are a group of high school students sponsored by the Alpha Phi Alpha Fraternity, Theta Tau College Chapter, and Epsilon Upsilon Lambda Graduate Chapter. Members of the two chapters work tirelessly and collaboratively to prepare young African American men for their futures by instituting a strong sense of self-worth. The chapter members serve as tutors, mentors, and friends to the Alpha Esquires. The program sponsors annual tours to historically black colleges and universities such as Florida A&M and Howard University. The Alpha Esquires program has been honored with the Governor's Service Award.

The enormity of the social-pathological issues affecting the typical life circumstances of young African American males begs for more concentrated, deliberate, and immediate efforts. Our new president, Barack Obama, best articulated the immediacy and urgency of an *agenda of change* in the development of African American males:

How many times in the last year has this city lost a child at the hands of another child? How many times have our hearts stopped in the middle of the night with the sound of a gunshot or a siren? How many teenagers have we seen hanging around on street corners when they should be sitting in a classroom? How many are sitting in prison when they should be working, or at least looking for a job? How many in this generation are we willing to lose to poverty, violence, or addiction? How many? (Fathers' Day Address, June 15, 2008, *New York Times*)

I gave a keynote address during the educational summit sponsored by EMU's College of Education and Office of Urban Education and Educational Equity, entitled "The State of the African American Male in Michigan: A Courageous Conversation," which spawned the development of this publication. My address, though prepared for a general audience, had particular relevance to African American male students and their parents. I tried to show the clear connection between obtaining postsecondary education and access to certain forms of economic, human, social, and cultural capital that will have far-reaching impacts on their personal lives and the well-being of their community. I began by reflecting on my own humble circumstances and upbringing.

I was born in Detroit. At the age of five, I moved to Cassopolis, Michigan. Cassopolis had a population of 1,500 in the 1950s. My dad had a third-grade education and lost his left arm just above his elbow in a car accident before I was born. My mother had a high school education.

Cassopolis, which is in Cass County, was a stop on the Underground Railroad. My father could not find work. The country did not have the Americans with Disabilities Act at the time, so he worked for a man who owned a tool-and-die shop in South Bend, Indiana. My dad made seventy-five dollars every two weeks for six months of the year and thirty-seven fifty for the other six months of the year.

During my formative years, my parents made it very clear that whatever I wanted to achieve in life, education would be essential. Although limited in their personal educational development, they were unyielding in their insistence that I go to college. The world today is broad, flat, and competitive, and competition is not limited to Ypsilanti, Ann Arbor, Detroit, or any city or village in Michigan. Our competition, and the competition that an African American male must be prepared to confront, is the *world*.

In 1983, the African American population in the United States was about twice that of the Hispanic/Latino population. However, in 2003, the Census Bureau reported that the Latino/Hispanic population was the single largest ethnic group in the nation with 13.2%, and the African American population was second at 12.7%. In 2004, the Census Bureau projected that the Hispanic/Latino and Asian communities would triple in population by the year 2050. Consequently, by the year 2050 the Hispanics/Latinos would represent one-third of America's population, which means that social scientists and demographers believe that by the year 2042 the majority of people in the United States will be people of color. My view is that America needs to get over this issue called *race* in America.

Although we need to focus on Michigan because that is where we live, the reality is that when we send our young African American men out to compete, the competition is no longer limited to just Michigan or the United States. The competition is worldwide.

Today, there are over 300 million people in the United States. By contrast, China has some 1.3 billion people. India has just over 1 billion people. The point is the world in which we live and compete is a world that is already made up of a majority of people of color. Thus, diversity and understanding diversity are good for business. If a U.S. company attempts to establish business relations in China or India, those respective governments will want to know how that company works with people of color in America, and how that company is organized and managed. There is serious interest in whether international companies influence in a positive way the lives of people of color in America. If a would-be international company does not have a story to tell about their efforts to hire people of color in America, they are likely to have problems doing business in China or India. The argument is simple: if an American company cannot demonstrate an ability to do business in the United States with people of color, then why should China or India do business with such a company? Diversity, frankly, is good for business.

The United States has 2.5 million people incarcerated in our federal and state prisons, which is the largest incarceration rate in the free world. Forty percent are African American and 23–25% are Hispanic. African Americans represent just over 13% of the U.S. population, but the African American and Hispanic prison incarceration rate is between 63 and 65%. Stunningly, 95% of these 2.5 million people will be released. Approximately 650,000 come out of prison every year and about one-third of them will return.

Why do I mention this waste of human capital? The incarceration rate among African American males is one of the most important aspects of the state of the life conditions of African American males. I have never met anyone that is perfect. If someone goes to prison and pays his debt to society, we need to wrap our arms around him and help him transition back into society. How unfortunate it is to see so many African American males waste their lives. Those wasted lives cannot be separated from the lives of their children and families they abandon. Regrettably, all too often African American males think it is manlier to stand on a corner and brag about how they got someone pregnant, as opposed to considering how to compete in the global marketplace. When they leave their children and and their childrens' mothers, there are several losers.

However, there is hope. I am encouraged that absentee fathers are central components of the courageous conversation we have begun. If a poor kid can grow up in Cassopolis, Michigan, without running water or an indoor toilet, and yet achieve success in life, then our young African American males can do the same. There are many opportunities for those who want to go into business and be successful. Despite the economy, one can still obtain capital to start a business. The African American community is virtually unlimited in its potential. There is absolutely no reason why we cannot be successful, but African American males must be supported in realizing their highest potential in society.

You might ask how Archer can be so smug about the conditions of African Americans. We only need to think back to a time when we, as a people, were enslaved in this country. It was against the law for us to read or write, but our ancestors taught some of us to do so by using a stick on a dirt floor and by reading from books that were either borrowed or lifted. Moreover, before the Civil Rights Era, we had our own African American businesses.

If we want to engage in a truly courageous conversation about the state of African Americans, we can begin with this edited volume. There are those of us in the African American communities who are in positions to open a door, reach behind, and pick somebody up—not as a handout, but as a hand up. I was raised to believe that I had to be twice as good as my majority counterparts just to be considered equal. Can you imagine what that is like knowing that you are good, knowing that you are better and still facing the challenges we faced simply because of our color? It does not have to be that way today. America is constantly evolving, and opportunities do not have to be limited. However, my friends, if we do not follow the directions and the programs of the kind set up by Dr. Polite, which were initiated and encouraged by the Kellogg Foundation, then the future for us will be very limited. If we do not convince young people to go to college and stay out of prison, if we don't cause the dropout rate to shrink immediately, then the future for us will always be what some of you are thinking and what most of us know. If the current trend continues, the future will not be bright. That is why Dr. Polite and the Kellogg Foundation brought us together.

Robert Kennedy once talked about how he took a rock and tossed it in the water, and he could see the ripples going away from where the stone entered the water. You could be that stone, the catalyst. You have great skills; you are a great people with a big heart, and you understand what must be done.

The question is, do you have the will? Are you ready? I believe that you are, but it requires honesty and it requires some "give and take" in our community. I so care about African American men that I established a scholarship foundation. I started out at Wayne State University and I graduated from Western Michigan University. I bestow $100,000 in scholarships every year. $5,000 each goes to ten Western Michigan University students, and to ten Wayne State University students. My scholarships are given to students who would otherwise have to work ten to twenty hours a week, and all I ask is that they have at least a 2.5 grade point average. Why? Because I want them to know that I care about them and that I and others in the community want them to succeed. My Rolodex is full of outstanding mentees because I care. You do not need a title or key position in the community to talk to young African American men who desire guidance. You would be amazed how helpful it is to go into a school on "career day," share with young men your career path, and answer their questions. I have personally interviewed many young people who come to my office and talk about law school and about wanting to be a mayor or politician. That is because someone, somebody took the time to go into a school and talk about his or her career. Put your hands on the shoulder of a youngster, an African American boy or girl and say, "You know that's a great question, you ought to be a lawyer." I have seen many outstanding young African American men and women who came from single-parent households who rose from their meager existence to become important leaders in Detroit. If does not matter if you have a mom or dad, or if one is a single parent. You can make a difference by simply caring or letting that youngster know that you care.

I will also tell you that as mayor of the city of Detroit, we accomplished a lot because of philanthropic foundations. Key among them was the W. K. Kellogg Foundation. I want to thank the foundation for all they have done and continue to do for Detroit, especially while I served as mayor. Kellogg, collectively with other foundations, invested almost $400 million over the eight years I was mayor of the city. For their support, I am eternally grateful.

Young African American boys can achieve whatever they can envision. Help them to see. Having this courageous conversation is absolutely needed, but also understand that if you have that courageous conversation there will be those of us—white, black, Christian and Jews—who really care, who will open up the door for African American males to walk through successfully. We frankly have no choice.

Preface

While our children are the most valuable natural resource, in spite of No Child Left Behind (NCLB), the education of African American boys is still not a national priority. The conditions affecting African American males in schools and society remain highly complex and astonishingly problematic irrespective of meager gains in achievement and graduation rates in recent years. Examples of the more salient conditions that are all too familiar and all too lamentable include high rates of school dropout and suspensions, high incidents of crime and incarceration, overrepresentation in special education, poor access to higher education, gender and masculine identity issues, and other health crises. These areas of concern adversely affect the quality of life for African American males in and near urban enclaves. In short, there are a myriad of historical and causal factors proffered to explain the disparate conditions of African American boys and men in contrast to their peers of other racial/ethnic backgrounds. However, there is a need to move beyond these problem elements to begin considering solutions in the form of educational imperatives and initiatives

African American and *Black* are used interchangeably in this text.

that can positively affect African American communities and schools, as forces that bear considerable influence on the educational, cultural, psychosocial, economic, and political achievements of African American males.

Given the scope of the dilemmas facing African American males, greater attention to them is warranted and acutely needed. There is a critical need for nationwide discourse among key stakeholders from state to state with an eye toward revamping policies and practices that adversely affect the schooling and community contexts of African American males. For nearly three decades, many states that have sizable urban centers (e.g., rust belt cities) where African Americans migrated following World War I have experienced and continue to experience severe losses in manufacturing jobs that have adversely impinged on African American men and their families. Historically, African American men played an integral part in their families and community life. This role is contrary to the widely held contemporary notion that a viable and adaptive presence of African American men failed to develop and flourish in their communities. Hence, the aim of this text is to bring into focus issues from both national and state perspectives, as well as critically examine the condition of African American boys and men from a variety of perspectives.

The central tenets of this book contend that at the core of the African American males' experiences in school and society is persistence, resilience, and triumph—a pattern of behavior that has been overshadowed by literature and discourse that focus on the social pathology of African American males. This core conception is based on the common experiences of ordinary African American males in schools and families, leading everyday lives in stable families and communities. Education is no exception. Despite the context of risk, scores of African American males have survived and progressed successfully. Although many African American males achieve at commendable levels and navigate the academic and social currents of their lives, their experiences are often posited as anomalies, often going unnoticed.

This volume endeavors to stimulate dialogue and initiate action in rectifying the unique societal barriers facing African American males, particularly as K–12 and postsecondary education are microcosms of larger society in perpetuating challenges for African American males. Each chapter highlights particular dilemmas facing African American boys and men. *The State of the African American Male* will provide fodder for the reader who wants to begin disentangling the conditions addressed in the book.

The text is organized in three parts; part 1 initiates a crucial conversation regarding the state of African American boys in k–12 education. In the first chapter, Deborah A. Harmon and Donna Y. Ford discuss the causal factors of underachievement in African American males. The authors contend that a village approach that uses all members of the community to advocate for and support African American males is required to address the underachievement of African American boys. Furthermore, their chapter examines the causes of the gap between the performance of African American and White middle-class students on achievement tests. Additionally, Harmon and Ford suggest ways to improve the academic gains and overall achievement of African American males. The second chapter, authored by Gilman W. Whiting, also discusses the achievement gap, taking readers on a brief journey through past influences on the present situation. Whiting illuminates the achievement gap and places research findings in the context of special education. He examines the overrepresentation of African American males in special education, placing the topic in a personal perspective and sharing how he came to study this issue. He also offers recommendations for change.

The next chapter deals with the state of mathematics and science achievement among African American males. Scott Jackson Dantley and Jacqueline Leonard deliberate on why fifty years after landmark cases like *Brown v. Board of Education* African Americans are still underachieving, especially in critical areas like mathematics and science. They explore the ramifications of feminization in education and recent legislation such as welfare reform and NCLB in the progress of Black males in school and in the workforce. In addition, the authors analyze data on perceptions of mathematics and science education in the African American community and offer recommendations to amalgamate cultural identity and socialization in learning mathematics and science.

While mathematics and science are chief gateways to understanding and maximizing technology, there is little specific data available regarding access to information communication technology (ICT) by African American males. Although there is a dearth of information regarding access to ICT, there is much that can and should be done in ensuring that African American males have the requisite technological skills for the 21st century. In the fourth chapter, Toni Stokes Jones and Nancy Copeland wrestle with the issue of technology access in U.S. schools and homes as well as abroad. The authors address issues of digital equity as it relates to African American students and their global counterparts. They offer suggestions regarding the best means of educating faculty and parents or guardians on how to integrate and use technology to support learning as well as for communication, by facilitating learning through authentic tasks that utilize ICT. The chapter concludes with recommendations that include seeking corporate, federal, and state funding to obtain computers for classrooms, lower student-to-computer ratios, and provide access to emerging technologies and ICT via broadband.

The last chapter in the section, by Vernon C. Polite, Cheryl Price, and Kristy Lisle explores the challenges facing the latest high school reform movement and its projected impact on African American males. The authors rely upon longitudinal data generated by traditional qualitative research approaches in data collection and analysis; in particular, personal narratives, which document in the voices, experiences, and concerns of African American males in a typical Michigan high school. This chapter offers implications for practice and concludes with policy recommendations designed to address issues distinctively linked to the academic future of African American males and their communities.

Part 2 of this book addresses African American male well-being relative to cultural, psychosocial, and sociopolitical contexts. The first chapter in this section, authored by Eboni M. Zamani-Gallaher and Yvonne Callaway, encourages school counselors and educational leaders to make cultural adjustments in educating African American males. The central aim of their chapter is to review the extant literature on school outcomes in K–12 and postsecondary environments for African American males in terms of critically/culturally responsive education. More specifically, the authors address issues plaguing Black boys and men within an educational and counseling context; and articulate relevant policies and practices that may yield culturally competent praxis that is germane to the overall effectiveness of educational practitioners and school counselors.

One quandary relative to the psychosocial development of African American males is public perception about violent behaviors among high school students. Anthony Troy Adams explores several questions related to school violence in the next chapter. Among his queries are the following: How do we define school violence? What is the prevalence of school violence in Michigan? What are the indicators of factors linked to school violence? Which traditional theories of deviance are useful for explaining violence in schools? How do schools manage violence (e.g., exclusionary disciplinary techniques, medicalization of discipline)? And what is the status of African American youths in Michigan? The chapter closes with policy recommendations that may stimulate a dialectical and a courageous conversation.

In a postindustrial global economy, where most core urban schools are racially segregated, concerns about the racial makeup of schools are not loudly heard. For these urban communities, school will be predominantly an African American experience. The chapter written by James Earl Davis tackles the intersection of race, gender identity, and urban education reform for African American males. Davis problematizes the uneasy ties of schooling and identity, asserting that is important to consider this nexus in light of current efforts at education reform aimed at increasing educational outcomes for African American males. The chapter specifically centers on race and gender identity in urban education reform, examining research on, and policies affecting, African American males. Particular attention is given to school-based interventions, early schooling, the role of teachers in identity development, as well as how research and practice complicates reform efforts. In short, the author addresses achievement and performance lags in addition to highlighting strategies and reforms to increase African American male students' opportunity to learn.

The next chapter, authored by Derrick L. Anderson and Robert W. Simmons III, addresses how HIV/AIDS has disproportionately affected the lives of African Americans throughout the United States and how Michigan mirrors the national epidemic, with the African American community representing more than 50% of HIV/AIDS cases in the state. This chapter uses current epidemiological data, journal articles, and other relevant information sources to examine the state of HIV/AIDS in the African American male community, both nationally and statewide. Anderson and Simmons argue that socio-environmental and cultural conditions shape attitudes in the African American community toward groups with particular vulnerability, especially in relation to HIV/AIDS public policy and care/prevention practices. The authors give voice to the issues that define the HIV/AIDS epidemic among African American men nationally and in the state of Michigan. The chapter concludes by discussing implications of the disproportionate impact of HIV/AIDS upon African American men and calls for community organizing to empower all at-risk groups to act in new ways that might begin to change the dynamic that now is so devastating to the African American community.

In the last chapter in this section, the influence of hip-hop culture on the status of young African American males is investigated by Marwin J. Spiller and Roderic R. Land. At the core of their discussion is an urgent longing to grapple with the bleak realities of an expanding population of young African American men who are disconnected from the mainstream society. The authors hold that unlike their female and White male counterparts, young Black men by most indictors have been left behind in the labor market, miseducated by the school system, and disproportionately incarcerated or placed on parole and probation. Yet largely through the medium of hip-hop culture a number of young Black men have been able to turn some of these negatives into positives. Without question, the power of hip-hop has been its capacity to give young Black men a louder voice in a society that has often silenced and marginalized them. Spiller and Land utilize the General Social Science Surveys (GSS) Cumulative Data File, 1972–2004, to examine hip-hop's role in and influence on the plight of African American men, particularly when it comes to educational attainment levels, labor market experiences, attitudes about race, and personal and financial well-being.

The final portion of the text, part 3, covers issues of access, equity, and post-secondary education. Gersham Nelson's chapter addresses the roots of the African American male challenge and calls for action in Michigan. The author provides a historical context for the current status of race and equity. Nelson outlines the federal government's failure to enforce the Fourteenth and Fifteenth Amendments, with the result that the Dred Scott decision of 1857 maintained legal primacy; this status quo was codified in the *Plessy v. Ferguson* (1896) decision until *Brown v. Board of Education* introduced a new doctrine of integration. The author discusses the antecedents that shaped modern-day challenges to access and equity. This historical backdrop leads to his discussion of the University of Michigan's effort to pursue diversity under the banner of affirmative action and how it is linked philosophically to the doctrine of integration. The chapter closes with an appeal for Michigan to launch a major initiative similar to those of Ohio and Indiana, developing and actualizing the latent talents and skills of African American males necessary to help provide the creative energy needed for state renewal and development.

M. Christopher Brown II and T. Elon Dancy II detail the research on African American male experiences in higher education. The out-of-class experiences of African American men and the ways in which they are shaped by college social environments, as influenced by institutional norms, values, ideas, and attitudes, are reported in the research literature. Brown and Dancy believe that Michigan can buttress African American male enrollment, engagement, and retention in college. The authors note that the in-class experiences of African American men are shaped by the norms, values, ideas, and attitudes within the classroom and other academic settings.

The next chapter highlights the work of William A. Smith in forwarding our understanding of misandric microaggressions and racial battle fatigue among African Americans in historically White institutions. Via focus group interviews, this chapter draws attention to a study of the experiences of 36 Black male students enrolled at Harvard University, Michigan State University, UC Berkeley, University of Illinois, and the University of Michigan. The author reveals active and passive denial mechanisms that allowed victims of Black misandry to coexist with oppressors, even when the hopes for racial improvement on campus are slim. This chapter clarifies what many young African American men enrolled in Michigan universities and other historically White institutions experience as race-related stressors that take the form of anti-Black male stereotyping and marginality (or Black misandry), which causes the hyper-surveillance and control to which young Black men are subjected. Black men are stereotyped and placed under increased surveillance by community and local policing. This chapter sheds important light on the experiences of an often overlooked, erroneously studied, and pathologized group: young African American men.

The concluding chapter in this book, written by Wallace Bridges, is on empowering African American male students. Bridges emphasizes the necessity for each of us to make a personal commitment to the academic advancement of African American males. In this chapter, he stresses his own personal commitment as a father, teacher, and theatre artist and how he has influenced his son, students, and other theatre artists. The chapter explores sources that examine the condition of African American males in American educational institutions as well as samples from the theatre and literary worlds that may promote change. These sources include excerpts from poems and plays, statistics from studies, models from news articles and websites and Bridges's own personal experience as a father, educator, and theatre artist.

The chapters in this volume document ways in which African American males continue to be affected by the legacy of inferior and segregated educational opportunities. This volume is yet another reminder that education is critical to all members of society, as changing demographics suggest we can ill afford to have a throwaway group. Critical to strengthening the fledgling state economy in Michigan are the school and community experiences of African American males. As Governor Jennifer Granholm and the State Board of Education in Michigan establish more rigorous standards for high school students, we remain hopeful that a paradigm shift will also occur in the policies, practices, and ethos of care needed to transform the educational experiences of African Americans males.

This book is for anyone who wishes to understand the etiology of Michigan's and nation's struggles with African American males across various areas of social life. Written with the interests of these excluded boys and men at its center, this text ardently rallies support for strategies that endeavor to assist African American males to self-actualize and achieve. America can no longer afford to turn its back on the millions of African American boys and men who should be poised (given the access to quality education, employment opportunities, and so forth) to become the next generation of educators, entrepreneurs, scientists, policymakers, and leaders in other arenas of civic life. Without further ado, we invite you to engage with the content to follow as we embark on a "courageous conversation" regarding the state of African American males.

Acknowledgments

This special edited volume is a result of an educational summit sponsored by the College of Education at Eastern Michigan University during the spring of 2006 on its main campus in Ypsilanti. There were more than 400 participants who engaged in a one-day dialogue focused around a myriad of issues affecting African American males in Michigan, issues that similarly affect African American men and their communities nationwide. Among the invited participants were representatives from public and private K–12 schools, community and religious organizations, criminal justice agencies, mental health and social service providers, and public and private institutions of higher education. The educational summit occurred only because numerous individuals and organizations from across the state provided generous financial and human resources, for which we are truly grateful.

The educational summit and this edited volume would not have been possible without the financial support provided by the W. K. Kellogg Foundation. The W. K. Kellogg Foundation was established in 1930 to help people help themselves through the practical application of knowledge and resources to improve their quality of life and that of future generations. Its programming activities center on the responsibility for self, family, community, and societal well-being. We are pleased that the Kellogg Foundation and its representatives recognized, by their generous support of this summit, the importance of the African American nuclear families and communities in Michigan. We are indeed grateful for the support provided by Dr. Marvin McKinney, a former program officer with the Foundation, as we developed our proposal for funding.

The financial support of several other donors must be acknowledged, as their contributions provided the additional force needed to bring the summit from a mere vision to an important reality: Comerica Bank; the C. S. Mott Foundation; Dr. W. Scott Westerman Jr., former Dean of the EMU College of Education; Dr. John W. Porter, former EMU President; and Dr. Vernon C. Polite, Dean of the College of Education.

The minds and hands required to secure the facilities, coordinate activities, and prepare documents and various related communications were numerous. We extend a special thank-you to the following individuals, organizations, and auxiliaries: The Department of Teacher Education; the Department of Leadership and Counseling; the Department of Special Education; Continuing Education; Dr. Nora Martin, faculty emeritus; Ms. Gail Getz, of the President's Office; Dr. Deborah Harmon and the staff of the Office of Urban Education; staff of the College of Education; Dennis Beagan, Special Assistant to the Provost and the Division of Academic Affairs at Eastern Michigan University. The greater Ypsilanti Community was well represented among the supporters of the summit, including Reverend Keith Peters, the Ypsilanti Chamber of Commerce, and Huron Valley Printing. Governor Jennifer Granholm's Special Education Advisor, Ms. Sue Carnell, provided important support during the planning phase. At the national level, Dr. Sharon Robinson, President, Ms. Jeannette Knight Mills, and Ms. Norma Mumford, from the American Association of Colleges of Teacher Education, were tremendously supportive.

Finally, we would like to give a special note of thanks to each of the contributors to this important body of work, who have remained committed to this project from its inception through its many phases. Without their scholarly contributions, this final important phase of the "courageous conversation" would be thwarted.

K–12 Educational Challenges

The Underachievement
of African American Males
in K–12 Education

Deborah A. Harmon *and* Donna Y. Ford

To be young and African American in the urban areas of the United States is to be subjected to all the harshest elements of oppression at the most vulnerable period of one's life.

» Robert Staples, *Black Masculinity*, 1982

To understand the underachievement of African American males in public education today, one must first examine the history of educational discrimination African Americans have experienced. That history begins with the peculiar institution of American slavery, in which Africans imported to the New World were forbidden to learn how to read and write. After the Civil War and the emancipation of America's enslaved populations, African American families were largely forced to live in segregated communities, where their children attended segregated schools. With the 1896 Supreme Court's ruling in *Plessy v. Ferguson,* such schools were deemed legal, if they offered "separate but equal" educational facilities and experiences to their students (Orfield, 2001). During the era of segregation, African American schools, though lacking in infrastructure compared to Whites-only schools, were staffed primarily by African American teachers who generally lived in the neighborhoods served by the schools. Because of funding inequities, African American schools were hard-pressed to acquire up-to-date instructional materials, but their teachers infused their curricula with lessons on the accomplishments and history of people of African descent to bolster their students' senses of self-esteem, group pride, and individual self-efficacy.

According to William Julius Wilson (1987), family involvement, or the participation of family members in tandem with classroom teachers to meet the learning needs of students, was less of a challenge for African American schools during segregation than it is currently. This was because these schools were centrally located within an essential part of African American communities. African American families from lower, middle, and upper socioeconomic levels all lived together in those communities, and they typically knew each other well enough to support each other's mutual educational interests. As a result, African American children frequently observed firsthand the impact of education on the lives of both laborers and professionals within their midst.

With the *Brown v. Board of Education of Topeka, Kansas* decision in 1954 came court-ordered desegregation. African American and White students were bused to the same schools in an effort to achieve numerical racial balance and equity in education. The face of schools across the nation eventually changed as African American students joined Whites in classrooms across the land. With desegregation came new challenges for African American students. Most of their new classes were taught by White teachers. Their new curriculum was Eurocentric and not inclusive of African American culture or history. African American family involvement in the schooling process declined as African American families typically did not live near their children's new integrated schools, and many African American parents found it increasingly difficult to attend school conferences and events.

During the 1970s, African American students at many of the newly desegregated schools realized gains in achievement test scores, but their test scores began to decline in the late 1980s. Today, after about 20 years of experimentation with busing and other integration methods, school districts across the nation have dismantled efforts to desegregate schools. Subsequently, African American and White students have returned to their neighborhood schools. The resulting separation is referred to as the resegregation of American education (Orfield, 2001).

African American communities have changed. They no longer consist of families representing lower, middle, and upper socioeconomic levels. Given the improved economic and housing opportunities that resulted from the *Brown* decision and the passage of other federal civil rights laws, many upper- and middle-class African American families moved away from their traditional urban and rural communities to integrate into suburban White communities. With the decline of the urban industrial economy in the 1960s, many unskilled jobs in the nation's cities were eliminated, resulting in a decrease in the number of middle- and working-class African American families and a subsequent increase in the social isolation of African Americans in high-poverty inner-city communities.

As a result, many of the African American youth remaining in the nation's urban neighborhoods ceased to have contact with regularly employed individuals —especially African American males, who rapidly became a shrinking presence in the labor force, with disproportionate numbers of them experiencing long-term poverty. These young people only rarely were able to tap into job networks or other middle-class resources. Their increasing social isolation yielded a breeding ground for drug abuse, domestic violence, higher birthrates, health problems, and disproportionate numbers of arrests, incarcerations, and suicides. These ills in turn led to increases in crime, addiction, welfare dependency, school dropout, and unemployment for African Americans in U.S. urban areas (Wilson, 1987).

In the ensuing decades, African Americans additionally experienced declines in the number of two-parent families and increases in the number of households headed by women whose men were living illegal and dangerous lifestyles (Roach, 2000; Wilson, 1987). The lack of African American men who could demonstrate responsible, legitimate, adult behavior has had a profoundly negative impact on African American boys, who have since childhood been bombarded with pejorative images and stereotypes of African American males by newspapers, movies, television, and the Internet. Adding to this construction of the African American male are the deprecating images in rap music and hip-hop videos that glamorize pimps and gangsters.

Currently many states, Michigan among them, are experiencing resegregation, leading some researchers to declare that the United States is more segregated today than it was before *Brown* (Orfield, 2001). Not surprisingly, Michigan has been named one of the most segregated states in the nation (Tench, 2004). Its largest city, Detroit, has been identified as the second most African American city, after

Gary, Indiana; while Livonia—only 15 minutes away from the Motor City—has been identified as the nation's "Whitest" city (Trowbridge, 2002). African American students, particularly males, are not faring well in Michigan's public schools, as demonstrated in the disparity in achievement test scores between African Americans and Whites (Great Schools, 2007). The confounding reality, however, is that this underachievement spans African American students across all socioeconomic levels, with those living in highly educated college communities claiming scores at the farthest ends of the widest academic gaps between African American and White students (Noguera, 2001, 2003).

In Michigan and elsewhere, large differences in test scores have been noted between African and European American students, even at the top levels of performance. In 2001, the Center on Educational Policy (Kober, 2001) examined the development and history of the achievement gap and presented its findings in a report that indicated that a significant reduction in the achievement gap had been achieved from 1970 to the late 1980s. The report further claimed that the nation had undertaken a concerted effort to improve educational opportunities through its War on Poverty program, school reforms, and entitlement programs such as Title I and Head Start. Beginning with the 1990s, however, that achievement gap began widening again, and was evident even before African American students entered kindergarten. Racial-ethnic differences in family income were found to contribute to the achievement gap but did not entirely explain the gap in test performance between African American and White students. Indeed, the achievement gap was noted among African American students regardless of socioeconomic status (Kober, 2001).

A few years ago, in an attempt to understand the performance of African American students, Howard University hosted a symposium on African American male educational achievement and invited leading scholars and experts on the achievement gap to identify possible causal factors (Roach, 2000). Table 1 summarizes the causes of the achievement gap between the performance of African American and White middle-class students on achievement tests that were identified at the Howard University symposium. Included in the table are suggestions for ways that each issue might be addressed. Also see the work of Barton and Coley (2009) for a more comprehensive review of 16 major correlates of the Black-White achievement gap.

The Howard University symposium brought to light several issues relating to the underachievement of African American male students in special education, regular education, and gifted education programs that required further study. It

TABLE 1. ADDRESSING THE ACHIEVEMENT GAP

FACTORS THAT CONTRIBUTE TO THE GAP	SCHOOL STRATEGIES THAT COULD HELP REDUCE THE GAP
• Limited participation of minority students in rigorous courses	• Challenging curriculum and instruction (multicultural/differentiated)
• Watered-down instruction	• Improvements in teacher preparation and professional development • Multicultural education • Differentiation
• Less-qualified or experienced teachers	• Experience with cultural diversity • Culturally competent teachers
• Teachers with low expectations	• Culturally competent training • High standards and accountability for subgroup performance
• Resource disparities between high-minority schools and other schools	• Equitable distribution of resources
• Concentrations of low-income and minority students in certain schools	• Sustained class size reductions in high minority schools
• School climate less conducive to learning	• Comprehensive school reform • Caring community based upon fostering resiliency
• Student performance anxiety • Stereotype anxiety	• Extended after-school and summer learning opportunities • Support groups • Counseling • Providing sanctuary
• Negative peer pressure • Antiachievement/acting White	• Support groups • Counseling • Sanctuary
• Disparities in access to high-quality preschools	• Expanded access to high-quality preschool
• Limited learning supports in homes and communities	• Improved social conditions
• Access to parenting education	• Parent education and involvement

also unearthed many concerns still unaddressed, grouping those challenges into four major categories: societal, family, school, and culture. Among the societal challenges raised at the symposium were those beliefs, practices, and conditions that negatively influence African American males' educational experiences, such as deficit-deprivation, social injustices and inequalities, and "the lure of the streets."

Deficit-deprivation theories propose the existence of inherent differences in intellectual ability among races. In effect, persons of European descent are deemed most intelligent, followed by Asians, Latinos, Native Americans, and last among all, African Americans. Teachers who subscribe to such beliefs hold low expectations of African American students' academic performance, which can result in poor performance, self-doubt, and the belief that academic achievement is the sole province of Whites (Ferguson, 1998). Structural inequalities refer to the differences in access, experiences, exposure, and enrichment that exist between schools and schooling at the middle and lower socioeconomic levels. Schools in high-poverty areas experience inadequate school resources, underfunding, large class sizes, less-qualified teachers, and high staff turnover. Moreover, these schools use White middle-class experiences as the standards and norms by which to measure their students. This practice privileges White middle-class students and puts students from lower socioeconomic levels at a disadvantage. Practices within the classroom also create social inequalities, including less rigorous teaching, emphasis on lower-level thinking skills, the provision of fewer opportunities to gain high-level academic skills, less-constructive feedback and encouragement, and infrequent referrals to Advanced Placement classes or gifted and talented programs (Ford & Moore, 2004; Harmon, 2004). The "lure of the street" refers to an unprincipled desire for material possessions and an emphasis on emulating what is colloquially called "thug life" or "gangsta" culture. Media and entertainment are the major forces transmitting these unflattering, anti-intellectual images of, and beliefs about, African American men to young people of all races and cultures. Exposure to these images can cause young African American males to have poor views of themselves and their communities as well as substandard achievement orientations toward and attitudes about their scholarly aptitude (Ford & Moore, 2004).

A substantial educational challenge for urban African American parents, the majority of whom are poor or working class, is overcoming or correcting the myth that they do not care about their children's schooling. This challenge exists because many teachers conceptualize and measure family involvement through a very limited paradigm. They complain about the frequently reported poor attendance of African American parents and other family members at school conferences and programs and conclude that African Americans today are disinterested in education. However, Ford and Moore (2004) suggest several reasons urban African American families often do not participate in school activities in the ways observed among other racial/ethnic groups. They note that for many such families fulfilling basic needs for food, clothing, and shelter often supersedes the need to participate more directly in the schooling process. Many do not have the funds to provide their children with the books, materials, and extracurricular activities that can enrich the educational experience; thus placing their children at a disadvantage when competing with students whose families have these resources and experiences. These shortcomings, Ford and Moore report, are often compounded with African American parents' own past experiences in desegregated schools. Many recall school as an unpleasant place and a hostile environment, and subsequently find it difficult to become involved with their children's schools and teachers. Some African American parents simply differ in how they show support for their children's education, and their alternate forms of involvement may not be recognized or valued by teachers.

Numerous school-based factors have been shown to influence the achievement of African American students, particularly males, in negative ways. Among them are tracking, the so-called Fourth-Grade Syndrome, cultural discontinuity, underprepared teachers, and low teacher expectations. Tracking is the practice of assigning students at the beginning of a school year to a fixed ability group and keeping them within that group regardless of their performance. Often, however, ability grouping in schools serving racially and ethnically diverse students is stratified not only by academic performance but also by race and ethnicity (Carter, 2005). Research has shown that typically African American students, especially males, are placed in the lower tracks. Students who find themselves in learning environments in which their educational needs are not being met often respond in one of two ways: withdrawing or acting out. It is precisely these kinds of behaviors that cause African American males to be targeted for referral to special education programs (Hallinan & Sorenson, 1983; Lucas, 1999; Oakes, 1985). Tracking reinforces racial boundaries and discourages African American students from enrolling in more challenging, Advanced Placement, or gifted education classes, as evidenced in the overrepresentation of African American males in special education and the underrepresentation of African American males in gifted and talented programs. Additionally, the prospect of being the only African American student in a higher-tracked class or program is a deterrent for group-identified African American students and leads them away from opportunities to develop their abilities (Ford, 1996).

Many American students experience a drop on their achievement tests, especially in reading and writing, during the fourth grade (Harmon & Jones, 2005). For African American male students, however, this declining academic performance typically begins before the fourth grade, when disproportionate numbers tend to "check out" of the schooling process completely. Unlike their White counterparts, many of these African American boys do not recover academically, thus marking the beginning of a downward slide toward negative achievement as they proceed through elementary, middle school, and high school (Lloyd, 1978).

Cultural discontinuity refers to a mismatch between the home culture and the school culture and, in many cases, the culture of the teacher. In most U.S. schools, the classroom environment—including the communication style, instructional style, and curriculum—are based upon the needs and norms of dominant-culture or White middle-class American students. African American male students typically find themselves to be "cultural misfits" in the schools they predominantly attend. Nowhere is this difference in culture more apparent than in the way teachers interact and develop relationships with African American male students (Irvine, 1999).

Research continues to suggest that African American students must have meaningful relationships with their teachers if they are to succeed academically (Bridgeland et al., 2006; Ferguson, 2005; Perry, Steele, & Hillard, 2003; Polite, 1992). Ferguson reports that African American students more often seek to please their teachers than do White children, while students from the dominant culture, who also enjoy meaningful relationships with their teachers, are motivated more by the need to please their parents than to please their teachers. African American students, Ferguson further contends, also more consistently identify teacher encouragement as a motive for their efforts and indicate that their teachers' encouragement is even more motivating for them than teachers' demands. In the absence of relationships characterized by supportive, nurturing, and encouraging interactions with teachers, African American students more frequently report that their teachers do not "care" about them (Ford & Moore, 2004; Harmon, 2004; Polite, 1992).

Underprepared Teachers

The majority of the U.S. teaching force is White, middle-class, and female (National Center for Education Statistics, 2007; U.S. Bureau of Statistics, 2007). These teachers generally are not knowledgeable about African American culture and the learning needs of African American students, as they have limited contact with African American communities. The lack the cultural awareness and understanding necessary for developing meaningful relationships with and effectively teaching African American students, especially males. Because of this lack of cultural competence, they often unknowingly create a hostile learning environment for African American students (Harmon, 2004; Ford & Moore, 2004).

Teacher Expectations

Teacher expectations refers to the beliefs and attitudes teachers hold about their students. Research on the impact of teacher expectations on student achievement overwhelming reveals that they have powerful implications for student achievement. They dictate teachers' behaviors and interactions with students, with the result being either high achievement or underachievement (Harmon & Jones, 2005; Harmon, 2002; Ferguson, 2001).

Experimental studies examining teacher expectations and student achievement confirm that teachers often consider race when forming opinions about their students and their students' potentials. As such, it is not unreasonable to assert that White teachers' expectations about their African American students, especially African American males, are influenced to varying degrees by the many negative beliefs and stereotypes that exist about African Americans. It is also likely that such pejorative viewpoints and attitudes may affect the way teachers interact and behave toward African American students (Carter, 2005; Ford & Moore, 2004; Fordham & Ogbu, 1996; Harmon, 2004).

Ferguson (2001) investigated the expectations and attitudes of White teachers toward African American students and found that "on average, [White] teachers probably prefer to teach whites, and on average they probably give whites more plentiful and unambiguous support" (298–99). Ferguson further maintains that White teachers tend to perceive their African American students as less willing to put forth the effort needed to succeed academically. This early perception can have a detrimental effect on African American students' future educational experiences. Beliefs held about older African American students when they are young often have a lasting impact on the students' educational experiences (Carter, 2005; Ferguson, 2001).

Other research concludes that teachers often perceive low-performing African American students as more difficult than low-performing White students and provide them with less support (Carter, 2005; Ferguson, 1998; Ford & Moore, 2004; Fordham & Ogbu, 1996; Harmon, 2004). Teachers view these difficult students as distractions and troublemakers, and indicate that they would rather spend their time attending to those students they perceive to be willing and interested in learning. On the other hand, higher-performing African American students are often perceived as "less difficult" than White students are and thereby receive more teacher support.

Low teacher expectations lead to classroom practices and interaction between teachers and African American students that affect the achievement of African American students. They also contribute to African American students' relatively low enrollment in Advanced Placement courses because teachers are less likely to recommend or admit African American students to those programs (Sadowski, 2001). Ferguson (1998) goes so far as to state that "teachers' perceptions, expectations, and behaviors probably do help to sustain, and perhaps even expand, the African American-white test score gap" (313).

Cultural Factors

The research literature also suggests that African American students experience school differently than Whites (Carter, 2005; Ogbu, 1994; Polite, 1992). For example, African American students report they feel less connected to school than do their White peers; many African American students contend that they are forced to participate in a system that has little regard for their culture, values, beliefs, and cultural-specific behaviors. Moreover, the belief that their academic performance is compared to a standard based upon White, middle-class society and culture is common among African American students. African American male students report feeling particularly vulnerable because of the preponderance of negative stereotypes and perceptions of African American men perpetuated by the media. Many African American males' negative attitudes toward school are based upon their perception that they receive worse punishment for inappropriate or unacceptable behaviors than do their White peers, and the research supports this belief.

Other culturally based or influenced factors have been shown to affect the achievement of African American students, particularly males. One such factor, according to Perry, Steele, and Hilliard (2003), is stereotype threat, a phenomenon experienced by African American students in academic settings heavily populated by peers and teachers who are likely to perceive them as embodying negative stereotypes. Stereotype threat, Steele contends, leads African American students to believe that they cannot perform as well as European Americans academically and, subsequently, not to try.

Fordham and Ogbu (1996) identify another cultural tendency among African American students to either (*a*) succumb to the notion that they must reject their African American culture and culturally based behaviors—that is, to "act White"—in order to succeed academically, or (*b*) to resist those impulses and assert their "African Americanness" by rejecting academic achievement. Fordham and Ogbu contend that the belief that achievement of academic success requires one to give up one's culture and adopt White middle-class culture leads sizable numbers of African American students, especially those from middle-class, educated communities, to adopt an anti-achievement ethic as an act of resistance (Ogbu, 1981). Ogbu posits that African American students may asset their "African Americanness" by rejecting the values that they perceive White students and teachers place on academic achievement and racelessness.

Majors and Billson (1993) contend that African American male students frequently attempt to counter pressures to "act White" by engaging in a behavior he dubs "cool posing," characterized by aloofness, lack of emotion, fearlessness, and detachment manifesting in unique ways of speaking and walking. To these students' detriment, however, many behaviors associated with cool posing are perceived as negative, rude, and inappropriate in academic settings and can lead to these males facing additional challenges in the classroom.

Conclusion

In most schools across the nation, African American male children spend full days in classrooms that can only be characterized as hostile environments—environments that are not designed for and that do not accept, validate, or channel the ways these male children think, speak, or behave into constructive learning and developmental experiences and skills. In these classrooms are teachers who typically know very little about African American males and how to teach them effectively. The curricula they use neither affirm nor include African American history or culture and are delivered in ways that are often incongruent with the ways research has shown African American males prefer to learn (Harmon, 2002; Ferguson, 2001; Ford, 1996; Irvine, 1991; Noguera, 2003). The damaging results of these cumulative negating experiences are apparent in the following statistics:

- Although about 50% of the U.S. public school population is comprised of students of color, 17% is comprised of African American students, and only 8.3% is comprised of African American males, African American students constitute almost 40% of the students placed in special education. (U.S. Department of Education, 2007; National Center for Education Statistics, 2007)
- If an African American child is placed in special education, 80% of the time that child will be male. (National Center for Education Statistics, 2007; U.S. Department of Education, 2007)
- Only 8% of the students placed in gifted and talented programs are African American students; of those, only 3.5% are male. (U.S. Department of Education, 2007)
- Fewer than half of African American males graduate from high school within four years after entering the ninth grade. (*OCR Elementary and Secondary School Survey*, 2002)

The challenges facing African American males in schools and society are enormous, and the causal factors behind their academic underachievement are numerous. Assessment of these dilemmas makes it evident that a comprehensive and collaborative effort is needed to address them. The "it takes a village" approach, which calls upon and enlists all members of society—from the local to the global community—to advocate for and support African American males thus seems highly reasonable.

REFERENCES

Barton, P. & Coley, R. J. (2009). *Parsing the achievement gap II*. Washington, DC: Educational Testing Services (ETS).

Bridgeland, J. M., Dilulio, J. J., Jr., & Burke Morison, K. (2006) *The silent epidemic: Perspectives of high school dropouts.* Washington, DC: Civic Enterprises.

Carter, P. L. (2005). *Keepin' it real: School success beyond black and white.* New York: Oxford University Press.

Ferguson, R. (1998). Teachers' perceptions and expectations and the black-white test score gap. In C. Jencks and M. Phillips (Eds.), *The black-white test score gap,* 273–288. Washington, DC: Brookings Institution.

Ferguson, R. (2001). Cultivating new routines that foster high achievement for all students: How researchers and practitioners can collaborate to reduce the minority achievement gap. *ERS Spectrum, 19*(4): 1–16.

Ferguson, R. (2005). Teacher perceptions and expectations and the black-white test score gap. In O. S. Fashola (Ed.), *Educating African American Males: Voices from the field,* 79–125. Thousand Oaks, CA: Corwin Press.

Ford, D. Y. (1996). *Reversing underachievement among gifted black students: Promising practices and programs.* New York: Teacher College Press.

Ford, D. Y. & Moore, J. L. (2004, Summer). The achievement gap and gifted students of color. *Understanding Our Gifted,* 3–7.

Fordham, S. & Ogbu, J. (1996). African-American students' school success: Coping with the "burden of 'acting white.'" *Urban Review, 18,* 176–203.

Great Schools (2007). *Data news.* Retrieved July, 11, 2009 from http://data. greatschools.net/2007/09/2006-2007-michi.html.

Hallinan, M. T. & Sorenson, A. B. (1983). The formation and stability of ability groups. *American Sociological Review, 48,* 838–51.

Harmon, D. A. (2002). They won't teach me: The voices of gifted African American inner city students. *Roeper Review, 24*(2), 68–75.

Harmon, D. A. (2004, Spring). Improving test performance among culturally diverse gifted students. *Understanding Our Gifted,* 18–22.

Harmon, D. A. & Stokes-Jones, T. (2005). Elementary education: A reference handbook. In D. Weil (Ed.), *Contemporary education issues,* 89–112. Santa Barbara, CA: ABC-CLIO.

Irvine, J. J. (1991). *Black students and school failure: Policies, practices, and prescriptions.* New York: Praeger.

Irvine, J. J. (1999). Preparing teachers for urban classrooms. *Blacks Issues in Higher Education, 16* (20), 30–33.

Kober, N. (2001). *It takes more than testing: Closing the achievement gap..*

Washington, DC: Center on Education Policy.

Lloyd, D. N. (1978). Prediction of school failure from third grade data. *Educational and Psychological Measurement, 38,* 1193–1200.

Lucas, C. J. (1999). *Teacher education in America: Reform agendas for the twenty-first century.* Palgrave Macmillan.

Majors, R. & Billson, J. M. (1993). *Cool pose: The dilemmas of black manhood in America.* New York: Lexington Books.

Noguera, P. (2001). Racial politics and the elusive quest for excellence and equity in education. *Education and Urban Society, 34,* 18–41.

Noguera, P. (2003). The trouble with black boys: The role and influence of environmental and cultural factors on the academic performance of African American males. *Urban Education, 38*(4), 431–59.

Oakes, J. (1985). *Keeping track: How schools structure inequity.* New Haven: Yale University Press.

OCR Elementary and Secondary School Survey (2002). Retrieved July 11, 2009 from http://ocrdata.ed.gov/ocr2002rv30a/.

Ogbu, J. (1982). Societal forces as a context of ghetto children's school failure. In L. Feagan and C. C. Farran (Eds.), *The language of children reared in poverty: Implications for evaluation and intervention,* 117–138. New York: Academic Press.

Ogbu, J. (1994). Racial stratification and education in the United States: Why inequality persists. *Teacher College Record,* 96, 264–98.

Orfield, G. (2001). *Schools more separate: Consequences of a decade of resegregation.* Cambridge: Civil Rights Project, Harvard University.

Perry, T., Steele, C., & Hillard, A. (2003). *Young, gifted and black: Promoting high achievement.* Boston: Beacon Press.

Polite, V. C. (1992, April). *All dressed up with no place to go: A critical ethnography of African American male students.* Paper presented at Annual Meeting of the American Educational Research Association, CA: San Francisco.

Roach, R. (2000). Explaining the achievement gap. *Black Issues in Higher Education, 17*(22), 22–24.

Sadowski, M. (2001, May–June). Closing the gap one school at a time. *Harvard Education Letter,* Retrieved on July 11, 2009 from http://www.edletter.org/past/issues/2001-mj/gap.shtml.

Staples, R. (1982). *Black masculinity: The black male's role in American society.* San

Francisco: Black Scholars Press.

Tench, M. (2004). Desegregation goals seen unmet in schools. *Boston Globe,* January 18. Retrieved August 7, 2007, from http://www.boston.com/new/ local/articles/2004/01/10/desegregation_goals_seen_unmet_in_schools/.

Trowbridge, G. (2002, January 14). What the numbers show: Racial divide widest in U.S. *Detroit News,* Retrieved August 7, 2007, from http://www. detroitnews.com/speciareports/2002/segregation/b02-390166.htm.

U.S. Bureau of Statistics (2007). School enrollment. Retrieved July 11, 2009 from .

U.S. Department of Education (2007). *Institute of education sciences common core of data.* Retrieved July 11, 2009 from http://nces.ed.gov/ccd/tables/ 200930502.asp.

U.S. Department of Education. National Center for Education Statistics (2007). *Common Core of Data, Public Elementary/Secondary School Universe Survey: School Year 2006–07.* Retrieved July 11, 2009 from http://nces.ed.gov/ ccd/pubschuniv.asp

Wilson, W. J. (1987). *The truly disadvantaged: The inner city, the underclass, and public policy.* Chicago: University of Chicago Press.

Overrepresentation of African American Males in Special Education

A CLARION CALL FOR ACTION AND CHANGE

GILMAN W. WHITING

On a Personal Note: Setting the Tone

While conducting qualitative, in-depth interviews for my doctoral dissertation, I made a conscious effort to remove myself from the population I was studying. After three years of being "trained" to observe and write from an etic perspective, I became very interested in a few theories concerning qualitative methodology. Not getting the definitive answers I sought from my quantitatively focused dissertation committee, I decided to seek primary sources on the topics of self-efficacy, qualitative interviewing, and case study design. Hence, I called Professors Albert Bandura, Irving Seidman, and Robert Stake—three renowned experts in these fields—and spoke with them directly to get the information and insights I needed. I learned a great deal from each of these thinkers and researchers.

Bob Stake said something to me that changed the way I think about my work even today. Before we spoke, I was grappling with the notion that I, as a researcher, was not involved in any meaningful way with the lives, stories, and circumstances of those who were the subjects of my research; rather, I was just observing. Stake told me, "Gil, don't take yourself out of the equation. You are more than just a researcher. You are an important part of getting to the meaning of the phenomena." Likewise, Professor Seidman reminded me that, because of the nature and time involved in successfully carrying out in-depth, qualitative work, one must have an emic, or culturally meaningful, perspective. This chapter has been written with these scholars' wise words in mind. Thanks to them, I care, then and now, about the students I study and subsequently acknowledge my role as not only a trained researcher but also one who is also emotionally connected to his subjects.

Researchers are expected to be several things—impartial, nonbiased, and objective. However, one has only to look into any special education class in America to understand that something is terribly wrong. If one does not understand, then I can only offer that something is terribly wrong with you. Of course, as an African American man, I have a stake in eliminating the disproportionately high placement of African American boys in special education. Thus, an opportunity to study this issue further is not simply a means to have my name on a publication. My goal is to remind policymakers, school administrators, teachers (special, general, as well as gifted and talented) and other school staff, families, and society that the issue of growing inequality in special education referrals and placements is real. For that reason, we all must continue to place special education disparities at the forefront of America's agenda in the battle for educational equity.

Special Education

A negative connotation is often associated with special education. Just saying the words *special education* conjures up feelings of failure. The words evoke images of kids who are not ready, of youngsters who are perceived as persons who will never be ready for mainstreaming. Although not many would move to abolish special education, eradicating the stigma attached to it should be the goal.

A closer look at special education across the country reveals that our nation's special education system is divided into many special needs areas. I call these areas objective and subjective regions. Objective regions include but are not limited to autism, speech, hearing, and visual impairments. Subjective regions include cognitive-related challenges, which are often couched in terms like *developmentally delayed* and *mental retardation,* and behavior-related problems such as *emotionally disturbed* and the catchall *multiple disabilities*. Black boys are statistically overrepresented in all of the subjective categories. Why is this? What can be done? Lastly, why should this overrepresentation be studied as a problem that matters?

In discussing any subgroup's current representation in education, whether one views that group's standing as positive or negative, one must consider the historical context and events that have led to the present reality. Most often, a cause-and-effect relationship exists between the subgroup's history and its contemporary academic achievement (grades, test scores, high school graduation rates, etc.). That being said, the phenomenon known as the "achievement gap" between the educational attainment of Africans Americans and European Americans has always existed. The gap is not due to genetics but rather to social and environmental realities, such as historic barriers to access and lack of parity in funding across institutional contexts.

John Ogbu (Ogbu, 2004; Ogbu & Simons, 1998) asserts that the enslaved Africans were among America's first involuntary minorities. From the early 1600s and for almost 300 years, African Americans were prohibited from accessing educational opportunities, from basic literacy to formal schooling. This educational opportunity gap created what we now call the academic achievement gap. In short, European Americans have always had the advantage in education vis-à-vis African Americans. This is nothing new. The question, however, is this: Does America now possess the will and courage to "fix" this gap and eliminate it for good?

Historically, African Americans have experienced discrimination in this country, not only in education, but also in housing, employment, health care, and the justice system. Numbering approximately 33.5 million, African Americans are currently the second-largest minority group in the United States (the Hispanic/Latino population surpassed them in the 2004 census). With a median age of less than 31 years, African Americans are also one of the youngest racial/ethnic groups in the United States.

Much remains for African Americans to be apprehensive about and to protest against, but it is important to acknowledge that the past few decades have seen some relative progress in terms of education. For example, more African Americans now complete high school and go on to college than ever before (Mishel & Roy, 2006). In the current test-driven public school system, thanks in part to the 2001 No Child Left Behind Act, African American students' scores on standardized tests have risen, although those scores remain comparatively low. The number of African

Americans living below the poverty level has also declined, even though natural disasters, such as hurricanes Katrina and Rita, reminded America and the world of the poverty that many still endure.

Notwithstanding this progress, persistent performance gaps remain between Black and White children in the United States. On average, Black students score lower on standardized tests and have higher detention, suspension, and dropout rates than White students. Black fourth, eighth, and twelfth graders score lower than White students do on standardized math, reading, geography, and history tests (Barton, 2003; Barton & Coley, 2009; Ferguson, 2002). They also are more likely to attend segregated schools, despite the lives lost and battles fought to bring *Brown v. Board of Education* (1954) into being and despite the legalization of civil rights for Blacks in 1964. Recent research and educational reports show that segregation, oftentimes hidden in political agendas called "rezoning efforts," is, in many cases, on the rise. Gary Orfield, co-director of the Harvard Civil Rights Project and author of many books, articles, and reports on school segregation notes, "We are losing many of the gains of desegregation" (*Washington Post*, January 18, 2004). "We are not back to where we were before *Brown*, but we are back to when King was assassinated" in 1968 (Kozol, 2005; Orfield, 2001). But the problems do not end there. African American children are less likely than White or Latino children to live in families with two married parents, and they are more likely than White children to live in poverty. African American students are also more likely to be victims of crime, both violent and property-related, than their Latino or White counterparts. These social ills cannot be ignored in any discussion of special education; nor can we ignore the chronic low performance of the nation's urban school systems—one of the most challenging issues facing educators and policymakers today.

Public authorities, as well as charitable foundations and businesses, have poured resources, ideas, and talents into the task of improving and desegregating America's urban schools and programs. Sadly, the future continues to appear bleak for many children attending inner-city schools across the country. To be sure, urban school districts have had to manage extraordinary challenges over the past several decades. The students they serve are more than twice as likely to live in poverty as other children; more likely to move frequently and have English as their second language; and less likely to live in two-parent families. They also are almost twice as likely to be assigned to special education and far more likely to drop out of school entirely. Additionally, urban schools are more likely housed in deteriorating buildings, more frequently the recipients of inadequate teaching materials and technology, and more often faced with dwindling financial resources. Additionally, urban schools are plagued with shortages of qualified and committed teachers (teachers who are inundated with so much red tape and paperwork their stress levels keep them looking to other areas of employment), principals, and support staff (Kozol, 2005, personal communication, 2007; Barton & Coley, 2009). The impact of these conditions is clear: they disrupt students' schooling, thereby maintaining the achievement gap and placing Black males, in particular, at risk for over or unnecessary referral to special education because of low achievement.

Over the course of the 1990s, as a new round of education reform was under way throughout the United States, the lack of achievement by urban school students became a major concern among communities and educators. A 1995 poll conducted by the Council of the Great City Schools, a coalition of the nation's largest urban public school systems, is revealing. The poll, described in *Critical Trends in Urban Education—Fifth Biennial Survey of America's Great City Schools,* showed that academic performance and student achievement ranked as the highest priority of urban school leaders, while the provision of social services ranked lowest. A follow-up poll conducted in 1998 showed that the rank order of priorities remained the same years later. In its most recent poll, the survey found that improving student academic achievement is the number one pressing need in urban public schools for the fourth consecutive poll. Closing racial achievement gaps follows as the federal law, No Child Left Behind, intensifies the need for improvement (Council of Great City Schools, 2007). States and districts have created and implemented a variety of new and sometimes radical approaches to organizing and managing urban districts. These efforts include initiatives to break urban school systems into smaller units, to privatize urban district operations and redesign and/or privatize their top management structures, and to establish private-school voucher programs. States are using a variety of funding mechanisms to help induce change and improvement in urban school districts, including financial incentives, new accounting systems, support for restructuring, and increased support for Head Start and other school readiness programs. Additionally, nearly half of the states have established accountability mechanisms that allow state officials to monitor school district performance more closely and to intervene directly in the operation of low-performing districts (e.g., Education Commission of the States, 1995, 1997).

All of this discussion provides an important point of departure for the two topics I will describe next. First, I will focus specifically on the achievement gap, connecting correlative variables to special education. This discussion will be followed by a focus on Black male overrepresentation in special education.

The Achievement Gap

Reading achievement among 17-year-old Blacks climbed through the 1970s and 1980s, but standardized test score gaps between Blacks and Whites widened somewhat during the 1990s (Barton & Coley, 2009; Barton, 2003). The patterns in mathematics achievement among 13-year-olds are similar: the gaps separating Black from White students closed in the early 1990s, then began to widen. When did these disparities begin? The aforementioned gaps start early, often before many students even enter school. Economically disadvantaged children have been shown, for example, to start kindergarten with significantly lower tested cognitive skills than their more economically advantaged counterparts. Even before entering kindergarten, the average cognitive score of children in the highest socioeconomic status (SES) group is 60% above the scores of those in the lowest SES group (Hart & Risley, 1995). Moreover, average math achievement is 21% lower for Black children than for White children (Lee & Burkam, 2002). Thus, from birth onward, minority and poor students disproportionately face conditions—at home, at school, and in their communities—that are correlated strongly and stubbornly with poorer academic achievement. Which conditions are most strongly associated with the academic achievement gap? Which of these relevant conditions are most likely to respond to concerted public efforts to change them?

The gaps in academic achievement between racial/ethnics groups have been studied from numerous perspectives. I will discuss two that I believe are comprehensive and worth investigation, as well as several larger points of departure for future research. The first is Paul Barton, of the Educational Testing Services' Policy Information Center, who authored *Parsing the Achievement Gap: Baselines for Tracking Progress* (2003). Barton states in the opening of his report that "achievement differences in school among subgroups of the population have deep roots. They arrive early and stay late—beginning before the cradle and continuing through to graduation." Identified in Barton's report are what he called the 14 correlates for academic achievement. Barton segments these correlates into school and before-and-beyond-school groupings, with 6 relating to school context and the remaining 8 relating to the before-and-beyond-school environment or context.

Correlates Related to Gaps in School Achievement

School Context Correlates

- Rigor of school curriculum
- Teacher quality and preparation
- Teacher experience and attendance
- Class size
- Technology-assisted instruction
- School safety

Before-and-Beyond-School Correlates

- Low birth weight
- Lead poisoning
- Hunger and nutrition
- Parent participation
- Parent availability
- Student mobility
- Reading (to younger children)
- Television watching

Related to this stream of thinking, Harold Hodgkinson's *Leaving Too Many Children Behind* (2003) offers a demographic picture of children born in 2000, addressing their prekindergarten years and the factors influencing their ability to achieve in school. Like Hodgkinson, Barton synthesizes work from prior studies relevant to student academic achievement. The findings of Barton's study show that, for all 14 correlates (described in more detail below), gaps exist between minority and majority student populations. Moreover, in the 12 cases for which data were available, 11 reveal unambiguous gaps between students from low-income families and higher-income families. It is essential to note now that all of the achievement gap correlates affect student achievement, including test scores, a major factor in special education placement. Black males seem to be harmed or affected most by these correlates.

SCHOOL CONTEXT CORRELATES OF ACADEMIC ACHIEVEMENT

Rigor of Curriculum

Barton claims that the terms "challenging curriculum, academic environment, and academic press" typically are used to denote rigor (2003, 9). He maintains that the rigor of the curriculum is the strongest predictor of the achievement gap, asserting that Black males have the least amount of access to challenging courses, Advanced Placement (AP) classes, and gifted education classes. Conversely, Black males are well represented in special education, a field whose substance and rigor repeatedly have been called into question. How is rigor defined and ensured in special education? The answer to this question is especially relevant in light of the low expectations society and educators often hold for students with special needs (Raymond, 2004).

Teacher Experience and Attendance

Just as student attendance affects school performance, so too does teacher attendance. Teachers working with urban students often have higher rates of absence and turnover (Darling-Hammond & Sykes, 2003). This lack of consistency with regard to teachers (and subsequently curriculum and instruction) negatively affects the quality of students' education. Low achievement is often the outcome, and low-performing Black males are prime targets for special education referral and placement.

Class Size

Urban schools are most likely to have larger class sizes than high-performing suburban schools. The implications of large and crowded classrooms (and schools) for student achievement are clear: classroom management, time on task, and opportunities for individualized attention (even as stipulated in IEPs or individualized education programs) are all compromised. Though students with low-incidence disabilities generally are placed in smaller classes than those with high-incidence disabilities (Patterson, 2005; Raymond, 2004), few states regulate class size in special education (Council for Exceptional Children, 2003). Given that Black males are gravely overrepresented among students designated with high-incidence disabilities (Patterson, 2005), they are likely to be in larger classes and, therefore, do not receive the attention they require to be successful academically.

The so-called digital divide is real. Today, technology plays a role in almost all educational, employment, and recreational activities. Computer access has the potential to help people with disabilities complete their coursework independently, participate in class discussions, communicate with peers and mentors, enroll in distance learning courses, pursue high-tech careers, and lead self-determined lives (e.g., Burgstahler & Cronheim, 2001; Kaye, 2000; Waddell, 1999). Further, students with disabilities benefit from the same opportunities technology offers to everyone else, including word processing, Internet exploration, and database access. On the other hand, some special education students use technology to compensate for their inability to perform a specific function because of a disability. For example, a person who cannot speak with his or her own voice can use a computer-based speech synthesizer to "speak" for him or her.

Despite the powerful potential of technology, teachers in urban settings seldom have adequate numbers of computers for classroom use, and their students often work with the least updated technology. When computers are available, teachers working in special education settings do not appear to use them for instruction-related purposes (Barton, 2003). Thus, they do not use computers, technology, and the Internet to augment instruction and support learning, both of which facilitate and promote student achievement.

School Safety

In the same year, Barton (2003) posited that learning is more optimal when students feel safe, Hoover and Stenhjem (2003) noted a steady increase in the harassment of youth with disabilities. Students who feel unsafe or threatened in any way are not likely to perform at optimal levels.

BEFORE-AND-BEYOND-SCHOOL CORRELATES OF ACADEMIC ACHIEVEMENT

Low Birth Weight
The percentage of Black infants born with low birth weight is disproportionately high (Barton, 2003). According to Reichman (2005), these infants are more likely to

(a) sustain long-term disability; (b) have impaired motor and social development; (c) repeat a grade; (d) fail in school; and (e) require special education. Black males are disproportionately represented among this group.

Lead Poisoning

Compared to White students (6%), 22% of Black students live in older homes whose walls and other structures and fixtures contain higher concentrations of lead (e.g., lead-based paint and lead water pipes) (Barton, 2003). Lead exposure and poisoning has at least three consequences: (a) reductions in tested intelligence and attention span; (b) increased reading and learning disabilities; and (c) increased behavioral problems (Centers for Disease Control and Prevention, as cited in Barton, 2003).

Hunger and Nutrition

Many Black students, specifically those who live in poverty, come to school hungry (Barton, 2003). Children who are hungry or malnourished cannot learn at optimal levels nor appropriately concentrate on academic tasks (Barton, 2003). Clearly, adequate nutrition is important for the development of sound minds and bodies.

Parent Availability

Barton (2003) situates parent availability in the context of family structure—that is, living in single-parent versus two-parent families. Black students live in single-parent homes, most often those headed by mothers, in greater numbers than do White students. Single-parent families tend to have much lower incomes than two-parent families. Those income differentials account for nearly half the negative effects attributed to parent absence, which include poor health, substandard educational attainment and achievement, behavioral problems, and impaired psychological well-being—all of which are risk factors for special education referral and placement. What are the effects when Black males are being raised by families only?

Parent Participation

Family involvement differs across racial and cultural groups (Harry, 2002). Black families tend to be less involved physically in school settings than White families, especially if they are headed by single and low-income parents. This lesser involvement can include attending fewer school meetings, reading less to children, checking homework less often, not volunteering at school, and more. Regardless of the reason, when family participation is low, students (including Black males) experience more behavioral problems, poorer academic performance, and lower rates of school completion (Barton, 2003).

Student Mobility

Black students who live in poverty are more likely to transfer schools than are impoverished White students. This lack of stability, which results in students constantly having to catch up to keep up with their classmates, has a negative impact on school achievement. It also increases the probability that their school records, particularly IEPs in the case of special education students, will not follow them from school to school in a timely manner. Thus, Black special education students from poor families may be deprived of the individualized services they require to succeed in school.

Reading to Young Children

Black students are read to by their parents less often than are White students (e.g., Smith, Constantino, & Krashen, 1997). This unfortunate reality negatively affects Black students' language acquisition, literacy development, reading comprehension, and general success in school (Barton, 2003). Students who have poor reading skills are at high risk for special education referral and placement as learning disabled, mentally retarded, and developmentally delayed students (Raymond, 2004).

Television Watching

Few recent studies have argued that watching television has positive academic benefits for students. Unlike reading, watching television is high among Black students' lists of preferred activities (Ford, Grantham, & Whiting, in press), and this detracts from their learning and school progress. The direction in which high-stakes testing is going and the increasing demands for various literacies that our nation will require, coupled with low reading levels, have the potential to spawn a whole generation of Black males who have diminished opportunities to be included among the American workforce.

Black Male Overrepresentation in Special Education

African American males have been represented disproportionately in special education since its inception (Harry & Anderson, 1994). In 1968, Dunn reported that some 60% to 80% of the students in special education classes for the mildly mentally retarded were students of color and low-socioeconomic-status students. That same year, the Federal Office for Civil Rights began surveying special education placement in school districts (Artiles et al., 2002), a monitoring effort that is ongoing to this day because of continued findings of inequity and recurrent litigation.

Most of the literature on the representation of Black students in special education has not addressed gender issues, and those that do typically present data by race or gender, but not by race *and* gender. The studies that disaggregate data consistently indicate that Black males, more than any other group, are overrepresented in certain special education categories, especially the high-incidence test driven and subjective disability categories (e.g., Patterson, 2005). This finding holds true whether the research focuses on data from the 1980s (e.g., Chinn & Hughes, 1987) or more recent data (e.g., Harry & Anderson, 1994; Harry & Klingner, 2006; Kearns, Ford, & Linney, 2005). It also holds true whether the study examines data from the Office for Civil Rights or the National Center for Education Statistics or the Education Commission of the States; that is to say, all of their reports document the Black male overrepresentation.

When scholars assert that Black males are overrepresented in special education, they simply mean that a discrepancy exists between the percentage of Black males in our schools or society and their percentage in the various special education categories. Black males constitute approximately 8% of the U.S. school population but account for much more than twice that percentage in certain special education categories (U.S. Department of Education, 2004). The issue, however, is not about actual numbers, but about percentages, in relationship to placement. Harry and Anderson (1994) contend that, when examining and discussing the notion of "overrepresentation," the percentage of Black males in the regular school population or district relative to their percentage in their school district's special education is most salient statistic.

Artiles et al. (2002) maintain that the placement of students of color in special education classes is one of the most complex problems facing educators in the new millennium. The data are seemingly endless, pointing to the sad reality that many inequities exist in education, particularly the education of African American males. These inequities are evidenced in many ways—high dropout rates, high disciplinary action rates, and high suspension and expulsion rates—but certainly African American males' high special education placement rates are the unfavorable outcomes of a complex network of social factors that do not favor Black male achievement in school and society (Harry & Anderson, 1994).

The overrepresentation of Black students in special education has been the focus of numerous literature reviews, reports, and studies (e.g., National Center for Education Statistics, 2007; Harry & Anderson, 1994). Most often, these publications point to one dismal reality—compared to Black females, compared to White males and females, and compared to all other racial/ethnic and gender groups—Black males are sorely and consistently placed in special education programs at disproportionately high rates. In the final section of this chapter, I will review the major issues regarding this particular dilemma, focusing on four broad areas: (1) definition and terminology; (2) statistics; (3) explanations and contributing factors (beyond the achievement gap factors previously discussed); and (4) recommendations for change.

Prior to addressing these topics, several caveats are in order. First, it is my firm, unyielding belief that Black males' overrepresentation in special education is rectifiable. Second, I believe that this overrepresentation is most prevalent when educators' subjectivity is greatest; thus, teachers' perceptions of and expectations for Black males matter a great deal. Those educators who focus on deficits are less likely to see the strengths of this particular student group, hence their disproportionate (and inappropriate) referral of Black males for special education placement and services. Third, I contend that Black males' overrepresentation in special education exists because standardized tests are the basis of most placement decisions. Such tests are not infallible, and their efficacy at predicting with Black and other non-White students' academic aptitude is continuously called into question (Whiting, 2006; Whiting & Ford, 2006). Fourth, I believe that special education placement for Black males often results in some form of exclusion from rather than inclusion in the general education classroom. Thus, an aspect of de facto segregation persists in special education services to Black males. Finally, I steadfastly maintain that the argument over whether placement in special education is harmful or beneficial for African American male students is moot. Scant data point to the benefits of special education for Black males (e.g., more support to, and/or tailored services for, students with special needs, opportunities for individualized instruction, etc.), especially over the long term. Hence, it is essential for educators, administrators, and policymakers to give serious consideration to rectifying this problem by correcting variables that can indeed be corrected.

Special Education: Recalling Its Purpose

Special education was mandated by law in 1975 with the passage of the Education for All Handicapped Children Act, now called the Individuals with Disabilities Education Act (IDEA). The purpose of the IDEA and its predecessor was and is to provide specialized services to students who require additional supports and different services beyond what is offered in general education. IDEA was intended to both regulate and extend to the education of all American children, regardless of disability category and severity as well as demographic variables (e.g., race, ethnicity, gender, income, socioeconomic status), and to guide the provision of educational services that are specific to their needs.

The intent of the IDEA and other special education laws is unambiguous: to address the special and individual needs of students who do not appear to benefit from general education programs and services, including curriculum and instruction. Who would disagree that students with learning disabilities; those impaired by emotional disturbances and developmental or cognitive delays; and those with visual, hearing, and physical disabilities would not benefit from individualized programs and services? Yet one must ask, "What is it that makes special education 'special'?" According to Harry and Anderson (1994) and Harry and Klingner (2006), special education is not that special. Harry and Anderson (1994) argue that the entire special education process is suspect, seriously flawed, and biased against Black males, from referral to assessment to placement to services:

> For the vast majority of African American males, special education placement means relegation to a stigmatized land of no return, in which a watered-down curriculum and over structured social experiences have little parallel in either regular education or real life. (615)

As Harry and Anderson (1994) further contend, the "special" in special education has lost much of its appeal because Black students, and most often Black male students, tend to be placed unnecessarily in the areas of special education in which student outcomes are most disconcerting. For example, students placed in mentally retarded (MR) and emotionally disturbed and behaviorally disordered (EBD) classes have very poor graduation rates; very few of these students attend institutions of higher learning (Saulny, 2005). Likewise, those in classes for the developmentally delayed are often repeatedly retained in their present grade, thereby increasing their chances of dropping out of school.

Essentially, the issue of Black males' overrepresentation in special education classes raises at least two questions. First, what is the percentage of Black males in special education overall? This question focuses on the aggregate data. Second, what is the percentage of Black males in all special education categories? In this latter regard, one must pay close attention to discussions about which categories are the most subjective or judgmental, which rely heavily on tests, and which carry negative connotations. For example, whether we want to admit it or not, the *learning disabled* label is more positive, or less stigmatizing, than the label *emotionally disturbed*. Moreover, the methods of diagnosing visual, physical, and hearing impairments are less subjective than those for diagnosing mental or behavioral impairments. In the former category, students' scores on cognitive or intelligence tests are used more as corroborative data; in the latter category, such scores are used more for diagnosis purposes. Yet, as Harry and Anderson (1994) state, "The centrality of the role of judgment makes it a potential source of bias" (603). The disability categories deemed most susceptible to subjective judgments and bias are those pertaining to mentally retarded, speech impaired, and emotionally disturbed students, as well as those relating to behavioral disorders and specific learning disabilities.

The type of special education placement prescribed also matters, as already noted. According to Harry and Anderson (1994),

> Special education placement is a very serious matter for two reasons: the stigma attached to being designated disabled and the likely detrimental outcome of being removed from the mainstream of education and thereby losing the opportunity to catch up or return to the regular classroom. (606)

FACTORS THAT CONTRIBUTE TO OR EXACERBATE OVERREPRESENTATION

Multiple factors are entangled in this complex problem, with explanations ranging from the pervasive impact of poverty on children's development to individual and institutional discrimination that often lowers expectations and increases disproportionate referrals and overidentification of Black males for special education (Artiles et al., 2002). Earlier in this chapter, I focused less on poverty as a correlate and more on teacher expectations and the consequences of low expectations. Given that the first step in the special education process is teacher referral, it is critical that we examine the impact of teachers' expectations for Black males on this group's overrepresentation in special education.

DEFICIT THINKING AND TEACHER EXPECTATIONS

The literature on teachers' expectations for Black students has a long history. In an extensive paper, Ferguson (2002) summarized research on the Black-White academic achievement gap, frequently finding that teachers often focus on Black students' shortcomings (perceived or real) at the expense of looking at their strengths. This focus on deficits or disadvantages, Ferguson asserts, is blinding and myopic. He concludes that this deficit orientation increases teachers' referrals for and the subsequent placement of Black males in special education. It further hinders teachers' willingness, effort, and ability to recognize the strengths and potential of their Black male students. Deficit orientations also stop educators from accepting any blame or responsibility for the deplorable educational outcomes of Black males, including their overrepresentation in special education. Too often, educators interpret differences as deficits, dysfunctions, and disadvantages within students and their cultures (Artiles et al., 2002; Ford et al., 2002; Harry & Klingner, 2006; Kearns, Ford, & Linney, 2005); thus, many Black males are referred to special rather than gifted education (Ford, Moore, & Whiting, 2006).

I argue that educators must move beyond a deficit orientation to recognize the academic potential and strengths of Black males. Changing negative orientations about this group of students holds unlimited promise relative to decreasing special education referrals overall and providing equitable and culturally responsive learning environments for them and for all students.

ASSESSMENT ISSUES

After students are referred to special education, the next step is assessment. Although expectations are subjective, tests are often considered objective and neutral. Despite their purported neutrality, tests have a powerful influence on Black male overrepresentation in special education. As Artiles et al. (2002) note, the assessment process in special education has a controversial history. Although the IDEA mandates that this assessment process be multidimensional and nondiscriminatory, concerns about the placement tests persist. Major court decisions (e.g., *Diana v. State Board of Education,* 1970, and *Larry P. v. Riles,* 1979) have raised red flags and resulted in mandates calling for the use of culturally responsive procedures and tools when assessing Black students for special education referral and placement (see Ford & Whiting, 2006; Whiting & Ford, 2006). Both the litigation and the legislation call into question the efficacy and fairness of standardized tests for identification and placement purposes with Black students.

Concerns about assessments often relate to whether intelligence quotient (IQ) tests are biased against Black students. A myriad of questions abound in this regard: What contributes to the lower IQ scores of Black students? More specifically, how appropriate are the questions or items asked and the acceptable answers to them? Do Black males respond differently than White students on IQ test items? How should the lower test scores of Black males be interpreted? What effect does the examiner have on test scores? Is the testing situation supportive for and welcoming to Black males? How useful is the information gained from the tests?

According to Harry and Anderson (1994): "The entire testing process is biased by virtue of placing at a disadvantage those students whose cultural and social experiences do not include the kinds of information and skills tested by these instruments" (613). Thus, a test that is valid and reliable for one racial, cultural, and gender group may not be valid and reliable for another group. Hilliard (1992) went so far as to charge that standardized tests hold little instructional validity, thus calling into question their usefulness.

TOWARD CHANGE

Clearly, school educators, administrators, and leaders must develop a collaborative approach to improving the nation's special education system. The reformation of big-city schools in the United States is being built around a broad consensus regarding which strategies are the most effective in turning around failing schools. Recommended strategies include setting fewer, but strategically clear and focused, goals targeting high academic standards, and strengthening classroom support for teachers and school leaders. It is necessary to develop school climates that are more conducive to learning, while establishing stronger accountability for teacher and student performance, as well as increasing community involvement and public support for urban schools. Additionally, increasing the level of financial investment made in schools and improving the effectiveness of the use of those funds in urban schools can build the capacity of urban centers of learning.

TEACHER PREPARATION FOR CULTURAL COMPETENCE

Teacher education programs and professional development efforts must prepare teachers to work with culturally diverse students and particularly with African American males (Whiting, 2006). They must focus on teachers' expectations in their myriad forms and address biases, stereotypes, and fears about these students so that deficit thinking and orientations are reduced and, ideally, eliminated. Part of this preparation must focus on giving teachers a solid understanding of culture, cultural differences, and how culture affects learning, behavior, and attitudes. It must address ways of helping teachers to become both culturally aware and culturally competent (see, for example, the specific recommendations of Banks, 1999; Banks & Banks, 2004; Boykin, 1994; Cross & Vandiver, 2001; Storti, 1998). Such enhancement can help to raise teachers' expectations about their students' academic potential, raise the level of teaching expertise, and reduce special education referrals. In conjunction, teachers must participate in ongoing, substantive self-reflection about their biases and expectations of Black males.

CULTURALLY RESPONSIVE, NONBIASED ASSESSMENT

It is imperative that the assessments used to determine special education placement be examined for biases and disparate impact. Ford and Whiting (2006) recommend discontinuing the use of many testing instruments currently available in favor of culturally responsive tests—namely those containing the fewest biased items (e.g., tests found to be more valid and reliable for Black males).

EQUITABLE POLICIES AND PROCEDURES

The policies and procedures governing special education referral and placement must be reexamined. How fair and equitable are teacher referrals (Ford, Grantham, & Whiting, 2008)? How appropriate are the cutoff scores used to categorize students? Schools must, in this regard, reevaluate their data. Do White teachers refer Black students more than they refer other students? Do White teachers refer Black males more than do non-White teachers? What are the specific circumstances cited in the referrals? Are the referrals unwarranted—that is, are they too subjective and not rationally sound? Do certain teachers show a pattern of over-referral and inappropriate referrals?

IMPROVED TEST-TAKING SKILLS

It is equally important that Black males be helped to improve their test-taking skills and confidence. As Steele (1997, 2003) reports, Black students often suffer from "stereotype threat" or the fear of taking tests and doing poorly because of their awareness of teachers' and others' negative attitudes about their test-taking ability. Steele contends that many Black students who are otherwise confident in their academic abilities lose that confidence when they are being assessed. He further asserts that this culturally specific form of test anxiety is debilitating and contributes to Black students' overall lower test scores. When test scores are low, Black males are especially vulnerable to low expectations and over-referral and over-placement.

EDUCATING BLACK FAMILIES

Educators cannot reduce or eliminate the overrepresentation of Black males in special education by themselves. Black families must play a key role in that effort. Thus, adults in the African American community must be made aware of this overrepresentation, and then collaborate on a formal, ongoing, and professional basis to learn how to promote their children's academic achievement at home. Workshops on literacy, for example, have been found effective in this regard, as are workshops that show parents how to become involved in their children's education in substantive and meaningful ways at home and school (see the many publications by Beth Harry and Gwendolyn Cartledge for specific recommendations).

PROMOTING A "SCHOLAR IDENTITY" AMONG AFRICAN AMERICAN MALES

At the outset of this chapter, I mentioned that three scholars helped shape my research vision and direction, but I only discussed the impact of two of them. I have saved the last, Albert Bandura (1977), for a separate focus because his social learning theory, a main construct of which is self-efficacy, has had an especially significant influence on my thinking. Bandura's theory is the basis of the "Scholar Identity" model for young Black males that I have been developing for most of my professional life (Whiting, 2006). This model theorizes that if one truly wishes to decrease the overrepresentation of Black males in the nation's special education programs, one must change or enhance these students' view of themselves as academics, as learners. It further holds that, just as many Black males have unshakeable confidence in and see themselves as superior in athletic and entertainment arenas based on their proficiencies in these areas, Black males who are highly competent in reading, math, science, and other school subjects must acquire and exude that same air of confidence and superiority. This proficiency must entail developing academic programs and strategies that target nine objectives:

1. Improve self-efficacy
2. Target their future aspirations
3. Increase their willingness to make sacrifices
4. Enhance their academic self-concept
5. Improve their need for achievement
6. Increase their self-awareness
7. Change their beliefs about the power of effort
8. Enhance their concepts of masculinity
9. Nurture their sense of racial/ethnic pride

Role models and mentors can facilitate this development, as can curricular changes and multicultural literature. Although this chapter is not the place for a full discussion of that theory and the Scholar Identity Model and program, those readers who are interested in learning more about it are encouraged to examine "Promoting a Scholar Identity among Black Males" (Whiting, 2006).

Conclusion

Those who profess to favor freedom, and yet deprecate agitation, are men [and women] who want crops without plowing up the ground; they want rain without thunder and lightning. They want the ocean without the awful roar of its waters. This struggle may be a moral one; or it may be a physical one; or it may be both moral and physical; but it must be a struggle. Power concedes nothing without a demand. It never did, and it never will. Find out just what any people will quietly submit to and you have found the exact measure of injustice and wrong, which will be imposed upon them, and these will continue till they are resisted. The limits are prescribed by the endurance of those whom [others] oppress. Men [and women] may not get all they pay for in this world, but they pay for all they get. If we ever get free from the oppressions and wrong heaped on us, we must pay for their removal. We must do this by labor, by suffering, by sacrifice, and if needs be by our lives and the lives of others.

—Frederick Douglass, 1857

Delivered nearly 150 years ago, and when the orator was less than 20 years out of slavery, these timeless words, espousing the ideology of "No Struggle, No Progress," illuminate the plight of today's African American male students. Far too many of these young men and boys are locked in a cycle of deprivation that leads to nowhere good, positive, or constructive. Special education has become little more than a warehouse for storing their minds, bodies, and spirits. Each year, fewer Black boys graduate from America's schools, while more enter America's prisons. This path is statistically clear and morally wrong. It *can* be rectified. It *must* be rectified.

As I move across this country and witness the dearth of Black children, and Black boys in particular, in gifted/talented programs, in honors and Advanced Placement classes, and among those destined and prepared to address the next challenges of higher education, I am reminded of Douglass's words: "Power concedes nothing without a demand." Equally, when I observe the multitude of seemingly wandering Black male bodies, heading in no particular direction, without any sense of self-efficacy or future focus, and in many cases despising, to a degree, the education process, I recall Douglass's enjoinment that these states "will continue till they are resisted." Yet, I wonder, how long will it be before our nation takes up the mantle to support sustained efforts to reverse these persistent trends?

REFERENCES

Artiles, A. J., Harry, B., Reschly, D. J., & Chinn, P. C. (2002). Over-identification of students of color in special education: A critical overview. *Multicultural Perspectives, 4*, 3–10.

Bandura, A. (1977). *Social learning theory.* Englewood Cliffs, NJ: Prentice-Hall.

Banks, J. A. (1999). *Introduction to multicultural education* (2nd ed.). Boston: Allyn & Bacon.

Banks, J. A. & Banks, C. A. M. (Eds.). (2004). *Multicultural education: Issues and perspectives.* Hobeoken, NJ: John Wiley & Sons.

Barton, P. E. (2003). *Parsing the achievement gap: Baselines for tracking progress.* Princeton, NJ: Educational Testing Service, Policy Information Center.

Barton, P. E. & Coley, R. J. (2009) *Parsing the achievement gap II.* Princeton, NJ: Educational Testing Services, Policy Information Center.

Boykin, A. W. (1994). Afro-cultural expression and its implications for schooling. In E.

Burgstahler, S. & Cronheim, D. (2001). Supporting peer–peer and mentor–protégé relationships on the Internet. *Journal of Research on Technology in Education, 34*(1), 59–74.

Chinn, P. C. & Hughes, S. (1987). Representation of minority students in special education classes. *Remedial and Special Education, 8*(4), 41–46.

Cross, W. E., Jr. & Vandiver, B. J. (2001). Nigrescence theory and measurement: Introducing the Cross Racial Identity Scale (CRIS). In J. G. Ponterotto, L. A. Suzuki, & C. M. Alexander (Eds.), *Handbook of multicultural counseling* (2nd ed.), 371–93. Thousand Oaks, CA: Sage.

Council for Exceptional Children. (2003). *Teacher-pupil ratio in special education.* Arlington, VA: Author.

Council of Great City Schools. (2007). *Critical trends in urban education—Fifth biennial survey of America's Great City Schools.* Retrieved September 19, 2007 from http://www.cgcs.org/newsroom/press_release20.aspx.

Darling-Hammond, L. & Sykes, G. (2003). Wanted: A national teacher supply policy for education: The right way to meet the "Highly Qualified Teacher" challenge? *Education Policy Analysis Archives, 11*(33). Retrieved September 20, 2007, from http://epaa.asu.edu/epaa/v11n33/.

Douglass, F. (1985). The significance of emancipation in the West Indies. In J.

W. Blassingame (Ed.), *The Frederick Douglass Papers, Series One: Speeches, Debates, and Interviews (Volume 3: 1855–63)* (p. 204). New Haven: Yale University Press.

Dunn, L. (1968). Special education for the mildly mentally retarded: Is much of it justifiable? *Exceptional Children, 23,* 5–21.

Diana v. State Board of Education. (1970). Civil Action No. C-703RFP (N.D. Cal., Jan. 7, 1970 & June 18, 1973).

Education Commission of the States. (1995). *The new American school district.* Denver: U.S. Department of Education.

Education Commission of the States. (1997). *Redesigning the urban high school.* Denver: U.S. Department of Education.

Ferguson, R. (2002). Addressing racial disparities in high-achieving suburban schools. *NCREL Policy Issues, 1,* 3–11.

Ford, D. Y., Grantham, T. C., & Whiting, G. W. (2008). Another look at the achievement gap: Learning from the experiences of gifted Black students. *Urban Education, 43,* 216–39.

Ford, D. Y., Harris III, J. J., Tyson, C. A., & Frazier Trotman, M. (2002). Beyond deficit thinking: Providing access for gifted African American students. *Roeper Review, 24*(2), 52–58.

Ford, D. Y., Moore, J. L. III, & Whiting, G. W. (2006). Eliminating deficit orientations: Creating classrooms and curriculums for gifted students from diverse cultural backgrounds. In M. G. Constantine & D. W. Sue (Eds.), *Addressing racism: Facilitating cultural competence in mental health and educational settings,* 173–93. Hoboken, NJ: Wiley.

Ford, D. Y. & Whiting, G. W. (2006). Under-representation of diverse students in gifted education: Recommendations for nondiscriminatory assessment (Part 1). *Gifted Education Press Quarterly, 20*(2), 2–6.

Harry, B. (2002). Trends and issues in serving culturally diverse families of children with disabilities. *Journal of Special Education, 55*(3), 131–38.

Harry, B. & Anderson, M. G. (1994). The disproportionate placement of African American males in special education programs: A critique of the process. *Journal of Negro Education, 63*(4), 602–19.

Harry, B. & Klingner, J. (2006). *Why are so many minority students in special education: Understanding race & disability in schools.* New York: Teachers College Press.

Hart, B. & Risley, T. R. (1995). *Meaningful differences in the everyday experience of young American children.* Baltimore: Brookes Publishing.

Hilliard, A. G. III. (1992). The pitfalls and promises of special education practice. *Exceptional Children, 59*(2), 168–72.

Hodgkinson, H. L. (2003). *Leaving too many children behind: A demographer's view on the neglect of America's youngest children.* April. Washington, DC: Institute for Educational Leadership.

Hollins, J. King & W. Hayman (Eds.), *The school achievement of minority children.* Hillsdale, NJ: Lawrence Erlbaum.

Hoover, J. & Stenhjem, P. (2003). Bullying and teasing of youth with disabilities: Creating positive school environments for effective inclusion. *National Center on Secondary Education and Transition Issue Brief, 2*(3), 1–6.

Kaye, H. S. (2000). *Disability and the digital divide* (Disability Statistics Abstract Report No. 22). Washington, DC: U.S. Department of Education, National Institute on Disability and Rehabilitation Research.

Kearns, T., Ford, L., & Linney, J. A. (2005). African American student representation in special education programs. *Journal of Negro Education, 74*(4), 297–310.

Kozol, J. (2005). *The shame of the nation: The restoration of apartheid schooling in America.* New York: Crown.

Larry P. v. Riles. (1979). C-71-2270, FRP, Dis. Ct.

Lee, V. E. & Burkam, D. T. (2002). *Inequality at the starting gate: Social background differences in achievement as children begin school.* Washington, DC: Economic Policy Institute.

Mishel, L. & Joy, J. (2006). *Rethinking high school graduation rates and trends.* Washington, DC: Economic Policy Institute.

National Center for Education Statistics. (2007). *The condition of education.* Washington, DC: U.S. Department of Education.

Ogbu, J. (2004). Collective identity and the burden of "acting White" in Black history, community, and education. *Urban Review, 36*(1), 1–35.

Ogbu, J. & Simons, H. D. (1998). Voluntary and involuntary minorities: A cultural ecological theory of school performance with some implications for education. *Anthropology and Education Quarterly, 29,* 155–88.

Orfield, G. (2001). *Schools more separate: Consequences of a decade of resegregation.* Cambridge: Civil Rights Project, Harvard University.

Patterson, K. H. (2005). Increasing positive outcomes for African American males in special education with the use of guided notes. *Journal of Negro Education, 74*(4), 311–20.

Raymond, E. B. (2004). *Learners with mild disabilities: A characteristics approach* (2nd ed.). Needham Heights, MA: Allyn & Bacon.

Reichman, N. (2005). Low birth weight and school readiness. *School Readiness: Closing Racial and Ethnic Gaps, 15*(1), 91–116.

Saulny, S. (2005). Study on special education finds low graduation rate. *New York Times*, June 3. Retrieved September 20, 2007 from http://www.nytimes.com/2005/06/03/education/03dropout.html.

Smith, C., Constantino, R., & Krashen, S. (1997). Differences in print environment for children in Beverly Hills, Compton, and Watts. *Emergency Librarian, 24*(4), 8–9.

Steele, C. M. (1997). A threat in the air: How stereotypes shape intellectual identity and performance. *American Psychologist, 52*, 613–29.

Steele, C. M. (2003). Stereotype threat and African-American student achievement. In T. Perry, C. M. Steele, & A. G. Hilliard III (Eds.). *Young, gifted and Black: Promoting high achievement among African-American students*, 109–30. Boston: Beacon Press.

Storti, C. (1998). *Figuring foreigners out.* Yarmouth, ME: Intercultural Press.

U.S. Department of Education. (2004). *Twenty-sixth annual report to Congress on the implementation of the Individuals with Disabilities Education Act.* Washington, DC: U.S. Government Printing Office.

Waddell, C. D. (1999). The growing digital divide in access for people with disabilities: Overcoming barriers to participation in the digital economy. Retrieved July 7, 2002, from http://www.icdri.org/CynthiaW/the_digital_divide.htm.

Whiting, G. W. (2006). Promoting a scholar identity among Black males. *Gifted Education Press Quarterly, 20*(3), 1–6.

Whiting, G. W. & Ford, D. Y. (2006). Under-representation of diverse students in gifted education: Recommendations for nondiscriminatory assessment (part 2). *Gifted Education Press Quarterly, 20*(3), 6–10.

The State of Mathematics and Science Achievement among African American Males

Scott Jackson Dantley *and* Jacqueline Leonard

Underachievement among African American students in mathematics and science is a national dilemma. From early childhood to secondary educational settings, many schools have failed to provide students of color with high-quality instruction in mathematics (Berry, 2008; Martin, 2003; Rousseau & Tate, 2003) and science (Oakes, 1990; Warren et al., 2001). African American students have consistently lagged behind their white counterparts in mathematics and science achievement. National Assessment of Educational Progress (NAEP) results from 1990–2007 show significant increases in mathematics for all demographic groups in grades four and eight (Lubienski & Copur, 2009). However, the data resemble pairs of parallel lines when it comes to achievement differences between black and white students at these grade levels. These parallel lines will never meet as long as opportunities to learn for black and white students continue to be drastically different. Furthermore, within group differences on NAEP show black females outperform black males slightly, whereas white and Hispanic males outperform white and Hispanic females, respectively (Lubienski & Copur, 2009).

These data contradict the common belief that males outperform females in mathematics and science (Noguera, 2005). When it comes to African American students, the reverse outcome occurs when you couple gender with race; that is, African American males perform less well in mathematics and science courses than do African American females (Leonard, 2001; Lubienski & Copur, 2009). A brief summary of national and Michigan standardized tests results reveal the stark contrast between black and white and male and female students' mathematics and science achievement.

National Standardized Results in Mathematics and Science

AMERICAN COLLEGE TEST (ACT)

On a national level, females from all racial and ethnic groups who planned to major in the sciences consistently outscored males on the ACT Mathematics and Science Reasoning test (ACT, 1994). However, African American students, in general, score the lowest on the ACT test in mathematics and science. Although African American students are the lowest-achieving group of students in science, those students who declare science as a major and enroll in high science and mathematics courses tend to outperform their peers who do not take advanced courses. Yet African American and Mexican American students represent the lowest percentage of students completing advanced courses in mathematics and science among science and nonscience majors. There is some evidence that the college entrance and advanced placement scores of underserved students taking more high school science courses have increased in recent years (Dantley, 2004). Increasing the number of minority and female students enrolled in science courses should continue to receive national attention.

NATIONAL ASSESSMENT OF EDUCATIONAL PROGRESS

Results of the 2007 National Assessment of Educational Progress (NAEP) show that achievement gaps in mathematics have narrowed between black and white students. Specifically, the gap in mathematics achievement has narrowed at all levels, except for white and Hispanic 17-year-olds (National Council of Teachers of Mathematics [NCTM], 2005). "The most significant difference was between white and black 13-year-olds" (NCTM, 2005, 10). The gap decreased from 46 points in 2004 to 27 points in 2005 for eighth graders taking the NAEP, which is the smallest gap since 1973 (NCTM, 2005). However, the gap between whites and blacks increased again in 2007 to 31 points. Furthermore, mathematics test results on the NAEP have not changed since 1973 for 17-year-olds despite an increase in the number of students taking advanced mathematics courses. Furthermore, the number of African American students enrolled in advanced mathematics courses remains dismal. Mathematics teachers must have high expectations of all students enrolled in advanced mathematics classes and do more to challenge and assist African American students (Berry, 2008; Rousseau & Tate, 2003).

In terms of science, NAEP reports the largest gap in mean proficiency is between Caucasian and African American students, with a 55-point difference across areas by age 17. Females outperformed males at age 9, but by ages 13 and 17, males, in general, had the advantage. Although gender differences on average proficiency NAEP scores have been decreasing, males, in general, have had higher scores at all age levels since 1970. However, Rodriguez (1997) found no significant gender differences in the performance of males and females in science courses. Rodriguez (1997) cautions against using data from national studies to interpret results based on race and ethnicity because the scores are not disaggregated by gender within racial and ethnic groups. For example, it is difficult to know if African American females outperformed African American males, which has been shown to be the case.

THE MICHIGAN SCIENCE REPORT CARD

Current achievement data about individual schools, districts, and cities in the state of Michigan are available on the state government's website. The percentage of students at or above proficiency in mathematics in Michigan during the 2003–4 academic year were:

- GRADE 4: 70.5% of all students and 51.0% of Black, non-Hispanic students;
- GRADE 8: 61.4% of all students and 33.3% of Black, non-Hispanic students; and
- 51.2% of all students and 22.4% of Black, non-Hispanic students. (*Michigan School Report Card*, 2006)

These data parallel national achievement data such as NAEP, which show improvement at the elementary and middle school levels but flat or declining scores at the high school level (National Center for Education Statistics [NCES], 2004). No Child Left Behind required assessment in science beginning in 2007, and reports in Michigan on science achievement have been promising. Science scores in 2000 were as follows:

- GRADE 4: Average scaled score for students in Michigan was 154 compared to a national score of 148;
- GRADE 8: Average scaled score for students in Michigan was 156 compared to a national score of 149; and
- The percentage of students who performed at or above the proficient level was 37 percent compared to the national average of 30 percent. (*Michigan School Report Card,* 2006)

However promising these results may be, there is still much work to be done to increase the proficiency of African American males in science and mathematics. Previous studies (Brookover & Erickson, 1969; Coleman et al., 1966; Morrow & Torres, 1995) show African American males' academic performance mirrors their experiences in the larger society. Rather than focusing on achievement gaps (Ladson-Billings, 2006), researchers and policymakers need to focus on the reasons African American males are disproportionately represented in the lowest-performing academic categories in mathematics and science-related fields.

The Plight of Young African American Males

Recently, the plight of young black men has been in the forefront. On Thursday, April 20, 2006, Cornel West graced the city of Philadelphia to discuss the topic at the University of Pennsylvania. Quoting W. E. B. Dubois, West spoke to an audience of more than 300 on the theme: "Poor, Young, Black, and Male: A Case for National Action" (Campbell, 2006). Just what are the issues that affect young, black men today? According to a *New York Times* article by Erik Eckholm, "The huge pool of poorly educated black men is becoming evermore disconnected from the mainstream . . . and to a greater degree than white or Hispanic men" (2006, n.p.).

Policy decisions made to reduce the welfare rolls put women on the fast track, but black men have been left behind. Even though the labor market in the 1990s was the best in 30 years, it was a bad decade for young black men. In 2000, 65% of black male high school dropouts in their twenties were jobless, not seeking work, or incarcerated. By the year 2004, "The number grew to 72%, compared to 34% of white and 19% of Hispanic dropouts" (Eckholm, 2006, n.p.). Fifty percent of black men in their twenties were jobless in 2004 compared to 46% in 2000. Incarceration rates for black men are also on the rise. "In 1995, 16% of black men in their twenties who did not attend college were in jail or prison; by 2004, 21% were incarcerated" (Eckholm, 2006, n.p.). Statistics show that by their mid thirties, 60% of black men who have dropped out of school have spent time in prison. Yet, in our inner cities more than half of all black men do not finish high school (Campbell, 2006).

When we examine the literature, it is clear that poverty remains a constant factor that increases the risk of low academic performance in school (Gabarino, 1999). In fact, poverty negatively influences student learning; these negative influences are exacerbated if a child is impoverished from birth. Impoverished children often experience poor health care, lack of good nutrition, parents with minimum education, and poor social services. According to Noguera (2005), addressing the lack of support services is not enough to ensure the academic prosperity of African American males because in the educational system they "take on" self-defeating characteristics. Noguera (2005) suggests that institutions take a systematic approach to alleviate the problems that plague black males, going beyond correcting policies and practices but also addressing the adaptive behaviors of these individuals.

Ogbu (1987), Fordham (1996), and Noguera (2005) define the negative adaptive behaviors of some black males as their ability to ignore the importance of educational success as a cultural phenomenon. Basically, to succeed in school is seen as "acting white" or "uncool" (Ogbu, 2003). Other black males may experience what is called stereotype threat (Smith, Sansone, & White, 2007). Essentially, stereotype threat supposes that a "competence-related stereotype can, in and of itself, lead to poorer task performance" (Smith, Sansone, & White, 2007, 99). In other words, some blacks may be underachieving in mathematics and science simply because they accept the stereotype that their performance is below par in these subject areas. Thus, their motivation and persistence to succeed in these subjects are severely hampered. Furthermore, some black males may suffer internalized oppression, viewing their blackness as a source of debilitation or helplessness (Speight, 2007). To explain this concept, Du Bois (1969) described a double-conscious dilemma:

The Negro is a sort of seventh son, born with a veil, and gifted with second sight in this American world,—a world, which yields him no true self-consciousness, but only lets him see himself through the revelation of the other world. It is a peculiar sensation, this double-consciousness, the sense of always looking at one's self through the eyes of others, of measuring one's soul by the tape of a world that looks on in amused contempt and pity. One ever feels his twoness,—American, a Negro; two souls, two thoughts, two unreconciled strivings, two warring ideals in one dark body, whose dogged strength alone keeps it from being torn asunder. (1969, 45)

On the one hand, to succeed in school is to assimilate and prepare oneself to live in society as it is. On the other hand, to rebel and act out in school is to resist the status quo but often results in a lack of preparation and poor achievement.

Using the social sciences as a theoretical basis, low attainment among black males might be perceived as being either a cultural or a structural phenomenon (Noguera, 2005). If it is cultural, the solution is to examine individual and family values as well as dispositions towards educational advancement. For example, if the individual and family place no value on obtaining a college education, then being successful in school and beyond is not a part of the end goal. Therefore, just improving facilities, hiring better-educated teachers, and offering additional support services will not enhance achievement and educational attainment. However, if the problem were viewed from a structural perspective, then addressing high-risk factors, such as the lack of teachers with degrees in the content area (e.g., mathematics or science), poor health care and nutrition, poor housing, and inadequate schools, would minimize the overall effect of poverty and begin to address achievement gains. The importance of school culture cannot be dismissed as a common thread that repeatedly suggests that the African American male can be successful in playing sports but not at excelling in science or mathematics.

Care must be taken with either approach because some African American males may employ their own "individual choice or agency" in interpreting what constitutes success for them, thereby either accepting or rejecting any interventions. Ogbu (1987) and Fordham (1996) contend that African American males can exhibit oppositional behavior towards achievement. For example, some African American males engage in behavior that marginalizes their success for fear of being perceived as being smart, which ultimately undermines their level of achievement in any subject. Dr. Malveaux puts it best in her article "Culture and Context: The Plight of Black Male Students":

> The same young brothers who scoff at scholarship when they hang out with their "posse" are likely to go home and furtively study, hoping for a ticket out of their stark reality. Too bad they can't lose face enough to invite their friends to study with them. (Malveaux, 2006, 27)

Two studies (Noguera, 2001; Weinstein, Madison, & Kuklinski, 1995) found that African American males, in particular, value how their teachers perceive them. In others words, there is a direct correlation between how students thought their teachers viewed them, either negatively or positively, and the likelihood of success. Male students who had teachers who expressed an interest in them were more likely to succeed. However, finding teachers who can relate to African American males is another issue.

Shortage of Male Teachers

When one examines the history of the teaching profession, we learn that the opportunity for women to teach increased sharply in the nineteenth century because of a fast-growing population and the absence of men during the Civil War (Montecinos & Neilson, 1997; Wiest, 2003). Marked by low salaries and low status, teaching came to be viewed as women's work (Carrington, 2002; Skelton, 2003). Concerns continue to be raised over the "feminization" of teaching and how it may adversely affect the education of boys (Montecinos & Neilson, 1997; Skelton, 2003). There is a need for male teachers in early childhood programs and elementary schools to serve as role models, especially for African American children reared in single-parent homes where the mother is the head of household (Lynn, 2002; Shreffler, 1998).

In a postmodern society that is concerned about diversity in the workforce, we continue to find a shortage of male teachers. Men make up approximately 15–17% of the elementary teachers in the United States, but only 2% of this number work in early childhood settings (birth to age eight) (Carrington, 2002; Cunningham & Watson, 2002; Montecinos & Nielsen, 1997; Skelton, 2003; Wiest, 2003). Lack of recruitment efforts is often cited for the shortage of male teachers at the early childhood and elementary levels (Cunningham & Watson, 2002; Montecinos & Nielsen, 1997). However, societal stereotypes and negative perceptions of male teachers continue to have an impact on the decision of men to teach younger children (Cunningham & Watson, 2002; Dantley, Leonard, & Scott, 2009; Skelton, 2003; Wiest, 2003). The shortage of African American male teachers has an impact on high school dropout rates among African American males (Lynn, 2002).

Dilemmas and Possibilities in Mathematics Education

More than a decade of rhetoric about mathematics equity has not led to equity for students of color and poor students (Martin, 2003). As a result, these students begin to disappear from the mathematics pipeline as early as elementary school (Martin, 2000). Of the numbers that enroll in advanced high school courses, a remnant chooses to major in mathematics at the college level. In 2002, only 0.5% of black college freshman majored in mathematics and only 3.9% (a 33% increase from 2001) of all U.S. Ph.D.s in mathematics were black (Kirkman, Maxwell, & Rose, 2003). While mathematics achievement gains in elementary and middle school are commendable, progress is still very slow.

Unequal resources, lack of high-quality teachers, and tracking (students to vocational and lower-level courses) have a negative impact on standardized test scores and contribute to low achievement in mathematics (Gamoran & Weinstein, 1998). In one study, Rousseau and Tate (2003) examined secondary mathematics teachers' practice in diverse classrooms. They found that white teachers responded to African American males in mathematics classrooms differently than they responded to other students. African American males, in particular, were marginalized and not given help unless they specifically asked for it. They were also not allowed to get help from other students. One African American male was observed simply sitting in class doing nothing for an entire mathematics period. Such differential treatment perpetuates subtle racist practices.

Martin (2000) conducted a qualitative study of middle school students at one school in Oakland, California. He observed three teachers, one female and two males, who used a reform-based curriculum with predominantly African American students. Observations of 35 students throughout the school year revealed different reactions to the school and the mathematics curriculum. Interviews with 7 of the 35 students revealed divergent attitudes about the school environment and their mathematics instruction. One African American male student described his perception of mathematics:

> Math is basically where you're adding things, and subtraction, and dividing. I don't think that in math you're drawing pictures. That's for art. —Carl, seventh grade (Martin, 2000, 103)

This view of mathematics often develops when students' experiences in mathematics classrooms are limited to computation and basic skills. Poor students and students of color are more likely to experience this type of mathematics education (Martin, 2000). When these students are presented with reform-based curriculum or nonroutine problems, they are more likely to shut down and find it difficult to think and reason for themselves (Lubienski, 2000). However, other studies have shown that African American students are motivated to learn mathematics when it is culturally relevant and contextualized in everyday experiences (Leonard, 2008; Malloy & Jones, 1998; Strutchens, 2002). Malloy and Jones (1998) found that middle school students in a summer program were motivated to solve real-world nonroutine word problems that were contextualized in the culture of the community. While some of these problems were very difficult, students persisted and exhibited behaviors that were consistent with those of mainstream students (Malloy & Jones, 1998). Moreover, Berry (2008) found several black male middle school students were successful in mathematics when their parents advocated for them and insisted that they had access to rigorous mathematics courses. Berry's study reveals that social factors, such as family and community support systems, encouraged black males to persist and succeed even when their teachers doubted their ability.

Furthermore, Kitchen, Depree, Celedón-Pattichis, and Brinkerhoff (2007) identify several schools and programs that have been highly effective in educating poor students of color. Their research findings show that middle school students outperform high school students, and charter school students outperform non-charter school students. Observations in high-poverty schools revealed that high achievement outcomes were linked to a close alignment with standards-based instruction. Moreover, teachers tended to actively engage students in learning math in middle and charter schools in comparison to their counterparts in high schools and noncharter schools. These data concur with the findings of Selby (2007), who found that high school teachers in Palm Beach County, Florida, did not engage in standards-based practices in their classrooms even though they believe these practices are advantageous for students. Likewise, Leonard (2002) found that African American students who attended charter schools were generally more motivated and interested in learning because both students and parents had higher expectations of a charter school education.

Specifically, Kitchen, Depree, Celedón-Pattichis, and Brinkerhoff (2007) found that teachers at two charter schools covered mathematics more in-depth and engaged students in high levels of mathematics discourse. Discourse practices such as chorus responses and call and response (Hollins, 1996; Stiff & Harvey, 1988) encourage African American students to communicate and learn in styles that are familiar to them. However, educational inequities, tracking, and lack of cultural relevance do not explain why some poor minority children achieve despite these adverse circumstances (Martin, 2000; Ogbu, 2003). Additional research that investigates the use of culturally specific pedagogy to engage students of color in mathematics at high levels is needed to study the impact of such practices on African American males and females (Leonard, 2008).

Dilemmas and Possibilities in Science Education

In the next 10 years there will be a dramatic change in the demographics of the workforce, where the training of underrepresented groups will become a major endeavor. It is estimated that 1.9 million workers in science will be needed by 2016 (Garcia, 2002; National Science Board [NSB], 2002). As of 1998, only 12% of the total science, technology, engineering, and mathematics (STEM) degrees were awarded to underrepresented groups, including African Americans, Latinos, and Native Americans (NSB, 2002). Although these statistics are alarming, we still grapple with the lack of interest in pursuing STEM careers among all groups. Currently, Caucasian males express the greatest interest and pursuit of careers in science. Regardless of the interested group, there are common criteria that all groups must have to be successful in STEM fields. They include high SAT mathematics scores and high school GPAs, in addition to taking advanced courses in science and mathematics while in high school (Seymour, 1992).

Research studies clearly suggest that having an interest in science is a critical factor in improving African American students' enrollment in science courses. However, a cultural identity that is oppositional to school success will clash with basic preparation in science. For many students, regardless of race or ethnicity, science is a subject that is strange or foreign (Aikenhead, 2001). Yet the culture of science and its basic tenets promote individualism and competition among those who are successful (Dantley, 2004), which is in direct conflict with African American learning styles that tend to promote communalism and cooperative learning (Boykin & Toms, 1985).

Another issue for STEM majors is retention across all groups. Among all fields, science in particular has the lowest retention rates (NSB, 2002). One explanation of the problem lies with the lack of prior science and mathematics preparation in high school. This is especially true for African Americans, a large percentage that take their STEM courses either at community colleges, because of low performance in high school, or in intensive remedial courses at four-year colleges (Feuers, 1990). According to the National Science Foundation (1996), 35% of ethnic minorities who graduated with degrees in science, mathematics, and engineering took science courses at community colleges.

Addressing issues of gender and ethnicity, Garcia, Yu, and Coppola (1993) unpack the psychological factors that could affect gender and ethnic differences associated with science achievement. The sample in their study included 557 college students taking a two-semester sequence of organic chemistry. When gender and ethnic differences in science performance are considered, what stands out are academic preparedness, motivation, and learning strategies (Garcia, Yu, & Coppola, 1993). Findings reveal that the strongest correlates for African American and Hispanic students were prior achievement and motivation. Moreover, Eccles (1984; 1987) found that coupled with a task, motivation becomes the mediator of gender differences in achievement. Haynes, Comer, and Hamilton-Lee (1988) assert that motivation is a strong predictor of achievement for both male and female African American students. In general, motivation or interest in particular educational domains may be the best predictor of persistence in the end (Smith, Sansone, & White, 2007).

Historically, African American males have struggled while moving through the educational system. In science in particular, they show measurable differences on high school GPA, SAT scores, grades on chemistry placement tests, and overall end-of-course grades (Dantley, 2004). All of these variables are strong correlates for success in science. Overall, for African American males and females, background preparation was the most critical factor and predictor for success in science.

According to Aikenhead and Jegede, "The transition from a student's life-world into a science classroom is a cross-cultural experience for most students" (1999, 271). In order to increase African American representation and retention in science courses, teachers need to become cultural brokers to help these students cross cultural borders into school science (Aikenhead, 2001). Crossing cultural borders involves "flexibility, playfulness, and a feeling of ease" on the part of students (Aikenhead & Jegede, 1999, 284). In order to cross borders, collateral learning (the ability to hold two or more conflicting beliefs simultaneously) and resolution of cognitive conflicts (e.g., conflict between Christian faith and evolution) must occur. Studies are needed of how teachers of African American students can create conditions in which these students can cross cultural borders into the culture of science.

Recommendations for Improving Math and Science Achievement

A recent study of predominately African American and Latina/o high school dropouts in the federal Job Corps program revealed that difficulties with mathematics were the primary cause of dropouts (Viadero, 2005). In addition to limited resources, poor instruction, unchallenging work, and tracking into low-level classes, a primary reason for student disaffection and poor performance in mathematics has been the disconnect between the curriculum and students' cultural orientations (Ladson-Billings, 1994; Leonard & Hill, 2008; Malloy & Malloy, 1998). Given these compelling factors, as well as their grave practical consequences (lack of access to jobs, high school attrition, poor literacy rates, etc.), there is a need for programming to address the needs of underserved students (Leonard & Hill, 2008).

One recommendation for raising the mathematics literacy standard is a college preparatory sequence of mathematics for all students in high school (Moses & Cobb, 2001). In order to improve male African American students' achievement and course-taking patterns, mathematics must be purposeful and relevant to their lives, taught in innovative and non-traditional ways, appreciated by the community (families, social groups, churches, and civic organizations), and seen as a road to economic success (Leonard, 2008; Martin, 2003). Children often emulate the beliefs and values of caregivers and the community. Thus, it is incumbent upon the entire community to help African American children develop mathematics identity and mathematics socialization. All institutions in the African American community must cooperate to dispel the notion that achieving in mathematics is synonymous with "acting White" (Martin, 2000; Ogbu, 2003). This view must be obliterated from all aspects of African American life.

Other ways to enhance the development of mathematics identity and mathematics socialization in the African American community are numerous. They include involvement of the Black church, which can play an integral role in mathematics socialization by "mathematizing" Sunday school lessons and sermons whenever the opportunity presents itself (Leonard, 2008). A list of recommendations that can be incorporated with school and home culture include making explicit connections between mathematics and the following:

- Black historical figures (such as Benjamin Banneker and Bessie Coleman)
- Music and art
- Children's literature
- Sports
- Games such as chess and dominoes. (Leonard, 2008)

Clearly, mathematics is in everyday life, and mathematical activity occurs on a daily basis. However, values and beliefs alone cannot reverse the trend of underachievement in mathematics and science among African American males. In addition, policymakers must address disparities in educational opportunities and ensure equitable school funding for poor and African American children (Morris, 2004). Then the spirit of *Brown vs. Board of Education* will be realized, and all children, including African American males, will achieve at higher levels in mathematics.

In terms of science, the National Science Board (2002) recommends that policymakers and curriculum developers revamp the undergraduate STEM curriculum to include more investigative learning, collaborative work, infused technology, and laboratory activities that promote experiences that are culturally relevant to African Americans. In addition, stronger partnerships with two- and four-year colleges should be established to address the retention rates of African Americans in science and mathematics. All of foregoing activities will begin to address the social support that African Americans males and the population, in general, will need in order to be successful in STEM fields.

When one examines the results of NAEP, ACT, and SAT scores, they all indicate the same pattern, that is, poor students consistently attain lower scores than children from more affluent households. Research shows underachievement among African American students even when socioeconomic status (SES) is controlled (Tate, 1997). Moreover, scores generally decline over time, implying that the longer students, regardless of race, are in school the worse they perform. While African American males and females have the lowest achievement in mathematics and science, gender and ethnicity become less important when one examines the impact of high-quality academic preparation, increased motivation, and use of culturally relevant strategies to facilitate successful science and mathematics achievement. More research is needed to identify the instructional practices and contextual factors that can affect underrepresented students by the time they reach middle school and continue through high school (Bruschi & Anderson, 1994).

Specifically, there is a need to study whether curriculum, instructional, and assessment models found in highly effective, high-poverty middle and charter schools are transportable to low-achieving schools with similar demographics across the state of Michigan and the nation (Kitchen, Depree, Celedón-Pattichis, & Brinkerhoff, 2007). In addition, innovative research, such as the use of computers and emerging technology, is crucial in learning how to improve mathematics and science outcomes among underachieving African American students (Leonard, 2008; Leonard & Hill, 2008). Additional funding for research that examines gender outcomes in relation to technology is needed to examine the motivation and performance outcomes of African American males. In summary, improving the performance of African American males in mathematics and science is no panacea. Educators, administrators, researchers, policymakers, and the African American community must collaborate to ensure that African American males are not left behind.

REFERENCES

ACT. (1994). Are our high schools graduates prepared in mathematics and science? (ERIC Document Reproduction Number ED 383 545).

Aikenhead, G. S. (2001). Students' ease in crossing cultural borders in school science. *Science Education, 85*(2), 180–88.

Aikenhead, G. S. & Jegede, O. J. (1999). A cognitive explanation of a cultural phenomenon. *Journal of Research in Science Teaching, 36*(3), 269–87.

Berry, R. Q., III. (2008). Access to upper-level mathematics: The stories of successful African American middle school boys. *Journal for Research in Mathematics, 39*(5), 464–88.

Boykin, A. W. & Toms, F. D. (1985). Black child socialization: A conceptual framework. In H. McAdoo & J. McAdoo (Eds.), *Black children: Social, educational, and parental environments,* 33–51. Beverly Hills, CA: Sage.

Brookover, W. B. & Erickson, E. L. (1969). *Society, schools, and learning.* Boston: Allyn & Bacon.

Brown v. Board of Education. (1954). 347, U.S. 483.

Bruschi, B. A. & Anderson, B. T. (1994). Gender and ethnic differences in science achievement of nine, thirteen, and seventeen year old students. (ERIC Document Reproduction Number ED 382 751).

Campbell, D. (2006, April 21). Addressing the plight of young black men. *The Philadelphia Inquirer,* B1, B10.

Carrington, B. (2002). A quintessentially feminine domain? Student teachers' constructions of primary teaching as a career. *Educational Studies, 28*(3), 287–303.

Coleman, J., Campbell, E., Hobson, C., McPartland, J., Mood, A., & Weinfeld, F. (1966). Equality of educational opportunity. Washington, DC: Government Printing Office.

Cunningham, B. & Watson, L. W. (2002). Recruiting male teachers. *Young Children, 57*(6), 10–15.

Dantley, S. J. (2004). Leaving No Child Left Behind in Science Education. *Black Issues in Higher Education, 21*(8).

Dantley, S. J., Leonard, J., & Scott, W. D. (2009, Spring). Exploring male preservice teachers characteristics and perceptions and teaching elementary school. *The National Journal of Urban Education and Practice,* 2(4), 201–13.

Du Bois, W. E. B. (1969). *The souls of black folk.* 1903; New York: New American Library.

Eccles, J. (1984). Sex differences in achievement patterns. In T. B. Sondereger (Ed.), *Nebraska Symposium on Motivation: Psychology and Gender,* 97–132. Lincoln, NB: University of Nebraska Press.

Eccles, J. (1987). Gender roles and women's achievement-related decisions.

Psychology of Woman Quarterly, 11, 135–72.

Eckholm, E. (2006, March 20). Plight deepens for black men. *New York Times.* Retrieved on April 17, 2006 from http://www.nytimes.com/2006/03/20/nationa12oblackmen.html?r=1&th&emc=th&oref=slogin.

Feuers, S. (1990). Student participation in mathematics and science programs. In D.P. Gallon (Ed.), *Regaining the edge in urban education: Mathematics and sciences.* Washington, D.C.: AACJC Community College Press.

Fordham, S. (1996). *Blacked out: Dilemmas of race, identity, and success at Capital High.* Chicago: University of Chicago Press.

Gabarino, J. (1999). *Lost boys: Why our sons turn to violence and how to save them.* New York: Free Press.

Gamoran, A. & Weinstein, M. (1998). Differentiation and opportunity in restructured schools. *American Journal of Education, 106*(3), 385–415.

Garcia, T. (2002). *Women and minorities in the science, mathematics and engineering pipeline.* (ERIC Document Reproduction Number ED 467 855).

Garcia, T., Yu, S. L., & Coppola, B. P. (1993). *Gender effects in academic cognition, motivation, and achievement.* (ERIC Document Reproduction Number ED 359 235).

Haynes, N. M., Comer, J. P., & Hamilton-Lee, M. (1988). Gender and achievement status differences on learning factors among Black high school students. *Journal of Educational Research, 81,* 233–37.

Hollins, E. R. (1996). *Culture in school learning: Revealing the deep meaning.* Mahwah, NJ: Lawrence Erlbaum.

Kirkman, E. E., Maxwell, J. W., & Rose, C. (2003). 2003 Annual Survey of Mathematical Sciences. [Electronic version]. *Notices of the AMS, 51*(2), 218–33.

Kitchen, R. S., Depree, J., Celedón-Pattichis, S., & Brinkerhoff, J. (2007). *Mathematics education at highly effective schools that serve the poor: Strategies for change.* Mahwah, NJ: Lawrence Erlbaum.

Ladson-Billings, G. (1994). *The dreamkeepers: Successful teachers of African-American children.* San Francisco: Jossey-Bass.

Ladson-Billings, G. (2006). From the achievement gap to the education debt: Understanding achievement in U.S. schools. *Educational Researcher, 35*(7), 3–12.

Leonard, J. (2001). How group composition influenced the achievement of sixth-grade mathematics students. *Mathematical Thinking and Learning, 3*(2&3), 175–200.

Leonard, J. (2002). The case of a first-year charter school. *Urban Education, 37*(2), 217–38.

Leonard, J. (2008). *Culturally specific pedagogy in the mathematics classroom: Strategies for teachers and students.* New York: Taylor & Francis.

Leonard, J. & Hill, M. L. (2008). Using multimedia to engage African American children in classroom discourse. *Journal of Black Studies, 39*(1), 22–42.

Lubienski, S. T. (2000). Problem solving as a means toward mathematics for all: An exploratory look through a class lens. *Journal for Research in Mathematics Education, 31*(4), 454–82.

Lubienski, S. T. & Copur, Y. (2009). *What do national data tell us about equity in mathematics education? Symposium—Equity research a decade in review.* Paper presented at the National Council of Teachers of Mathematics Research Pre-Session, Washington, DC, April 20, 2009.

Lynn, M. (2002). Critical Race Theory and the perspectives of black men teachers in the Los Angeles Public Schools. *Equity & Excellence in Education,* 35(2), 119–30.

Malloy, C. & Jones, G. (1998). An investigation of African American students mathematical problem solving. *Journal for Research in Mathematics Education,* 29(2), 143–63.

Malloy, C. E. & Malloy, W. M. (1998). Issues of culture in mathematics teaching and learning. *The Urban Review, 30*(3), 245–57.

Malveaux, J. (2006). Culture and Context: the Plight of Black Male Students. *Diverse, 23*(5), 27.

Martin, D. B. (2000). *Mathematics success and failure among African-American youth: The roles of sociohistorical context, community forces, school influence, and individual agency.* Mahweh, NJ: Lawrence Erlbaum.

Martin, D. B. (2003). Hidden assumptions and unaddressed questions in *Mathematics for All* rhetoric. *The Mathematics Educator, 13*(2), 7–21.

Michigan School Report Card. (2006). Retrieved on May 20, 2005, from http://www.michigan.gov/mde/0,1607,7-140-22709_25058—,00.html.

Montecinos, C. & Nielson, L. E. (1997). Gender and cohort differences in university students' decisions to become elementary teacher education majors. *Journal of Teacher Education, 48*(1), 47–54.

Morris, J. E. (2004). Can anything good come from Nazareth? Race, class, and African-American schooling and community in the urban south and midwest. *American Educational Research Journal, 41*(1), 69–112.

Morrow, R. A. & Torres, C. A. (1995). *Social theory and education: A critique of theories of social and cultural reproduction.* Albany: SUNY Press.

Moses, R. P. & Cobb, Jr., C. E. (2001). *Radical equations: Math literacy and civil rights.* Boston: Beacon Press.

National Center for Education Statistics. (2004). *The nation's report card.* Retrieved June 16, 2009, from http://nationsreportcard.gov/math_2007/m0009.asp.

National Council of Teachers of Mathematics. (2005). Young students gain on NAEP, scores unchanged for teens. *News Bulletin, 42*(2), 1, 10.

National Science Board. (2002). *Science and engineering indicators—2002.* Report No. NSB-02-1. Arlington, VA: NSB.

National Science Foundation. (1996). *Women, minorities, and persons with disabilities in science and engineering: 1996.* Report No. NSF 96-311. Arlington, VA: NSB..

Noguera, P. (2001). Racial politics and the elusive quest for equity and excellence in education. *Education and Urban Society, 34*(1), 27–42.

Noguera, P. (2005). The trouble with black boys: The role and influence of environmental and cultural factors on the academic performance of African-American males. In F. Olatokunbo (Ed.), *Educating African-American Males: Voices from the field,* 51–78. Thousand Oaks, CA: Corwin Press.

Oakes, J. (1990). *Multiplying inequalities: The effects of race, social class, and tracking on opportunities to learn mathematics and science.* Santa Monica, CA: Rand.

Ogbu, J. U. (1987). Opportunity structure, cultural boundaries, and literacy. In J. Langer (Ed.), *Language, literacy and culture: Issues of society and schooling,* 42–57. Norwood, NJ: Ablex.

Ogbu, J. U. (2003). *Black American students in an affluent suburb: A study of academic disengagement.* Mahweh, NJ: Lawrence Erlbaum.

Rodriguez, A. (1997). *Counting the runners who don't have shoes: Trends in student achievement in science by socioeconomic status and gender within ethnic groups.* Madison: National Institute for Science Education, University of Wisconsin–Madison.

Rousseau, C. & Tate, W. F. (2003). No time like the present: Reflecting on equity in school mathematics. *Theory into Practice, 42*(3), 210–16.

Selby, S. W. (2007). Instructional practices that influence students' mathematical assessment on the FCAT: A study of secondary teachers' practice. Doctoral dissertation, Temple University, 2007.

Seymour, E. (1992). "The Problem Iceberg" in science, mathematics and engineering education: Student explanations for high attrition rates. *Journal of College Science Teaching, 21*(4), 230–38.

Shreffler, M. R. (1998). Raising a village: While male teachers as role models for African American male students. *Journal of Negro Education, 67*(2), 91–95.

Skelton, C. (2003). Male primary teachers and perceptions of masculinity. *Educational Review, 55*(2), 195–209.

Smith, J. L., Sansone, C., & White, P. H. (2007). The stereotyped task engagement process: The role of interest and achievement motivation. *Journal of Educational Psychology, 99*(1), 99–114.

Speight, S. L. (2007). Internalized racism: One more piece of the puzzle. *Counseling Psychologist, 35*, 126. Retrieved on September 17, 2007, from http://tcp.sagepub.com/cgi/reprint/35/1/126.pdf.

Stiff, L. & Harvey, W. B. (1988). On the education of black children in mathematics. *Journal of Black Studies, 19*(2), 190–203.

Strutchens, M. E. (2002). Multicultural literature as a context for problem solving: Children and parents learning together. *Teaching Children Mathematics, 8*(8), 448–54.

Tate, W. F. (1997). Race-ethnicity, SES, gender, and language deficiency trends in mathematics achievement: An update. *Journal for Research in Mathematics Education, 28*(6), 652–79.

Viadero, D. (2005). Transition mathematics project. Retrieved August 12, 2005 from http://www.transitionmathproject.org/marketingarticle.asp.

Warren, B., Ballenger, C., Ogonowski, M., Rosebery, A. S., & Hudicourt-Barnes, J. (2001). Rethinking diversity in learning science: The logic of everyday sense-making. *Journal of Research in Science Teaching, 38*(5), 529–52.

Weinstein, R. S., Madison, S., & Kuklinski, M. (1995). Raising expectations in schooling: Obstacles and opportunities for change. *American Educational Research Journal, 32*(1), 121–59.

Wiest, L. R. (2003). The current status of male teachers of young children. *Educational Forum, 68*(1), 62–70.

Access to Technology in the Twenty-first Century

IMPLICATIONS OF THE DIGITAL DIVIDE
FOR AFRICAN AMERICAN MALES

Toni Stokes Jones *and* Nancy Copeland

Legislation such as No Child Left Behind requires that all American students have access to technology and that all their teachers be prepared to utilize technology in the classroom so that their students can be technology literate by the time they finish the eighth grade (U.S. Department of Education, 2006). Infusing technology into education is also a pressing issue for educational leaders in other developed countries (e.g., Canada, European Union, United Kingdom, France, Australia, and Italy) as well as less-developed countries (e.g., Philippines, Chile, Singapore, Costa Rica). This chapter addresses issues of digital equity as they relate to African American students and their global counterparts. It also examines students' information communication technology (ICT) access in schools and homes in the United States and abroad. This chapter will discuss African American males' access to ICT.

How Technology Influences the Digital Divide

Information communication technology (ICT) refers to desktop and laptop computers, handheld computers (or personal digital assistants/PDAs), and cell phones that allow access to the Internet via various methods (e.g., telephone lines, broadband or wireless connections). Many countries have made tremendous gains in providing students with access to ICT in schools, homes, workplaces, and public facilities. It is important to note, however, that the method by which ICT access is achieved is based on a number of factors, including economics, social status, geographic location, technological infrastructure, and in some cases race/ethnicity.

The United States is a leader in providing access to ICT, yet as more U.S. schools recognize the need to integrate ICT into their classrooms concerns over the unequal distribution of access to technology mount and grow. The phrase *digital divide* was coined to refer to this gap between the technology "haves" and "have-nots" (Norris, cited in Jackson et al., 2003). Affluent schools, typically in suburban areas, have already created technology-rich learning environments for their students, but schools in many urban and rural districts were late to join the digital revolution. Subsequently, students at ICT-poor schools have little or no access to the information technologies that were touted to substantially improve their academic achievement and better prepare them for the world of work in the twenty-first century. Worse still, the patterns of unequal access are typically seen along racial and economic lines, with urban and rural schools that have significant African American or high-poverty populations falling into the "have-not" category.

The digital divide exists in developing countries for similar reasons. In those nations, private schools are often better funded and as a result have access to state-of-the-art ICT, whereas public or government schools have less funding and less access. Moreover, the requirements for an adequate technological infrastructure are often not present in developing countries. Low rates of literacy are additional technology barriers in these nations and, as such, make it difficult for their school populations to engage in ICT. For example, in countries like South Africa, where the technological infrastructure is available and access to the Internet is growing, wealthy Whites—who comprise the minority—are the predominant "haves" (Kirkman, 2003).

Reasons for Including Technology in Education

In the United States, the Partnership for 21st Century Skills (2006) includes ICT literacy as one of six components necessary to improve the quality of education, make high school more rigorous, and enable high school students to "use technology to learn content and skills—so that they know how to learn, think critically, solve problems, use information, communicate, innovate and collaborate." Similarly, educational policy in Canada is set separately by each of the provincial and territorial legislatures, and both the central government and the various legislatures see the need for ICT in schools, and for many of the same reasons that are espoused in the United States. The Conference Board of Canada also maintains that ICT, especially the Internet, is a "valuable source of the information and knowledge [Canadian youth] need to improve their employability skills" (2001, 10–11). Likewise, Australia and the United Kingdom value the use of ICT to support student learning. According to Bruniges (n.d.), one of the goals of education in Australia is to have students leave school being "confident, creative and productive uses of new technologies." The United Kingdom's national curriculum requires that all students be "given opportunities to apply and develop their ICT capability, through the use of ICT tools to support their learning in all subjects" except physical education (Edwyn, 2001, 21). Each of the above-noted countries also aims to reduce its own national digital divide related to lack of access to ICT.

New Zealand has also recognized the need for ICT in schools and has a broad goal of enhancing "the development of students' knowledge, understandings, skills, and attitudes through the appropriate and effective use of ICT" (*ICT Strategy for Schools, 2002–2004: New Zealand,* 2004). Furthermore, the International School Manila (ISM)—a private, nonprofit, coeducational institution consisting of an elementary, middle, and high school in the Philippines—asserts that its "curriculum is technologically current for students" and that all its school personnel "use information technology as a learning tool" (Thew, 2000, 6).

The United World College of South East Asia (UWCSEA), a boarding school in Singapore, has similar aspirations for its students. Like ISM, the UWCSEA comprises elementary, middle, and high school grade levels. Technology is integrated into its curriculum to support UWCSEA's largely computer-literate student body, and "it is expected that by age 13 the majority of students will have basic knowledge and confidence in a full range of I.C.T. skills" (Thew, 2000, 12). Thew notes that another school in Southeast Asia, the Singapore American School, for Americans living in that nation, supports ICT as a part of its overall school environment. There, "The important place of I.C.T. is established, resourced and organized" (16). Similarly, both the Nigerian and South African governments recognize that ICT benefits students and teachers as well as families and nations. In 2001, the Nigerian government announced its intention to "to make Nigeria an IT [information technology]-capable country in Africa and a key player in the information society by the year 2005" (Kirkman, 2003). The South African government has also made significant strides in providing improved ICT access, albeit largely to wealthy Whites (Kirkman, 2003).

Clearly, both developed and developing countries see the need for integrating ICT into education. The developing country of Chile reasons that ICT supports a new society that requires new skills. As technology is prevalent in all aspects of life, ICT can help to enhance productivity and support efforts to "create more effective learning environments" (Hepp et al., 2004, 1). Cawthera (2002) cites two main reasons for computers in schools: (1) They provide a cost-effective way of improving the quality of and access to education; and (2) information communication and technology are important to the future of any economy and therefore demand attention in schools.

Access to Technology: Policy versus Reality

Many nations recognize the need for their students and teachers to utilize technology to support and enhance the quality and effectiveness of learning—and they all want to use ICT to do so. In these nations, families are encouraged to have ICT equipment (in particular, computers with Internet access) in their homes, but is this the reality or just policy? Data from the United Nations (2004) and the U.S. Central Intelligence Agency (2006) show that the number of Internet users in developed and developing countries increased overall from 2001 to 2005 (see table 1). Moreover, what about access to ICT in developing countries as it relates to gender? Little or no data regarding that are available. Indeed, mention of gender and ICT in developing countries most often indicates that girls have less access not only to ICT but also to education than do boys (Isaac, 2002; Key Literacy Statistics, 2006). For these reasons, this chapter will devote only minimal discussion to the access to technology according to gender, especially in developing countries.

Developing Country: Chile
Since 1992 Chile has been a leader in South America with regard to educational use of and access to ICT. In that year, Chile established a goal of providing Internet access to all 10,000 of its public schools. The Chilean Ministry of Education teamed

TABLE 1. NUMBER OF INTERNET USERS BY COUNTRY, 2001 AND 2005

	NUMBER OF INTERNET USERS		INCREASE
	2001*	2005†	
DEVELOPING COUNTRIES			
Chile†	3,102,200	5,600,000§	45%
Philippines	2,000,000	7,820,000	74%
Nigeria	200,000	1,768,700	89%
Jamaica†	100,000	1,067,000	91%
South Africa	2,890,000	3,600,000	20%
DEVELOPED COUNTRIES			
United States	155,000,000	203,824,428	24%
United Kingdom	24,000,000	37,800,000	37%
France	18,716,000	26,214,174	29%
Canada	15,200,000	20,900,000	27%
Australia	8,400,000	14,189,544	41%
Singapore	2,247,000	2,421,800	7%
New Zealand	1,908,000	3,200,000	40%

* Data is most often received from the Telecommunications Ministry or regulatory agency in each country in response to an annual questionnaire. Estimates are derived from Internet Service Provider (ISP) subscriber counts. When country data are not available estimates are obtained by taking old data from previous years or from market research and multiplying them by some factor to obtain an estimate of current Internet users. Most recent data: 2002. SOURCE: International Telecommunication Union, World Telecommunication Indicators (Geneva 2002). Retrieved from http://cyberschoolbus.un.org/infonation3/menu/advanced.asp, May 12, 2006.

† Statistics may include users who access the Internet at least several times a week to those who access it only once within a period of several months. SOURCE: Retrieved from http://odci.gov/cia/publications/factbook/docs/notesanddefs.html#2153 on May 12, 2006.

§ Data as of 2004.

up with telecommunications companies to ensure that over 90% of Chilean students had access to an Internet-accessible computer in their school. One outcome of these collaborative efforts was Enlaces, which implemented an ICT teacher-training program. Through Enlaces, "Staff members at more than 20 universities throughout Chile have helped train about 70,000 public school teachers in how to use technology to improve instruction" (Gehring, 2004, 3).

According to the 2002 Chilean national census, 20.5% of households had a computer in the home, yet only 10.2% had Internet access. By 2004, a substantial percentage of Chilean teachers used computers in the classroom as well as at home. Chilean teachers were provided training in the use of ICT to support student learning, which alleviated their own anxieties about using technology in the classroom. As a result, more students in rural schools had increased access to ICT and were engaged in learning content using ICT. Another program created by the Enlaces team is Wordarium, which supports the development of language arts skills for third- through eighth-grade students by enabling them to create a dictionary of words they use but are not found in dictionaries (Laval & Flores, 1995).

Another Enlaces program created in a Chilean school, For Knowing and Telling, is a language arts program that led to the publication of a widely distributed story that students from other schools were enlisted to finish (Laval & Flores, 1995).

The overall ICT picture in Chile is this: (1) the numbers of households with Internet access are not significant but growing; (2) most ICT is located in computer labs and not actual classrooms—that is, not every classroom or student has a computer with or without Internet access; (3) teachers' use of ICT can be categorized as communication, teaching, and technical; and (4) students' use of ICT can be categorized as communication, productivity, and recreation.

Developing Country: Jamaica

Jamaica, like many other developing countries, lacks the technological infrastructure to provide universal access to ICT. Jamaica has low digital literacy but high aspirations for digital access. Although Jamaica is a latecomer to integrating ICT in education, it is dedicated to fully integrating ICT into its system of education. Through the efforts of Jamaica 2000, a private-public partnership in education, 170 of 250 Jamaican high schools had computer labs in 2002 (Kirkman, 2003).

In January 2003, Jamaica's Berkman Center for Internet and Society, in collaboration with the Jamaican Ministry of Industry, Commerce, and Technology and other local organizations, initiated a computer-based learning pilot project in that island nation's schools. The goal of the project was to draw youth into technology through creative innovations (Berkman Center for Internet and Society, n.d.). In 2004, the National Housing Trust and the Jamaica Computer Society Education Foundation were responsible for ensuring that 19 schools each "received between 5 and 15 computers, air-conditioning units, desks and chairs, uninterruptible power supplies and training, among other benefits" (*NHT Computers in Education Project*, 2004).

Developed Country: United Kingdom

Increased access to ICT is becoming a reality for teachers, students, and families in the United Kingdom. Government initiatives have enabled more schools to have broadband connections and wireless laptops, provide teacher training to integrate technology in their curriculum, and identify ways to increase ICT access outside of schools. Reportedly, teachers in the UK are more confident teaching with technology, and students' achievement levels and engagement with ICT is increasing (Office of Her Majesty's Chief Inspector of Schools, 2002).

The 2002 inspector's report points out that during a literacy hour/lesson teachers enabled students to practice phonics with a focus on initial sounds and consonant-vowel-consonant words and then to work independently at their computers. That lesson, the report further states, "was directly linked to the National Literacy Strategy. The activities challenged pupils well, both in terms of increasing their literacy knowledge and understanding, and by reinforcing their ICT skills" (10).

Although government initiatives in the UK have had positive effects, they are not without problems. For example, "Too many schools still have difficulty in managing their ICT resources and struggle to increase pupils' ICT competence, let alone use this across the curriculum" (Office of Her Majesty's Chief Inspector of Schools, 2002, 13). Additionally, that report notes, lesson objectives are not always adequately supported by ICT, and students sometimes are left unattended at the computer for long periods, among other issues.

Developed Country: Australia

Most primary and secondary schools in Australia have Internet access (Kirkman, 2003). Australia's National Education Performance Monitoring Taskforce released positive findings regarding ICT in that nation's schools in 2000. Its findings indicated the following:

> 71 percent of Australian schools had a student-computer ratio of 15:1 or less and this ratio is decreasing each year; 37 percent of the computers in schools were in laboratories and 31 percent in classrooms; laptop computers comprised 16 percent of all computers used for educational purposes in schools—most of these in the non-government school sector; . . . secondary schools generally had lower student-computer ratios than primary, common applications in schools included integrated packages, reference CDs, educational games and virus protection. (Bruniges, n.d.)

The Australian Programme for International Student Assessment survey of 2000 also reported positive findings for Australia compared to other Organisation for Economic Co-operation and Development countries (i.e., developed countries).

For example, 85% of Australian students had access to computers at home almost daily, 9% reported never having access to computers at home, 43% used a computer almost daily at home, and a little over 31% accessed the Internet daily (Bruniges, n.d.). Moreover, most Australian teachers reported feeling confident integrating technology in their classroom and indicated they had been using ICT and participating in professional development on the subject for over five years.

One would think that these impressive findings about ICT access would extend to Australia's indigenous and disadvantaged population, but this is not the case (Blackmore et al., 2003). These students are faced with barriers to ICT access similar to those of their low-income, rural, and inner-city African American counterparts in the United States. Remote and rural living conditions, poor technological infrastructure, and low literacy rates contribute to the digital divide "down under." Classrooms and pedagogy that lack ICT integration, coupled with low parental involvement and dwindling employment opportunities, contribute to digital literacy and ICT access being in short supply for Australia's indigenous, special needs students. Each of these conditions leaves the students in disadvantaged circumstances. 'Disadvantaged' is better understood as the cumulative effect of a complex conjuncture of factors. Groups traditionally understood to be disadvantaged in Australia are rural and isolated students, Indigenous students, students with disability, children of non-English speaking background and girls. But it is not a disadvantage *per se* to be male or to be female, to be an Aboriginal, or to have physical or intellectual disabilities" (Blackmore et al., 2003). Moreover, teachers of indigenous students in Australia are often less comfortable integrating technology into the curriculum and have less access to professional development that would ensure their capacity to support the culturally favored modes of communication—music, word, and visual graphics—of indigenous groups.

Often the issues of ICT access in Australia (and across the global community) relate to socioeconomic disparities that intertwine with race/ethnicity and gender. However, the literature reveals a need for greater access for indigenous, special needs, and other disadvantaged students in Australia (Blackmore et al., 2003; Le@rning Federation, 2000). An example of integrating ICT in the curriculum with indigenous kindergarten and first-grade students in a community in Western Australia suggests that when given "frequent use of the computer and other technology (e.g., the digital camera) to enhance language learning, students demonstrated movement along the Reading and Writing First Steps Developmental Continuum (oral language, reading, writing and spelling)" (Blackmore et al., 2003).

Regarding gender, indigenous male students in Australia have been found to use computers differently from their female counterparts (Blackmore et al., 2003). Moreover, these boys report being especially interested in using and learning with ICT and often do well when learning with ICT. They also report being more comfortable using computers, are more engaged with ICT, and use it more often at home and in school when it is present.

Developed Country: United States

Although the United States is a leader in providing ICT access to its citizens, the conclusions of the U.S. Department of Education (2006), the U.S. Department of Commerce's National Telecommunications and Information Administration (1995, 1998), and other entities that focus on ICT access reveal a vast disparity among racial/ethnic groups and social classes in the United States. American schools serving primarily racial/ethnic minorities or high-poverty communities were found to have the least access to the Internet. Civil rights leader Jesse Jackson has likened this situation to "digital apartheid," reflecting the egregious social divides along racial lines of the past (Peters, 2001, 25). Pinkett (2001) suggests that providing all Americans with equal access to ICT resources could become a key civil rights issue of twenty-first-century America.

In the 1990s, concerned that the nation's poor and non-White communities would fall further behind in ICT access, President Clinton launched "a national mission to ensure that every student in every school will be technologically literate in the 21st century" (Riley, 1996). As a result, billions of dollars in federal funds were earmarked for U.S. schools to equip themselves with "modern computers, high quality educational software, trained teachers, and affordable connections to the Internet."

Since then, substantial progress has been made to ensure that all U.S. students have equitable access to ICT resources. Reports from the National Center for Education Statistics (2004) indicate that virtually every American public school (99.5%) has Internet access, including 93% of instructional rooms (classrooms, libraries, and computer labs), and that only a slight gap remains between the "haves" and "have-nots" in this nation. Student/computer ratios are an important gauge of student access to ICT. Averaging 4.4 computers per student, U.S. schools have ample

TABLE 2. PERCENTAGE OF U.S. SCHOOLS WITH INTERNET ACCESS, 2003

	IN SCHOOLS	IN INSTRUCTION ROOMS	STUDENTS PER INSTRUCTION ROOM COMPUTER
All schools	99.5%	93.0%	4.4
High minority schools (> 50%)	99.5%	92.0%	5.1
High poverty (> 75% free/reduced lunch)*	99.0%	90.0%	5.1

* Some data not available for all schools.

infrastructure to engage students with technology. Those enrolling large numbers of minority and low-income students also have considerable Internet access and similar student/computer ratios. Reports such as these fuel the belief that the digital divide crisis is over and should no longer be at the forefront of the national agenda (Arrison, 2002). Table 2 summarizes the U.S. ICT access data.

The picture is somewhat different, however, when access to ICT beyond schools is considered. In that regard, digital inequities along racial, economic, and educational lines are readily apparent:

- 60% of African Americans have a home Internet connection, compared to 74% of White Americans.
- 57% of African Americans report going online frequently, compared to 70% of Whites.
- 29% of Americans who have not graduated from high school, compared to 61% of high school graduates and 89% of college graduates, have never gone online. (Pew Internet and American Life Project, 2005)

Mossberger, Tolbert, and Stansbury (as cited in Mossberger, Tolbert, & Gilbert, 2004) found similar inequities in ICT access and use based on ethnicity, geographic location, and socioeconomic status. However, home access to ICT by gender was found to be virtually the same across all racial/ethnic groups with one exception: African American males use the Internet slightly less frequently (a difference of just two percentage points) than African American females (Mossberger, Tolbert, & Gilbert, 2004; U.S. Department of Education, 2006).

The prevalence of broadband may cause a new divide between those who have faster Internet connections (e.g., cable modems, DSL, wireless broadband) in the United States and those who have dial-up or no connectivity. According to a U.S. Department of Commerce (2004a) report, the American online experience is significantly enhanced with a faster connection:

> Broadband users are more likely to use the Internet more frequently and in a wider variety of ways. Among Internet users, those with broadband connections at home are more likely to be daily Internet users (66.1%) than those with dial-up service (51.1%). Persons with broadband at home also engage in more types of activities online.

American students use the Internet for a variety of school tasks including research, writing papers, homework help, and communicating with classmates (Levin & Arafeh, 2002). If access at home is limited to slower-speed connections, chances are that these students will use the Internet less frequently.

Socioeconomic status and locale are critical factors in understanding ICT inequities for urban African American males with high dropout and low literacy rates. When high-speed access is available—although the Pew Internet and American Life Project (2005) indicates that fewer than 25% of lower-income families have such access—Internet use may be limited because low reading comprehension (Mossberger, Tolbert, & Gilbert, 2004). Moreover, ICT access in public facilities such as libraries may also be limited because of decreased local funding and lower-quality services (fewer or older computers). Friends and relatives who have Internet service are another source of access, yet in lower-income communities individual social networks are more likely to include unemployed and less-educated members who also lack Internet access. Thirteen percent of African Americans had broadband connections at home in 2004 (Horrigan, 2004).

ACCESS TO TECHNOLOGY: STATE OF MICHIGAN

The overall level of ICT access in Michigan's schools parallels national trends showing increased computer and Internet access (see table 3); however, Michigan's high-minority and low-income schools do not fare as well (Park & Staresina, 2004). Virtually all schools in the state have Internet access (97%), as do nearly all instructional classrooms (89%); yet Michigan's high-minority schools have less access overall (95%) and specifically in classrooms (81%). Similarly, 95%

TABLE 3. PERCENTAGE OF SCHOOLS IN MICHIGAN AND NATIONWIDE WITH INTERNET ACCESS, 2003

TECHNOLOGY ACCESS	INTERNET		SCHOOLS W/ BROADBAND	STUDENTS PER INTERNET-CONNECTED COMPUTER
	IN SCHOOL	IN CLASSROOMS		
Statewide	97.0%	89.0%	73.0%	4.2
Nationally	99.5%	93.0%	95.0%*	4.4
Instructional classrooms	n/a	n/a	n/a	10.4
High-minority schools (> 50%)†	95.0%	85.0%	65.0%	5.5
High-poverty (> 75% free/reduced lunch)†	95.0%	81.0%	68.0%	6.0

NOTE: The high percentages may be the result of how data are reported.

† Some data not available for all schools.

of low-income schools in the state have Internet connections, yet only 85% of instructional classrooms have them. The ratio of students per computer for such schools also falls short of national (4.4:1) and statewide (4.2:1) levels.

According to a report presented at the Michigan State Policy Network Education Policy Forum (Bhanpuri, 2003), half of Michigan's 216 low-performing schools are located in urban areas, and 86% are high-minority schools. Detroit, the largest city in the state, houses a significant concentration of African Americans (84.5%); indeed, 14% of African Americans nationwide reside in the state of Michigan, and African American students comprise 20% of the Michigan public school student population. Students in high-minority schools in Michigan actually have fewer chances to use the Internet because they typically share their schools' computers with more students (6:1). This is also true of low-income schools (5.5:1). Given that technology is most effective when integrated into settings where learning occurs most—that is, in the school classroom—and because these students may share a computer with as many as 10 others, they therefore have fewer opportunities to use ICT resources to supplement their learning (Park & Staresina, 2004).

Although the exact nature of the impact of ICT on student achievement is difficult to determine given the numerous confounding factors involved, several studies have shown that improvement in student performance occurs when technology use is closely tied to curriculum standards (Center for Applied Research in Educational Technology, n.d.). This finding could present an opportunity for improving the annual yearly progress of low-performing schools in Michigan.

Michigan is one of only a handful of states to fund personal digital assistants

(PDAs) and laptops for schools, exceeding the national average by several percentage points: for example, respectively, it funds PDAs and laptops at 8.6% and 20.5% Michigan schools compared to 7.6% and 12.4% nationally (Park & Staresina, 2004). This may have positive implications for students of color if in fact their teachers are able to use the PDAs and laptops to increase student access in the classroom. Budgetary constraints have eliminated state-level funding for these resources (they were federally funded in 2004).

Data from the U.S. Bureau of the Census (2004) suggest that income and education also predict Internet use. In Michigan, 17% of African American households earn less than $25,000 and thus are considered low-income. Because poor households have less access to ICT and African American households are disproportionately poor, African American males are less likely to have a computer or Internet access at home or to have the skills necessary to use ICT resources effectively. One study of Internet use by 123 Michigan low-income adults, who received Internet access for the first time through the study, found race, age, and income to be strong predictors of use (Jackson et al., 2003). Lacking appropriate knowledge and skill, many of the study's participants became frustrated and subsequently limited their Internet use.

Increasingly, however, African Americans are going online, nationally and in Michigan. A 2000 survey of the state's residents reported 60% as having gone online (Wilson, 2000) This percentage is higher today. Presumably, increased access to computers, the Internet, and other ICT resources, in Michigan and elsewhere in the U.S., will continue to rise as the cost for equipment and Internet services lessens, narrowing the digital gap even further. Thus, educators, parents, community leaders, and other technology decision makers should rethink the traditional idea of digital equity that looks primarily at access. They should instead examine ways to foster inclusion by looking at the digital divide from a "use" perspective, determining the influence of culture and place on ICT attitudes and use, particularly for African American males.

Policy Recommendations and Implications for Practice

Although the data reported in this chapter were based primarily on findings from studies published earlier in the twenty-first century, we expect that ICT access and use in the United States will continue to grow. The following are our recommendations for improving ICT access and use for African American males and all others adversely affected by the digital divide:

- The most obvious recommendation, and perhaps the most difficult to accomplish, is that school districts seek supplemental funding either through corporate and philanthropic sponsors or through state or federal grants to help them lower the student-computer ratio—ideally to the 3:1 range—and provide students with access to state-of-the-art ICT, particularly emerging technologies.
- Although the digital divide has narrowed and African Americans are close to having ICT access equal to White Americans, steps must be taken now to address the new digital divide: that related to the use of ICT via broadband and wireless connections. These means of connecting to the Internet are crucial to fostering broader ICT access and supporting learning.
- The federal government and telecommunications providers alike should enter into pacts with the nation's public schools and their surrounding communities to facilitate quick and reliable universal access for students and their families.
- Funding for the Enhancing Education through Technology program should be restored to at least FY05 funding levels.
- More after-school and weekend programs that target and encourage African American males to be more proficient users of ICT should be established or expanded.
- ICT professional development opportunities for teachers should be expanded, specifically just-in-time professional development (JITPD) in the form of online training. An ideal solution is to provide teachers with on-site technology specialists trained in instructional design and technology integration who can offer face-to-face instruction during times convenient for most teachers.
- Teachers should be taught how to communicate the importance of ICT to minority parents, many of whom in urban areas are single females with multiple offspring. Schools should provide a small stipend, childcare, or meals for families whose parents participate in ICT training.
- Provide additional support to assist parents in purchasing computers, PDAs, Internet-ready cells phones, and other ICT equipment for students' home use.
- Improve the cultural diversity of the Internet—when students see resources and materials that reflect who they are and how they think and live, they are more apt to see the Internet as a credible resource.

- Scholars need to conduct more research on digital literacy (i.e., access, use, pedagogy, and economics) in African American and other culturally diverse communities.

One very disturbing reality is that improving access to and use of twenty-first-century ICT by and for African American males does not appear to be a priority item on any national, regional, or local educational reform agenda. Most of the extant research examines the use of ICT overall by race far more than by gender; and when looking at access by gender the focus is largely on girls, less on males, and even less on race *and* gender. More research is needed to determine exactly which digital equities exist for African American males. More urgently, however, more educators must assume responsibility for ensuring that inequities of any kind, especially for African American males, are extinguished.

REFERENCES

Arrison, S. (2002). *C/Net News.com.* Retrieved from http://news.zdnet.com/2100-9595_22-858660.html.

Berkman Center for Internet and Society. (n.d.). *Module III learning.* Retrieved May 19, 2006, from http://cyber.law.harvard.edu/bold/deve103/modules/episodeIII.html.

Bhanpuri, H. (2003). *Policies and programs to support Michigan's highest priority schools.* Michigan State Policy Network Education Policy Forum. Lansing, MI. Retrieved May 19, 2006, from http://www.ncrel.org/policy/states/files/mispf03.htm.

Blackmore, J., Hardcastle, L., Bamblett, E., & Owens, J. (2003). *Effective use of information and communication technology (ICT) to enhance learning for disadvantaged school students.* Retrieved May 19, 2006, from http://www.dest.gov.au/sectors/school_education/publications_resources/profiles/effective_use_technology_enhance_learning.htm.

Bruniges, M. (n.d.). *Developing performance indicators for ICT in education, New South Wales Department of Education and Training.* Retrieved May 11, 2006, from http://www.Unescobkk.org/fileadmin/user_upload/ict/e-books/

ICTindicators/ICTinEdchap41.pdf.

Cawthera, A. (2002). *Computers in secondary schools in developing countries: Costs and other issues.* Department for International Development, World Links for Development, and the Human Development Network of the World Bank.

Center for Applied Research in Educational Technology. (n.d.). *Topic: Student learning.* Retrieved May 19, 2006, from http://caret.iste.org/index.cfm?fuseaction=evidence&answerID=1%23references#references.

Conference Board of Canada. (2001). *Performance and potential 2000–2001: Seeking made in Canada.* Retrieved May 16, 2002, from http://sso.conferenceboard.ca/e-Library/LayoutAbstract.asp?DID=255.

Edwyn, J. (2001). *Learning to change: ICT in schools.* Paris: Organization for Economic Cooperation and Development.

Gehring, J. (2004). South America. In *Technology counts '04—Global Links: Lessons from the world.* Retrieved May 16, 2006, from http://counts.edweek.org/sreports/tc04/article.cfm?slug=35s_America.h23.

Hepp, P., Hinostroze, E., Laval, E., & Rehbein, L. (2004). *Technology in schools: Education, ICT, and the knowledge society.* Retrieved May 9, 2006, from http://www1.worldbank.org/education/pdf/ICT_report_octo4a.pdf.

Horrigan, J. (2004). *Trends in Internet adoption and use: Comparing minority groups.* Presented to Pew Internet & American Life Project, May 14, 2006. Retrieved May 20, 2006, from www.pewinternet.org/ppt/Horrigan.OTX.ppt.

ICT strategy for schools, 2002–2004: New Zealand. (2004). Retrieved May 9, 2006, from http://www.logos-net.net/ilo/150_base/en/init/nzl_2.htm#kuva.

Isaac, S. (2002, November). It's hot for girls! ICT as an instrument in advancing girls' and women's capabilities in school education in Africa. Paper presented at the United National Division for the Advancement of Women Expert Group Meeting "Information and Communication Technologies and Their Impact On and Use as an Instrument for the Advancement and Empowerment of Women," Seoul.

Jackson, L. A., Barbatsis, G., von Eye, A., Biocca, F., Zhao, Y., & Fitzgerald, H. (2003). Internet use in low-income families: Implications for the digital divide. *IT & Society, 1*(5), 141–65.

Key Literacy Statistics. (2006). *International statistics: Gender.* Retrieved May 14, 2006, from http://www.literacytrust.org.uk/Database/stats/keystatsadult. html#genderrelated.

Kirkman, G. (Ed.). (2003). *Global information technology report, 2001–2002: Readiness for the networked world—75 country profiles.* Berkman Center for Internet and Society: The World Bank Institute. Retrieved May 13, 2006, from http://cyber.law.harvard.edu/itg/libpubs/profiles.html.

Laval, E. & Flores, L. (1995). *Educational projects using networks in Chilean elementary schools.* Retrieved May 17, 2006, from http://www.isoc.org/ HMP/PAPER/138/html/paper.html.

Le@rning Federation, 2000, education.au limited, and Curriculum Corporation. (2000). *Strategy for Generating Online Curriculum Content for Australian Schools.* Retrieved May 20, 2006, from http://www.icttaskforce.edna. edu.au/icttaskforce/Jahia/home/pid/21.

Levin, D. & Arafeh, S. (2002). *The digital disconnect: The widening gap between Internet savvy students and their schools.* Pew Internet and American Life Project. Retrieved May 19, 2006, from http://www.pewinternet.org/pdfs/ PIP_Schools_Internet_Report.pdf.

Mossberger, K., Tolbert, C. J., & Gilbert, M. (2006). Race, place, and technology. *Urban Affairs Review, 41*(5), 583–620.

NHT computers in education project. (2004). Retrieved May 19, 2006, from http:// www.ict4djamaica.org/content/home/index.htm.

Office of Her Majesty's Chief Inspector of Schools. (2002). *ICT in schools: Effect of government initiatives—Pupil achievement.* Progress Report, 2002. Retrieved May 13, 2006, from http://www.ofsted.gov.uk/publications/docs/19.pdf.

Park, J. & Staresina, L. N. (2004,). Tracking trends: Technology counts 2004. *Education Week,* May 6. Retrieved May 18, 2006, from http://counts. edweek.org/sreports/tc04/article.cfm?slug=35tracking.h23.

Partnership for 21st Century Skills. (2006). *Results that matter: 21st-century skills and high school reform.* Retrieved May 8, 2006, from http://www .21stcenturyskills.org/.

Peters, T. (Ed.) (2001). *Spanning the digital divide: Understand and tackling the issues.* Published by bridges.org. Retrieved May 16, 2006, from http:// www.bridges.org/publications/65.

Pew Internet and American Life Project. (2005). *Digital divisions.* Retrieved May 16, 2006, from http://www.pewinternet.org/Reports/2005/Digital-Divisions.aspx.

Pinkett, R. D. (2001). Redefining the digital divide. *Teaching to Change LA, 1*(2). Retrieved May 16, 2006, from http://www.tcla.gseis.ucla.edu/divide/politics/pinkett.html.

Riley, R. W. (1996). U.S. Department of Education Secretary, personal communication to Chief State School Officer. Retrieved May 16, 2006, from *Archived Information* at http://www.ed.gov/Technology/TLCF/ltr.html.

Thew, E. L. P. (2000). Information and communication technology in schools: An international perspective—an investigation of school based technology programmes 2000. Minolta Report. Manurewa Central School, Manurewa, Auckland, New Zealand.

United Nations, (2004). *School cyberbus: Information advanced.* Retrieved May 12, 2006, from http://cyberschoolbus.un.org/infonation3/menu/advanced.asp.

U.S. Bureau of the Census. (2003). *Current population reports: Computer and Internet use in the United States.* Retrieved May 18, 2006, from http://www.census.gov/population/www/socdemo/computer.html.

U.S. Central Intelligence Agency. (2006). *The world fact book.* Retrieved May 12, 2006, from http://www.cia.gov/cia/publications/factbook/rankorder/2001rank.html.

U.S. Department of Commerce, National Telecommunications and Information Administration. (1995). *Falling through the net: A survey of the "have nots" in rural and urban America.* Retrieved May 14, 2006, from http://www.ntia.doc.gov/ntiahome/fallingthru.html.

U.S. Department of Commerce, National Telecommunications and Information Administration. (1998). *Falling through the net II: New data on the digital divide.* Retrieved May 14, 2006, from http://www.ntia.doc.gov/ntiahome/net2/.

U.S. Department of Commerce, National Telecommunications and Information Administration. (2004a). *A nation online: Entering the broadband age.* Retrieved May 18, 2006, from http://www.ntia.doc.gov/ntiahome/dn/index.html.

U.S. Department of Commerce, National Telecommunications and Information Administration. (2004b). *A nation online: How Americans are expanding their use of the Internet.* Retrieved May 14, 2006, from http://www.ntia. doc.gov/ntiahome/dn/index.html.

U.S. Department of Education. (2006). *Educational technology fact sheet.* Retrieved May 4, 2006, from http://www.ed.gov/about/offices/list/os/technology/ facts.html.

Wilson, M. I. (2000). *The knowledge economy and distressed communities III: Internet access and use.* Retrieved May 4, 2006, from https://www.msu. edu/user/wilsonmm/Smart/reports.htm.

All Dressed Up with
No Place to Go

HIGH SCHOOL GRADUATION REFORM AND
MICHIGAN'S AFRICAN AMERICAN MALES

Vernon C. Polite, Cheryl Price, *and* Kristy Lisle

Poor high school graduation rates are a matter of grave concern at both the national and state levels. Nationally, the high school graduation rate for European American students is 78%; for Asian American students, 72%; for African American students, 55%; and for Hispanic American students, 53%. At 48%, African American male students have the lowest graduation rates of any subgroup nationwide (Green & Winters, 2006). In the state of New York, only 43% of the 1.1 million students in public school districts graduate from high school (Green & Winters, 2006). In California, fewer than one in four, or 23%, of ninth-graders graduate from high school after completing the course sequence. Latino and African American students in that state are three times less likely to graduate with the essential skills diploma (Education Trust, 2003). In Georgia, 64,000 boys were part of the high school class of 2005 when classes began in fall 2001, but only 40,000 made it to their senior year. Sadder still, no one in the state of Georgia can really explain what happened to those 24,000 boys (Downey, 2006).

The aforementioned dismal figures are more staggering when one considers that a high school diploma is the threshold requirement for acceptance into college, the military, and many higher-paying careers (O'Neill, 2001). Students who find themselves without the benefit of a high school diploma have limited options in their adult lives. They are at an even more enormous disadvantage in terms of their school-to-work transition, potential for personal achievement, and—not least of all—self-esteem (O'Neill, 2001). Strident voices in the k–12 educational policymaking community have warned that poorer-performing groups of high school students (e.g., racial/ethnic minorities, low-income pupils, and students with disabilities) may experience increased grade retention and dropout rates as standardized testing and school-exit pressures change and increase. For example, one in four high school students in the state of California and one in three in Los Angeles drop out of school (Landsberg & Blume, 2008).

In several states, for example, New York, instead of receiving a high school diploma upon graduation, students who fail to master the course content but who perform adequately on the required exit examinations are offered a "certificate of attendance." Students who receive such certificates are at greater risk of not returning to school at some later time in their lives to earn their diplomas. The alternative for many of these students is to drop out of high school altogether rather than face the possibility of not graduating.

Many states that have instituted the new secondary education standards focusing on student and teacher accountability along with the revised high school graduation requirements legislated by the federal No Child Left Behind (NCLB) Act of 2001 have begun to realize the negative impact those requirements are having on a number of school districts, especially those that serve large numbers of students at the margins of society, including the poor, minorities, and the differently abled. School district personnel have much to consider and learn from states and districts that have already begun to experience the impact of the NCLB's high-stakes testing and revised graduation requirements. Research examining the outcomes of NCLB-mandated high school exit examinations has identified several areas that have become problematic for schools and students at the state level. For example, among the 24 states that currently require exit examinations driven by the new content standards for diploma candidates, 19 withhold diplomas from students until they retake classes to pass the examination (Ashford, 2003).

In Louisiana, 2,000 students left the New Orleans public school system in 2003 because they did not want to take the exit exams. California opted to delay its exit examination requirement for two years in 2003 because large numbers of its students were not graduating from high school. In Florida, 12,600 seniors failed that state's high school exit examination, the Florida Comprehensive Assessment Test (Ashford, 2003).

As school districts struggle to meet the NCLB mandates to raise academic achievement and revise high school graduation requirements, reform measures are surfacing in state departments of education across the nation. The current national trend among secondary schools is to infuse one or more of these reforms into strategies aimed at elevating successful high school exit rates to lessen the achievement gap. In the state of Michigan, Ackley (2005) has argued, the recent reforms mandated by the state board of education will enable Michigan to reclaim its prominence as a world leader in education and a producer of a highly skilled and competent workforce. Some of the salient components of the state board of education's reform plan include mandates calling for high academic standards and new roles for counselors and school administrators. Also included in the new Michigan high school graduation requirements is the added requirement that all students must take and pass the Michigan Merit Examination (MME). In the 2006–7 school year, the previous Michigan Educational Assessment Program (MEAP) high school exit test was replaced with this new school assessment system.

Previously Michigan's high school graduation requirement mandates were left to the good judgment of local educational agencies to determine. Subsequently, the only requirement was that students complete one unit of civics (e.g., a course in government).

The new requirements call for a more comprehensive course sequence that supports current content standards in English, health and physical education, mathematics, science, and social studies (see table 1). The overarching goal of these new state mandates, the state superintendent of Michigan public schools, Mike Flanagan, insists, is to ensure that every Michigan student is afforded the opportunity to acquire a useful skill set and a first-rate education.

In the year 2000, the average African American man earned 58% of the average White American man (National Urban League, 2007). Not only have African American men traditionally earned less than their White American counterparts, their unemployment rates have remained nearly twice as high (National Urban League, 2007). The precarious employment status of a large percentage of African American men adversely affects their families, communities, and society in general. In Michigan as elsewhere, the strength of the African American community depends

TABLE 1. NEW MICHIGAN HIGH SCHOOL GRADUATION REQUIREMENTS

SUBJECT	NUMBER OF CREDITS
Social Science	3
Government/Civics (½)	
Economics (½)	
U.S. History and Geography, World History and Geography (2)	
English	4
English 9	
English 10	
English 11	
English 12 or Humanities or CTE*	
Mathematics	4
Algebra 1	
Geometry	
Algebra 2	
One additional mathematics or math-related credit (Mathematics must be taken in senior year.)	
Science	4
Biology	
Physics or Chemistry	
One additional science credit*	
Health and Physical Education (each ½ credit)	1
Health, personal fitness, team sport	
World Languages	2
Credits earned in grades 9–12* OR an equivalent learning requirement	
for credit for students in grades experience in grades K–12	
Visual, Performing and Applied Arts	1
Vocal or instrumental music, art, music appreciation, art history,	
multicultural art, or readers' theater)	

NOTE: Prior to 2006, the only state-mandated requirement was one credit of Civics (Government); post-2006, incorporation of online learning experiences required in each of the mandatory credits).

in large part on the ability of schools to sufficiently engage African American males and prepare them to enter and succeed in the workforce. Education is key to securing the future of this challenged segment of the state's and the nation's citizenry. The mandates of No Child Left Behind call for a 90% graduation rate of all students across all school districts. However, the suspension and expulsion rates of Michigan's African American males (31%) will adversely affect the overall graduation rates of the school districts in Michigan where these students are most concentrated (Green & Winters, 2006).

Research has shown that promoting African American students' belief in their academic efficacy is a key component to curbing attrition (Martin, 2005). In educational contexts, caring has been found to stimulate enhanced academic learning, improve students' social abilities, and help students to recognize their own aptitudes and talents (Beck, 1994, 2004; Lyman, 2000; Marshall et al., 1996; Mayeroff, 1990; Noblit, Rogers, & McCadden, 1995; Noddings, 1992, 1995, 2002, 2003). Scholars have varying opinions, however, about what it means to truly "care," be caring or demonstrate caring behavior. The findings of this study suggest that providing a culture of care and support for Michigan's African American male students, who most likely will be the most adversely affected by new requirements, will be especially critical to the success of the state's recent school reform measures. Given Michigan's comprehensive new high school academic courses and exit examination requirements, creating a caring school culture that embraces the whole student and responds to the various obstacles to learning that African American male high school students encounter, both in school and in society, is a crucial prerequisite to these students' success. Relationships between teacher and student are fundamental to this equation, but these relationships are affected by many factors.

Looking through the lens of a single high school located in a predominantly African American, middle-income community in southeastern Michigan, this study focuses on the impact of the broad-sweeping revisions to Michigan's high school graduation requirements that have been proposed by Michigan superintendent Michael Flanagan (Ackley, 2005). The findings of this study suggest that Michigan educators must provide their African American students, and especially their male African American high school students, with a quality education within a caring cultural context. An excerpt extracted from one of this study's respondent narratives was especially telling in this regard. As we examined the effects of Michigan's comprehensive high school reform on its African American male students, this narrative provided rich insights into both the need for sweeping reforms and the possible ill effects of such reforms if implemented in the absence of an equally comprehensive caring school culture.

Caring as a Component of High School Reform

For teacher caring to have an impact, school administrators must construct a culture and community that supports genuine compassion. Teachers not only have to create caring relationships in which they are the caregiver, they also have a responsibility to help their students develop the capacity to care for others. Therefore, the school operation must be based foundationally on cooperation, shared relationships, effective communication, and an entire school community that takes caring seriously as an overarching purpose.

Caring can help to ensure the social and academic success of marginalized students; however, educators must first be able to understand the student and the context of his or her world "caringly." This means that educators must come to see with the student's eyes what the world is like and understand how students see themselves instead of viewing students from the teacher's perspective disconnected from the student's outlook. Thus, the teacher's interest, according to Mayeroff (1990), should be focused solely on the student. Only in that way will teachers be able to be responsive to their students' needs and development.

Beck (2004) describes how caring relationships are linked to living fully as a person. He offers two purposes or goals as basic to any caring action: (1) promoting human development and (2) responding to human needs. A third aspect of the caring framework is commitment (Beck, 2004). As Beck argues, the associations and commitments between people make caring possible. Gilligan emphasizes that those who care must recognize that they have a "moral imperative—a responsibility to discern the 'real and recognizable trouble' of this world" and to act to alleviate suffering caused by that trouble (2004, 8). On the other hand, Marshall et al. (1996) contend that responding to human needs is a situation- and person-specific way of performing in a world that requires individuals who care to be fully and sensitively attuned to the needs of those for whom they care. Noddings (1992) echoes this perspective of caring as relational, noting that it is common to think of caring as a virtue or an individual attribute rather than as a professional skill.

The literature overwhelmingly suggests that school administrators today must abandon the customs traditionally associated with leading a school in exchange for a model that emphasizes caring as fundamental to the lives of all students, staff, faculty, and administrators. Nonetheless, particularly in urban schools with high percentages of poorer-performing African American populations, the absence of a caring leadership model is too often accepted as commonplace by those who are comfortable with bureaucratic, fear-based school climates. As many researchers have found, however, when teachers possess the ability to create shared relationships, meet the needs of their students, and communicate with respect and cooperation, schools serving poor and racial/ethnic minority populations can positively influence student achievement (Foster, 1993, 1994; Haberman, 1995; Irvine, 1990). Lyman (2000) goes so far as to state that because caring affects learning and every other aspect of school life, school leadership using caring as a model should be a requirement. As Foster notes, focusing on the African American male's preference for successful teacher-student relationships: "When students were questioned about what made a 'good teacher,' the qualities most often cited were firmness, compassion, and an engaging style of teaching" (1999, 17). These students' best teachers, Foster contends, respected them, inspired them to work hard, and made learning interesting and relevant.

Marshall et al. (1996) suggest that an ethic of caring can provide school administrators with valuable perspectives to guide their moral reasoning and decision making, not as a model for educational leadership in and of itself but as an overarching ethical framework to guide administrative decisions. They further state that when making decisions, school administrators are best informed when they draw from other leadership models and combine the most appropriate aspects of those models in a culture of caring that guides their choices and administrative policymaking. That is, Marshall et al. posit that, by incorporating an ethic of caring, educational leaders can better determine which elements of a particular leadership model or models to use when faced with solving the many situation- and context-specific problems they confront each day.

Bolman and Deal identify additional indicators that suggest the power of caring leadership in the educational workplace. They explain that the pressures of immediate tasks and of satisfying the "bottom line" often crowd out the personal needs that people bring with them to their places of work. Yet caring, they contend, "brings with it knowing about others—[it] requires listening, understanding, and accepting" (1995, 103). Further, when a leader gives his or her workers power, authorship, love, caring, and significance, workers typically affirm the fundamental moral precepts of compassion and justice. When leadership is fused with the spirit of these concepts, Bolman and Deal maintain, the cornerstone of a purposeful and passionate community is cast.

Based on their work with African American male high school students deemed incorrigible in traditional school settings, Polite, Lisle, and Price (2006) have developed a comprehensive model for constructing a caring school climate (see figure 1). Their Caring School Climate Model for African American Youth details

FIGURE 1. A CARING SCHOOL CLIMATE MODEL FOR AFRICAN AMERICAN YOUTH

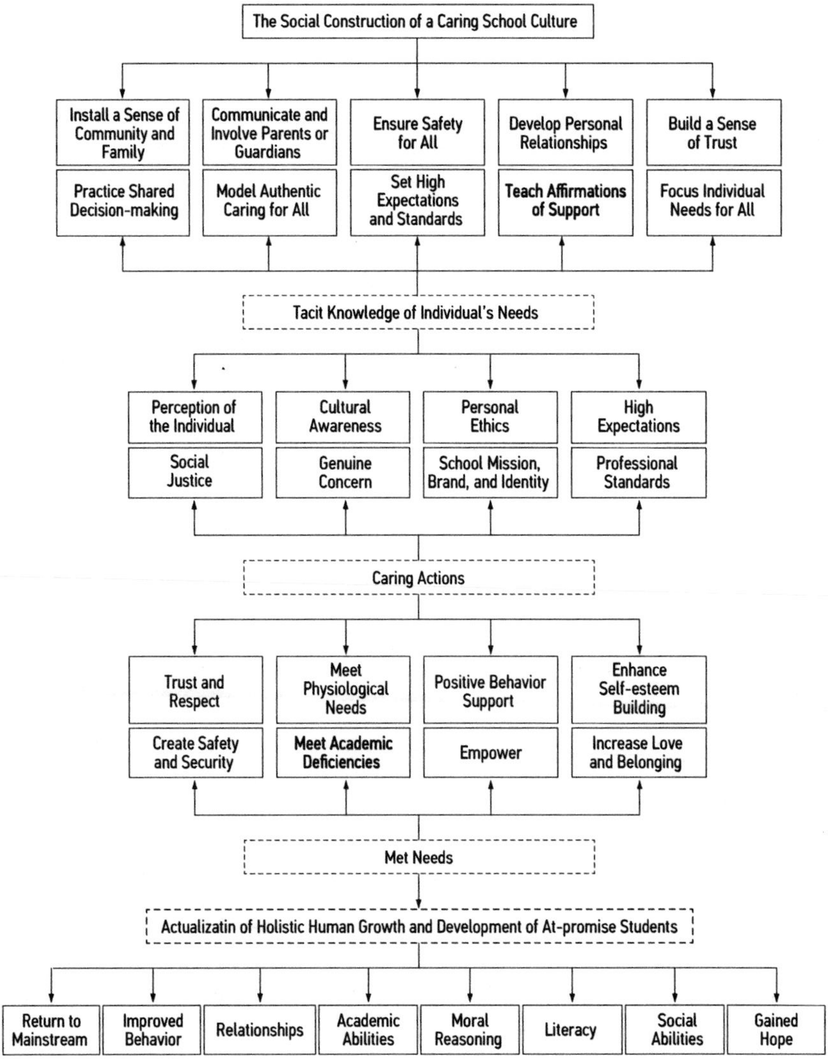

The Social Construction of a Caring School Culture

Install a Sense of Community and Family	Communicate and Involve Parents or Guardians	Ensure Safety for All	Develop Personal Relationships	Build a Sense of Trust
Practice Shared Decision-making	Model Authentic Caring for All	Set High Expectations and Standards	Teach Affirmations of Support	Focus Individual Needs for All

Tacit Knowledge of Individual's Needs

Perception of the Individual	Cultural Awareness	Personal Ethics	High Expectations
Social Justice	Genuine Concern	School Mission, Brand, and Identity	Professional Standards

Caring Actions

Trust and Respect	Meet Physiological Needs	Positive Behavior Support	Enhance Self-esteem Building
Create Safety and Security	Meet Academic Deficiencies	Empower	Increase Love and Belonging

Met Needs

Actualizatin of Holistic Human Growth and Development of At-promise Students

Return to Mainstream	Improved Behavior	Relationships	Academic Abilities	Moral Reasoning	Literacy	Social Abilities	Gained Hope

the wide array of elements that comprise the vital components of such settings. It also outlines the critical indicators for these students' success and their basic academic and social needs as well as provides examples of the impact of caring action on these far-too-often troubled youth.

African American Males and High School Reform in Michigan:
Up Close and Personal

The study reported in this chapter made full use of established qualitative research strategies such as those described by Bogdan and Biklen (2003). Included among these strategies were over 600 hours of on-site observations conducted among the African American male student population of Metropolitan High School (MHS; a pseudonym), a predominantly African American, middle-income community in southeastern Michigan. The lead author, a former administrator of a predominantly African American urban high school, also attended numerous African American–sponsored cultural events and social activities in the subject school community during the course of the study. His role as a participant-observer in this study was additionally compounded by his roles as both a researcher and administrative employee of the school district in question. This tripartite role offered the study a clear advantage—namely, access to the whole system, its policies, and its procedures. Follow-up interviews were conducted with a smaller subgroup of eight participants from the 1995 and 2006 cohort classes to determine the effects of schooling experiences on the work experiences of these students, who are now men in their mid-30s.

MHS was built with all the amenities of an upper-socioeconomic-level community high school of the late 1950s: complete with a radio station, planetarium, television station, theater, and both deep-diving and Olympic-sized swimming pools as well as rich academic programs. By the close of the 1980s, the MHS student population was predominantly African American. It was also ranked as one of the lowest-achieving schools in the state. While the school was seen as a haven of highly personalized classroom instruction and extracurricular and cocurricular interactions between teachers and students in 1970, by 1980 it was controlled by layers of rules and structures designed to control student behavior, primarily that of African American males. Table 2 offers a detailed look at the MHS African American male Class of 1989.

Although Metropolitan High always offered a comprehensive array of regular and Advanced Placement courses, and although numerous explanations have been offered for the academic failures of its "second-wave" students, the sad reality is that these latter-day students most often did not avail themselves of the opportunities provided by the school. Table 3 reveals the widespread avoidance of academic rigor

TABLE 2. DEMOGRAPHICS OF AFRICAN AMERICAN MALE STUDENTS IN THE MHS CLASS OF 1989

FACTOR	INCIDENTS	
	NUMBER	PERCENT
Graduated with class	60	69%
Graduated late	3	4%
Graduated below average	39	49%
Graduated above average	8	2%
Graduated with honors	4	5%
Took ACT exam	17	20%
Scored 16 or higher on ACT	4	5%
Dropped out through nonattendance	28	32%
Expelled by Board of Education	8	2%
Moved out of school district	8	2%
Earned a GED or adult education degree	4	5%
Killed	1	1%
Fate unknown	3	4%
Shot by gunfire	9*	10%
Incarcerated between 1986 and 1995	28*	32%

NOTE: $N = 115$; average age at time of study = 36 years.

* Known incidents

TABLE 3. MATHEMATICS COURSES COMPLETED BY AFRICAN AMERICAN MALE STUDENTS IN THE MHS CLASS OF 1989

SEMESTER COURSE	NUMBER WHO COMPLETED COURSE	PERCENTAGE WHO COMPLETED COURSE
Pre-Algebra 1	65	61%
Pre-Algebra 2	62	58%
Algebra 1	36	34%
Algebra 2	31	29%
Geometry 1	21	20%
Geometry 2	14	13%
Trigonometry 1	4	3%
Calculus 1	2	2%

NOTE: $N = 107$. Eight students who transferred to another school because of a change in residence are not included.

among the African American male students in the MHS Class of 1989 cohort. In the case of mathematics—the gatekeeping discipline for access to the present-day world of technology-rich employment—the majority of these students (60%) never completed Algebra 1, suggesting that by and large they were not prepared to enter the postindustrial era in which they currently find themselves as young men living in Michigan.

Billie (a pseudonym), a member of the MHS Class of 1989 cohort, offered the following rationale for this failure while reflecting on his high school academic experiences. At the time of the study, Billie was working in an unskilled position on the assembly line of a major factory and had attended the local community college part-time for two years. He shared the following insights on his years at MHS:

> I think the classes were offered there, but I don't think the students took them and nobody made [or encouraged] them. The challenging courses were offered, but nobody took them. . . . I don't think that's service to kids. All that school had was more rules and [they didn't] give you anything on the other hand. That doesn't work very well.

Another respondent, Benny (a pseudonym) was working part-time for a major factory and a clothing store at the time of the study. He had attended the local community college for one year, and was unemployed. Benny's comments typified the frustrations the study cohort faced when the realities of their poor choices in high school intersected with their school-to-work transitions:

> No one ever told me that I needed Algebra 1, 2, and 3; and geometry and trigo-nometry, calculus, and then all those sciences. I see now with my computer science [college classes] classes that you need to have a lot of math. I stopped at geometry. So it would have helped if I had gone a little farther, but I really didn't know that [when I was in high school] . . . If I were back in high school now, I would study advanced mathematics and electronics . . . electronics and computers 'cause that's the field that everything is moving towards: computers or electronics. I really didn't pay attention to it in high school.

The majority (85%) of the respondents interviewed built their high school programs around courses that had little relevance for their futures. For example, it was common for members of this group to have taken Ceramics 1, 2, 3, 4 and 5 and/or Photography 1, 2, 3, 4 and 5, while their mathematics courses, for example, consisted only of Pre-Algebra 1 and 2 and Algebra 1. It was shocking to learn, yet common, for these young men to articulate their lack of knowledge about the prerequisites for specific college programs and jobs. Many reported that while in high school they had postsecondary plans for careers in mathematics, electronics, the sciences, health careers, and so forth; yet the overwhelming majority had enrolled in courses that were clearly unrelated to those fields. Indeed, fewer than 10% had enrolled in traditional college preparatory courses in mathematics. Further, 80% of the respondents took the ACT college entrance examination during either their junior or senior of high school.

A large body of research suggests that attendance remains the most predictive determinant of student achievement (Lan & Lanthier, 2003; Lee & Burkam, 2003). One of the problems commonly related by the respondents regarding their high school attendance was that all too often they were not sufficiently involved in the academic process to warrant regular school attendance. Indeed, one out of three African American male students in the MHS Class of 1989 was expelled for lack of attendance. This lack of engagement was tied to many factors, among them social distractions, negative peer pressure, and lack of personal motivation.

The narrative of one student-respondent, Kyle (a pseudonym), provided particularly rich insights into both the need for sweeping reforms to address the past and present lack of engagement by Michigan's African American males in that state's educational system and the possible ill effects of such reforms if presented in the absence of an equally comprehensive caring school culture. As Kyle related:

> At 36 years of age, I have already been at the GM plant for the past 10 years as unit manager. I supervise 45 people who work largely with computers and robots. My job is to ensure that the robots are functioning and the production is maintained at a high level. Most of the persons that I supervise are White and many resent being supervised by a Black man.
>
> I graduated in 1989 from Metropolitan High School. I understand that there were about 115 African American males in my class between the tenth and twelfth grades. It is difficult to learn that out of that number only seven went to college following high school. I am really shocked to hear that news. What is

really difficult for me to comprehend is that only about 30% of those guys ever studied advanced mathematics in high school. And now that I think about it, there were very few Black guys in my math classes. They were in the school, but not in the same academic program that I followed.

You know, those were rough times at Metropolitan High! Many of the guys in my class were caught up with the drug culture and making a quick dollar. I know that many of them died as a result of their involvement with drugs and fast cash. Others are still in jail . . . from what I've heard.

I deliberately managed to escape a lot of the negative stuff while I was in high school. I had a lot of help from my counselors . . . who guided me throughout high school. You really need a strong counselor because you don't go in high school thinking, "Well, I'm going to take this math class or I'm going to take this science program." It depends on what your career goals are, and in high school obviously you have your standard classes that you have to take. Then, once you take them and do well, it's only practical to go to the advanced levels.

I was in Algebra, then Algebra 2, [then] Trig. I went on to Geometry and so forth. So, it was a natural progression for me with the support of good counseling. Of course I stayed close to my mentors and counselors. I was close to the assistant principal in the school and another Black male counselor who really helped me throughout the high school years. I just wanted something better for myself—those were my values.

It's interesting when I think back on some of the Black guys in my class. I think their focus was different. My number one focus was to continue my education. I was an athlete; I played basketball, and I enjoyed the sport. That was my true motivation—one of my highest motivations, second only to my family. Actually, my family was second to basketball because that was my love, and I knew in order for me to play, I had to be eligible; so it only made sense for me to stay in class and focus on my dream: to play for the NBA.

I don't know about the other Black guys or other students; their focus was obviously something different than mine. Maybe it [their focus] was making a lot of money right then and there. A lot of those guys were in the drug game. I grew up in the same neighborhoods. I found out that their parents were already into it [drug trafficking]; or someone close to them was already involved with "street pharmacy." So, it was only a natural progression for them to get involved too, being that was [their] family's way of life.

The economy was so bad with all the factory closings until drugs became a real viable way of life for some. You know, "We gotta get this money" and "We got the drug traffic," and "We got all of it in our favor." Some guys' kids are around it every single day. They come home from school and they see their parents or siblings in the basement cutting keys [preparing kilograms of crack or cocaine] and stacking money. So, yeah, the guys were curious and drawn into the game, and drugs were their primary focus in high school. The reality is the media . . . tends to focus too much attention on a small group of guys who are into crime, violence, and drugs. The sad truth is that most of the guys from my class who did not attend college or trade school are not in trouble with the law, but they are experiencing difficult times since it is almost impossible to get a real job in Michigan if you are a Black male without skills or a degree.

Yes, I saw some students driving those fancy cars. When I was in high school I didn't even have a car! I didn't get my first car until my freshman year in college . . . I had to save enough money to purchase it by working during the summer months.

As I said, my primary goal in high school was basketball. . . . Interestingly some of those guys in my class were better ballplayers than me, but because they were not [academically] eligible to play, they never saw the high school court. What a shame! [They were] really gifted ballplayers. Since they did not have their academics together, they were already destined to fail before they ever stepped on the court. The coach at Metropolitan High School at the time liked the clean-cut kids and would not waste his time with the losers. There were some exceptions, but you had to be really, really good.

When I was growing up, the positive men in life were my uncles. I didn't have a father to grow up with and to teach me all of the things that I know now. It was mostly my uncles that teamed up, and whenever it was their turn to put the time in [with me] they put the time in and made the best of it. I also think that my peers are some of the stronger men in my life—the positive ones. You know, people like yourself [referring to the lead author] when I was growing up, you know, going through high school. You were that ideal man in my life because you were one of those that helped shape me to become the person that I am. You know I never forgot about you or lost sight of you.

I go out there, and I mentor young kids in the city under one of the mayor's special initiatives. I assist in planning a number of social events for young kids such as sport events and fashion shows—keeping the kids busy and off the streets. My role is a volunteer event planner. . . . I try to stay involved in community events; everybody should have a charity in their life, some activity when you're actually helping others. I don't get paid for this work. It's my way of giving back and my way of relieving stress in my life. That's the only activity that I have other than working out at the gym. So volunteering is more satisfying than probably anything I could receive monetarily. I would love to be paid for my volunteer work, but I'm a firm believer that if you put forth maximum effort and you put out a good project and a good product, the money will chase you—you don't have to chase the money! You know as I get older, I wouldn't say I'm wise beyond my years, I think I just have a common sense about myself. I'm grounded. I'm not easily impressed. I can look from afar and say, "Wow, that's a really nice car. I could have that if I wanted it, but do I want that right now? Nah, you know it's just a ——." You've got to use your head! You've just got to have common sense and just not succumb to negative peer pressure. . . .

I'm just trying to seize the moment at this point! I'm 36, and I'm at a point now that I want to retire by age 40 and start my own business. The only work I'm going to do is truly for myself. I'm not going to work for anybody else, and I call the shots now [at the plant] so I might as well call them, truly, for myself.

Conclusion

The following policy recommendations are offered to address the unevenness in resources and schooling experiences typically faced by African American males in Michigan high school settings:

- Embrace the concept of caring school cultures and smaller learning communities as alternatives to settings that are insensitive to the special needs of African American male students
- Ensure equity in spending across school districts so that the high schools attended by the majority of Michigan's African American males—namely, those in some of the state's most challenging urban enclaves—have facilities, supplies, and equipment commensurate with high schools in the wealthier suburbs
- Recruit and provide incentives to attract highly qualified teachers from diverse

backgrounds to serve in those schools, especially those with credentials in the critical areas of mathematics, science, and technology

- Train or retrain school counselors and administrators across K–12 schooling to understand and respond to the academic and socio-psychological needs of African American males
- Address the disproportionate suspension and expulsion rates of African American males

The link between highly complex social issues and student achievement must become central to an ongoing discourse with school administrators and counselors who serve African American male student populations in Michigan. The findings of shared in this chapter suggest that for Michigan's African American male high school students to excel academically in the post-NCLB environment, several important variables must be present. First among these are explicitly articulated academic goals based on the proposed Michigan standards. Additionally, the provision of challenging curricula, extra instruction, and highly skilled instructional personnel are critical to creating the types of learning environments that can help African American males meet the demands of Michigan's new high-stakes testing and successfully graduate from high school.

Michigan educators must provide their African American students, and especially their male African American high school students, with a quality education within a caring cultural context. Constructing a caring culture in high schools that serve African American males is essential to success of the Flanagan plan for high school reform. It is also likely to be the most challenging aspect of the current reform movement.

REFERENCES

Ackley, M. (2005). *State board reviews Flanagan's recommendations for state high school graduation requirements.* November. Retrieved June 1, 2006, from http://www.michigan.gov/mde/0,1607,7-140-5373_5379-130312—,00.html.

Ashford, E. (2003). Rethinking the high school exit exams. *Education Digest,*

69(2), 51–55.

Beck. L. G. (1994). *Reclaiming educational administration as a caring profession.* New York: Teachers College Press.

Beck, L. G. (2004). Caring across racial barriers: A case study. Paper presented at the annual meeting of the American Educational Research Association, San Diego.

Bogdan R. C. & Biklen, S. K. (2003). *Qualitative research for education: An introduction to theories and methods* (4th ed.). New York: Pearson Education.

Bolman, L. G. & Deal, T. E. (1995). *Leading with soul.* San Francisco: Jossey-Bass.

Downey, M. (2006). *Help boys reach school finish line.* Retrieved June 1, 2006, from http://projects.accessatlanta.com/search/query/.Education Trust (2003). *African American Achievement in America.* Washington, DC: Education Trust.

Foster, M. (1993). Educating for competence in community and culture: Exploring the views of exemplary African American teachers. *Urban Education, 27*(4), 370–94.

Foster, M. (1994). Effective Black teachers: A literature review. In E. R. Hollins, J. E. King, & W. C. Hayman (Eds.), *Teaching Diverse populations: Formulating a knowledge base* (p. 242). Albany: State University of New York Press.

Foster, M. (1999). Teaching Black males: Lessons from the experts. In V. C. Polite & J. E. Davis (Eds.), *African American males in school and society: Practices and policies for effective education,* 8–19. New York: Teachers College Press.

Gilligan, C. (2004). Knowing and not knowing: Reflections on manhood. *Psychotherapy and Politics International, 2*(2), 99–114.

Green, J. P. & Winters, M. A. (2006). *Leaving boys behind: Public high school graduation rates.* New York: Center for Civic Innovation, Manhattan Institute.

Haberman, M. (1995). Selecting "star" teachers for children and youth in urban poverty. *Phi Delta Kappan, 76*(10), 771–81.

Irvine, J. J. (1990). *Black students and school failure: Policies, practices, and prescriptions.* Westport, CT: Greenwood Press.

Lan, W. & Lanthier R. (2003). Changes in students' academic performance and perceptions of school and self before dropping out from school. *Journal of Education for Students Placed at Risk, 8,* 309–32.

Landsberg, M. & Blume, H. (2008). 1 in 4 California high school students drop out, state says. *Los Angeles Times,* July 17. Retrieved August 3,

2008, from http://www.latimes.com/news/local/la-me-dropout17-2008jul17,0,1269326.story.

Lee, V. E. & Burkam, D. T. (2003). Dropping out of high school: The role of school organization and structure. *American Educational Research Journal, 40,* 353–93.

Lyman, L. L. (2000). *How do they know you care?* New York: Teachers College Press.

Marshall, C., Patterson, J., Rogers, D. L., & Steele, J. R. (1996). Caring as career: An alternative perspective for educational administration. *Educational Administration Quarterly, 32*(2), 271–94.

Martin, J. (2005). *Promoting students' belief in their academic abilities is key to curbing African-American high school dropout rates.* Washington University in St. Louis University Communications. Retrieved June 1, 2006, from http://news-info.wustl.edu/news/page/normal/5055.html.

Mayeroff, G. (1990). Getting to know a good middle school: Shoreham–Wading River. *Phi Delta Kappan, 71,* 505–13.

National Urban League (2007). *The state of black America 2007: Portrait of the black Male.* Washington, DC: National Urban League.

Noddings, N. (1992). *The challenge to care in schools: An alternative approach to Education.* New York: Teachers College Press.

Noddings, N. (1995). Teaching themes of care. *Phi Delta Kappan, 76,* 675–79.

Noddings, N. (2002). *Educating moral people: A caring alternative to character education.* New York: Teachers College Press.

Noddings, N. (2003). *Happiness and education.* Cambridge: Cambridge University Press.

Noblit, G. W., Rogers, D. L., & McCadden, B. M. (1995). In the meantime: The possibilities of caring. *Phi Delta Kappa, 76*(9), 680–85.

O'Neill, P. T. (2001). Special education and high stakes testing for high school graduation: An analysis of current law and policy. *Journal of Law & Education, 30*(2), 185–222.

Polite, V. C., Lisle, K., & Price, C. (2006) Caring Leadership for troubled African American adolescents: A case study. In L. Foster & L. C. Tillman (Eds.) *African American perspectives on leadership in schools: Building a culture of empowerment.* A special series offered by the University Council for Educational Administration. Lanham, MD: Rowman & Littlefield.

PART 2

Cultural, Psychosocial, and Sociopolitical Contexts of African American Male Well-being

The Call for Cultural Adjustments in Educating African American Males

IMPLICATIONS FOR SCHOOL COUNSELORS AND LEADERS

Eboni M. Zamani-Gallaher *and* Yvonne Callaway

American society is both "browning" and "graying." The present U.S. population contains both larger numbers of non-White racially/ethnically diverse persons (i.e., African Americans, Asian Americans, Hispanic/Latino(a) Americans, and Native Americans) and greater numbers of "Baby Boomers" who are approaching their retirement years. The bulk of U.S. population expansion over the last 20 years has been due primarily to the increased births and immigration of Hispanics at rates that have consistently outpaced those of other U.S. racial/ethnic groups. Demographers project that in fewer than five decades, people of color will comprise the majority of U.S. citizens, with White non-Hispanic persons projected to account for 47% of the population by 2050 (U.S. Bureau of the Census, 2002). In some parts of the country, the future is already here. For instance, Hispanic Americans, African Americans, and Asian Americans currently account for over half the population of California, making it the first to become a "minority-majority" state.

Although American society is more heterogeneous on the surface, it continually struggles with achieving parity for all of its citizenry—educationally, economically, socially, politically, and so forth. This is particularly true when examining the plight of African American males within U.S. institutions. Across racial/ethnic groups, African American males are more often considered at-risk, deemed outcasts, and stratified in relationship to educational and occupational mobility (Gibbs, 1988; Parham & McDavis, 1987; Rodriguez, 1997). Attendance and achievement patterns for African American males in K–12 schools, along with Black men's gainful employment in the workplace, receipt of health care, participation in the political arena, and other areas of social life are not reflective of parity with others in the populace.

The charge to develop policies and practices to reverse these patterns for African American males in Michigan is eminent. That charge calls for all educators and citizens who are concerned about and committed to resolving the cultural and gender disparities in educational outcomes plaguing African American males nationwide to take a stand. Concerned with the overall performance of all Michigan youth, in December 2003 Governor Jennifer Granholm announced plans to make the state secondary general curriculum tougher (Burke & Johnstone, 2004). The governor's intent was to encourage Michigan students to attend and graduate from college in an effort to attract new industries and strengthen the states' ability to compete in a knowledge economy. However, more stringent exit requirements will not prevent African Americans from being placed at the intersection of race, poverty, and gender. Michigan's Black males in particular are exposed to many inherent risks and few benefits in the state's K–12 educational system.

This chapter seeks to explore the literature on Black boys and men within K–16 educational and counseling contexts, and to address explicitly the issues plaguing these males as they progress from the elementary to the postsecondary pipeline. It also seeks to integrate as well as articulate processes, policies, and practices that may yield culturally competent praxis that has utility and that is germane to educational practitioners and school counselors in the state of Michigan.

Enrollment Trends for African American Males in K–12 Schools

Nearly all of the common educational challenges occurring in Michigan are reflected in the national data. Data reveal that in 1999–2000, African Americans made up 17% of the K–12 student population and 8% of the national teacher workforce (Toppo, 2003). Moreover, 38% of the nation's public schools did not have a teacher of color on staff; indeed, 84% of public school teachers countrywide were White, and an overwhelming number of those were women. Although, at 37%, Michigan ranks above average in the number of teachers of color it employs, it has not yet achieved a critical mass sufficient to garner better educational outcomes for its Black male students on a consistent basis.

A review of the literature about the current educational status and achievements of Black males in America reveals a systemic national failure. For example, in a study of U.S. school districts with 10,000 or more Black male students, the Schott Foundation for Public Education (2005) reported among 20 representative high schools across the country, graduation rates for Black males ranged from a low of 19% to a high of 34%, with only half of the schools achieving graduation rates above 30%. This pattern is documented throughout the literature (Brown & Davis, 2000; Polite & Davis, 1999; Varlas, 2005) and comes as no surprise given both historical evidence and recent research data that links racial, ethnic, and gender classroom dynamics to student achievement and to the consistent troubles Black boys face in K–12 public schools.

A CLOSER LOOK AT MICHIGAN

Michigan's demographic landscape is often a contradictory one. The state contains two of the most racially segregated metropolitan areas in the United States per capita: Detroit and Livonia. These cities are polar opposites in terms of Black/White residential ratio. Livonia, on one hand, is 98% White. By contrast, 82% of Detroiters are African American and only 12% are White (U.S. Bureau of the Census, 2002, 2006). The average age of Detroit residents, 30.9 years, parallels the national average for Blacks across the country (i.e., 30.6 years), yet this is five years younger than the median age of Whites nationwide (Hoffman, Llagas, & Snyder, 2003). By contrast, the overwhelmingly White residential community of Livonia has a mean age that is higher than the national average for Whites at 42.3 years old.

Show Me the Money: Educational Expenditures and High-Stakes Testing in Michigan

During the 2002–3 school year, African American students comprised 20.1% of students enrolled in Michigan public schools (Becker, 2002). Prior to that year,

TABLE 1. MICHIGAN'S BLACK AND WHITE (NON-HISPANIC) POPULATIONS BY GENDER, 1995–2025 (IN THOUSANDS)

	1995	2000	2005*	2015*	2025*
BLACK	1,379	1,435	1,486	1,594	1,705
Male	646	672	696	746	799
Female	733	763	790	848	906
WHITE	7,774	7,790	7,767	7,701	7,628
Male	3,803	3,818	3,813	3,795	3,777
Female	3,971	3,972	3,954	3,906	3,858

SOURCE: U.S. Bureau of the Census (2002).
* Projected.

the number of African American males enrolled had been increasing yearly, from 154,869 in 1999–2000 to 191,708 in 2002–3 (Becker, 2002); by 2003, however, African American male enrollment declined to 176,697. Although the state currently ranks among the top in the nation for per-pupil expenditures, 17.1% of all Michigan students matriculate in Title I, low-income-based schools, and 32.7% are eligible for free/reduced-price lunches (Becker, 2002).

The Michigan Educational Assessment Program (MEAP) is a standards-based test that is designed to measure how well students have mastered particular skills by grade level. Ideally, all Michigan students should meet or exceed the standards for each grade. Based on data collected in 2002, the percentages of students ranked as "low" performers on the MEAP reading and mathematics scales increased between elementary and middle school (Kids Count in Michigan, 2003). Fewer low-income students performed satisfactorily (i.e., >300 on reading test, >520 on math test), and the rates of increase for this group were consistently higher than the aggregate. Table 2 compares fourth- and eighth-grade MEAP scores for all Michigan students and for all Title I and Title I–targeted students in the state.

The Kids Count in Michigan *Data Book* (2003) provides county profiles of child and family well-being in the state for the 2002 fiscal year and offers a wealth of information about educational outcomes for Michigan's K–12 students. The *Data Book* notes an alarming achievement gap between Black and White students in fifth-grade mathematics. Consider, for example, for 2003, the Michigan black/white achievement gap for fourth-grade math is 35 points in contrast to the U.S. black/white gap for fourth-grade math of 27 points. Similarly, eighth-grade math scores on the 2003 MEAP test illustrate a 41-point black/white gap whereas the U.S.

**TABLE 2. PERCENTAGE OF STUDENTS RANKED AS LOW IN MEAP READING
AND MATH SCORES, 1999–2000**

STUDENTS	ALL	TITLE I	TITLE I TARGETED
READING			
Grade 4	18	20	32
Grade 7	21	26	37
MATH			
Grade 4	9	10	20
Grade 7	14	19	37

SOURCE: Kids Count in Michigan, 2003.

black/white gap for eighth-grade math is 35 points. There is a 39-point Michigan black/white gap for fourth-grade reading 2003. The fourth-grade reading U.S. black/white gap is 30 points. Among Michigan eighth-graders, 2003 MEAP reading scores reveal a 30-point black/white gap while the U.S. black/white gap for eighth-grade reading is 26 points (Coulson, 2005).

In 2001, $112 million in scholarships were awarded to high school graduates in Michigan based on MEAP scores. Of the 43,650 graduates in the state's high school class of 2002, 37% qualified for Michigan Merit Scholars (MMS) awards; 97% of them were eligible based on their MEAP scores. A five-year analysis of MEAP data indicates that White Michigan students were twice as likely overall to pass this state test as were Blacks. As a result, financial support for higher education, awarded on the basis of MEAP performance, was awarded to African American students, males in particular, at much lower rates.

The MMS program is four times more likely to benefit students in the highest income districts. Well over half of African American students (59%) fall in the low-income group of students least likely to score satisfactorily on the state achievement test or to benefit from the dollars earmarked for its graduating seniors' postsecondary expenses. In Michigan, African American students represent the highest number of poor students and are up to four times more likely than White students to live in poverty. Michigan continues to experience an unstable economy, with unemployment woes caused by the shrinking automobile manufacturing base carrying over into education and the home lives of the state's youngest residents (e.g., one out of every four young children under age five is living in poverty).

It is also important to consider the demography and residential patterns (e.g.,

TABLE 3. DETROIT PUBLIC SCHOOLS MEAP RESULTS: PERCENTAGE MEETING/EXCEEDING STANDARDS, 2004 AND 2005

	2005 STATE AVERAGE	DETROIT STUDENTS MEETING/EXCEEDING STANDARDS	
		2004	2005
READING			
Grade 4	81%	60%	67%
Grade 7	71	40	48
Grade 12	78	58	57
WRITING			
Grade 4	45%	33%	32%
Grade 7	52	26	34
Grade 12	57	35	29
MATH			
Grade 4	71%	55%	54%
Grade 8	60	32	35
Grade 12	57	25	24

SOURCE: Great Schools Inc., 2006.

rural, suburban, or urban) of Michigan's students when examining the state's Black-White achievement gap. Becker (2002) reports that the per-pupil spending gap between poor and affluent students in Michigan is the highest in the nation. Detroit, for example, features an urban school district primarily comprised of low-income students of color. Ninety-one percent of its students are African American, 6% are Hispanic American, and 72% receive free or reduced-price lunches. Clearly, average MEAP performance for Detroit's inner-city elementary, middle, and high school youth are below the state average performance (Great Schools, 2006).

Of the 141,406 students enrolled in Detroit's 261 public P–12 schools, the vast majority are African American (Great Schools, 2006). Over two-thirds of fourth-grade Detroit Public School (DPS) students met or exceeded the state standards for reading (compared to the statewide fourth-grade average of 81%). Forty-five percent of fourth graders across the state met or exceeded the standards for writing, compared to 33% of DPS fourth graders. Fifty-four percent of DPS fourth graders met or exceeded the state's mathematics standards; the state average was 71%. Similar achievement gaps in reading and writing were found in the MEAP performance of DPS students' vis-à-vis statewide averages at grade 7, grade 8 for mathematics, and grade 12 across all three subjects (Great Schools, 2006). The proficiencies of

TABLE 4. DETROIT PUBLIC SCHOOLS MEAP AND MME RESULTS: PERCENTAGE MEETING/ EXCEEDING STANDARDS, 2007–2008

| | 2008 STATE AVERAGE | DETROIT STUDENTS MEETING/EXCEEDING STANDARDS | |
		2007	2008
READING			
Grade 4	85%	70%	65%
Grade 7	73	57	39
Grade 11	62	32	36
WRITING			
Grade 4	45%	36%	24%
Grade 7	77	43	57
Grade 11	41	17	17
MATH			
Grade 4	86%	65%	64%
Grade 7	73	29	44
Grade 11	46	14	14

SOURCE: Great Schools Inc., 2008.

DPS students have not improved and in some cases are now worse, as 2007–8 data illustrate (see table 4).

A change in state law replaced the MEAP high school test with the Michigan Merit Exam (MME) to better align with the state's new high school graduation requirements, which are more rigorous. The junior class of 2007 was the first to take the MME. Given that the MME is an entirely new assessment, student results are not comparable to previous high school MEAP tests.

Counseling Considerations

While it is important for students to have a sense of agency, given the policy changes and politicized environment surrounding high-stakes testing, many students, particularly those enrolled in Detroit Public Schools, may feel voiceless. It is the role of the school counselor to act as a change agent and to advocate for students and for social justice. One of the tasks most central to this role is enhancing the quality of life and empowerment of students. This process is meant to be developmental, grounded in theoretical paradigms and best-practice models, and refined through action research. From this perspective, prevention rather than remediation is the intent of school counseling.

In Michigan, statewide planned school counselor interventions are identified as specific grade-level goals for cognitive, affective, and behavioral domains. Also known as the Michigan Comprehensive Guidance Model, this model, which has been used for many years, is meant to ensure that student development is addressed consistently and developed throughout K–12 education. However, an examination of the academic achievement and quality of life measures for African American males reveals that this group has not demonstrated outcome gains as a result of the state's comprehensive approach to school counseling.

It is critically important for counselors to be culturally competent; hence, teacher education, educational administration, and counseling education programs must purposefully design curricula to promote the cross-cultural knowledge and skills necessary to improve counselors' effectiveness in resolving the challenges facing African American males. Lee (1991) outlines how incorporating African American culture can facilitate the empowerment process for young Black males. Studies by Day-Vines and Day-Hairston (2005), Delpit (1996), and others also posit strategies by which educational and counseling personnel can integrate cultural dimensions (i.e., basic aspects of Black life) that typically are ignored in efforts to facilitate positive developmental experiences.

If educators and counselors are not equipped with an understanding of African American culture, if they lack sensitivity or knowledge regarding key tenets of Black male development, then Black males' academic and psychosocial problems will only worsen. Culturally focused counselors and educators should embrace being student-centered by advocating that the exchange of teaching and learning involve an understanding of the realities of the Black male perspective such that self-actualization for African American males can be fully enacted (Bailey & Paisley, 2004; Lee, 1991). As they grapple with cross-cultural issues, counselors and educators must delve even further to grasp the meaning of these students' multiple group memberships at the nexus of race and gender.

The Confluence of Racial and Gender Identity

Belgrave and Allison (2006) advocate the use of contemporary models that consider the value of the extended or collective self as an agent of change and positive resistance. They also establish the importance of supporting racial identity development for African American youth through messages about racial status and its meaning concerning behaviors and relationships within and outside of the racial group, cultural stereotypes, social realities, and strategies for overcoming racial barriers. Such messages, they contend, are most likely delivered by parents who are married, older, more educated, and living in more racially mixed neighborhoods. These messages tend to be gender-based in that they stress pride for girls and barriers for boys, and they are more often delivered by mothers than fathers.

As Belgrave and Allison further maintain, socialization messages provide the foundation for healthy racial identity development. Accordingly, a healthy Afrocentric identity includes the following:

1. Positive in-group identification and a sense of common connections and group fate, which result in the saliency of group norms and practices
2. Awareness of out-group perceptions and negative expectations as well as of the potential for such views to negatively affect African Americans' academic self-efficacy and vulnerability to stereotype threat
3. Viewing academic achievement as consistent with, important to, and embedded in one's ethnic identity

Belgrave and Allison (2006) articulate several benefits of a positive ethnic identity. They claim, for example, that for adolescents it is positively associated with strong self-concept, positive self-esteem, more and stronger parental connections, better coping skills, and more prosocial and sanctioned activities. They also suggest a positive relationship between developed moral reasoning and developed racial identity. Conversely, they posit a negative relationship between strong ethnic identity and problem behaviors such as drug use and violence. Although their macroanalysis of the research literature yields mixed support for the influence of racial identity on academic achievement, Belgrave and Allison uncover considerable support for the argument that children who are aware of racism perform better academically than those who are not. They conclude, thus, that awareness of racism can be connected to academic motivation and effort, and that more prepared students are less likely to be adversely affected by racist and discriminatory practices.

Belgrave and Allison's research can be used to inform the translation of counseling theories to practice with African American males. So too can Mary Howard-Hamilton's (1997) work examining developmental theories relevant to this population. Howard-Hamilton suggests alleviating Black males' salient educational and self-esteem concerns through personal development using counseling interventions. She cautions, however, that it is dangerous to apply traditional student development theories to this group without first examining the unique intersection of race and gender.

Howard-Hamilton's arguments concerning racial identity development are congruent with the aforementioned culturally framed approaches. Her Africentric Resistance Model operationalizes an Afrocentric worldview, the central proposition of which is that knowledge of one's cultural, historical, and racial roots generates a self-affirmative buoyancy to combat negative stereotypes. Additionally, strong cultural emphases on kinship, interdependence, collective responsibility, generosity, and spirituality are believed to counteract the experiences of racism and oppression through positive resistance. Moreover, the ability to recognize and cope with social inconsistencies, discrimination, and prejudice are critical to perceptions of self-worth and efficacy that influence African American male academic achievement. This is especially so in educational settings in which the dominant group's social norms and values are operative.

Self-Concept and Efficacy among African American Males

Constructs of the self, including gender and racial identities, worldviews related to interpersonal relationships, and awareness of others' perceptions of self are all viewed as contributing to the underachievement of African American males (Noguera, 2003). Self-efficacy theory stresses the existence of a reciprocal relationship between personal factors (e.g., self-perceptions, worldview, role and status assignments, age, gender, race, physiognomy), behavior factors (e.g., competencies, skills, and preferences), and the sociopolitical environment (e.g., individual and group power and role constraints, associational patterns and opportunities). These factors interact in a reciprocal fashion to shape behavior.

Bandura (1997) contends that as individuals develop concepts of self and of the environment, they are most likely to attend to and/or select certain experiences and filter out others. Both direct instruction and modeling have been demonstrated as effective technologies for developing self-efficacy, which may implicitly convey that one possesses the necessary capabilities to succeed. Self-efficacy has been shown to have predictive and interactive effects on goal setting and judgmental heuristics that moderate the nature, extent, and duration of problem solving and coping behaviors.

Osborne (1999) points to the relationship between African American males' identification with academics and their lack of support in schools as primary obstacles to these males' success in school. He argues that schools reinforce negative stereotypes of Black male youth, leading them to develop oppositional identities that reflect those stereotypes and make them agents in their own failure. Subsequently, these factors work together to support the Black male academic underachievement that consistently results in lower grades and test scores as well as higher dropout rates and less engagement in postsecondary endeavors.

Osborne references three prominent approaches to addressing educational achievement for African American males: Steele and Aronson's (1995) *stereotype threat model*, Ogbu's (1981) *cultural-ecological perspective*, and Majors and Billson's (1992) *"cool pose" theory*. These concepts focus on the symbolic interaction of African American males' identification with academics as a necessary condition for changing outcomes.

Stereotype threat theory posits that stress resulting from the perception that one is not able to meet the demands of a given situation can produce debilitating anxiety. This model proposes that minority-group students are at risk of lowered performance in situations where racial stereotypes regarding achievement are salient (Belgrave & Allison, 2006). Osborne (1999) suggests that Black students may be subject to such heightened anxiety in school situations that they often withdraw as a self-protective response. Withdrawal reduces the anxiety and perhaps, concomitantly, concern with evaluation in the school setting. Osborne also notes that African American students' self-esteem is more affected by home, family, and community than school.

Conversely, Ogbu (1981, 1986) argues from a cultural-ecological framework that African Americans either consciously or unconsciously interpret school learning as incongruent with and unrelated to their social identity, sense of security, and self-worth. He asserts that African American male students are aware that hard work does not necessarily pay off for them, and that those who do succeed are rarely accorded the same benefits as their White counterparts. This awareness, combined with peer and cultural pressure, may act against academic engagement. The cultural pressure to which many Black males react typically occurs within the context of White racism, which is a social construction based on negative affect for members of particular racial/ethnic groups. Arguably, racism places hierarchical values on race and demeans those without the status and power that are socially determined based on ascribed characteristics.

Taylor and Howard-Hamilton (1995) point to the social tendency for the poor to be seen as lazy and even immoral while the affluent are likely to be cast as esteemed and admired, and maintain that identical marginalization occurs along racial lines. Hence, racism, sexism, classism, and elitism commingle and are each important in the context of identity development. Traditional counselor training demonstrates adherence to and bias in favor of Western value preferences consistent with middle-class, Protestant ethics, Standard English, and a strong belief in the *notion* of meritocracy. Members of oppressed minority groups who endorse this worldview are predicted to suffer from group powerlessness, depression, and a negative sense of self-worth.

The hypothesis that African American males may assume a ritual masculine persona, or "cool pose," as a defense against threats of oppression and racism in society and schools has also emerged from the literature (Majors & Billson, 1992). Osborne (1999) notes that African American males' academic achievement is often obstructed by such psychological defenses. The adoption of a reactive masculine persona may induce anxiety regarding peer acceptance and group affiliations that are not supportive of a strong identification with academics. These conditions culminate in Black male students' lower levels of identification with academics, which have been shown to increase as they grow older. Behavioral manifestations of this cool pose—aloofness, fearlessness, and nonconformance—contribute to the underachievement of this group in two ways; (1) they lead Black males to withdraw from the academic environment and cause significant others in that environment to withdraw from or withdraw support for these students; and (2) they reinforce negative stereotypes of Black males.

Conceptual Underpinnings Related to Research on African American Males

SOCIAL LEARNING THEORY

Much of the research points to the potential of Bandura's (1997) social learning theory as an effective and culturally relevant intervention modality for African

American males in educational settings, and one that provides several specific recommendations for intervening. Social learning theory is specifically offered by Howard-Hamilton (1997) and alluded to by others as a modality for addressing salient concerns related to African American male students. Self-efficacy theory, developed as an extension of social learning theory, proposes that individuals' experiences and behaviors are largely the result of cognition (Bandura, 1997). Higher dissatisfaction for cognitive failure or substandard performance, combined with higher self-efficacy, is seen as generating greater efforts to succeed and make greater performance improvements. Conversely, being less efficacious and more satisfied (with failure or substandard performance) correlates with less effort and improvement in performance over time.

RESILIENCE

Although research has indicated that the socially learned behavior of racial/ethnic minorities illustrates lower coping self-efficacy with regard to perceived educational and career barriers than their White counterparts (Luzzo & McWhirter, 2001), one cannot discount the capacity Black men have shown, for generations, to overcome unthinkable obstacles. Arguably, African American males have triumphed mightily in the face of adversity. In the face of endangerment many have emerged resilient and strengthened by their experiences. Resilience is considered a critical factor in curbing the damaging effects of institutional and individual forms of racism, sexism, and classism that disenfranchised members of this society often face.

Studies have supported the impact of resilience-promoting behavior among marginalized race and gender groups. Borman and Overman (2004) identified individual characteristics that distinguished academically successful—or as they operationalized them, *resilient*—minority and low-socioeconomic-status elementary school students from their less successful or nonresilient peers. They formulated and tested four risk- and resilience-promoting school models: (1) effective schools, (2) peer group composition, (3) school resources, and (4) supportive school communities. Their findings indicate that racial/ethnic minority students from low-income backgrounds had increased risks and fewer resilience-promoting behaviors than did White students of similar backgrounds. Borman and Overman's study also supported implementation of uniformity and promotion of individual- and school-level academic resiliency models for all low-income students irrespective of race/ethnicity. It concludes that a supportive school community model is the most dynamic means of protecting children from harsh conditions and in turn promoting resiliency as required.

Warren (2005) examined resilience as a factor relating to how young African Caribbean men attending schools in London dealt with institutional racism. His study used rich qualitative methods employing the first-person narratives of 15 African Caribbean young men in three London schools. Warren concluded that these students engaged in what he deemed resilience by refusal—that is, they refused to be overregulated, overdisciplined, and treated more severely than their White counterparts. Captured in his study was a portrait of Black male students who embodied a sense of agency. Additional support for these students' participation in school-based mentoring programs was found to be an effective means of assisting them to cope with and counter the hegemony of the learning environments in which the subjects found themselves.

Implications for School Counseling and Educational Leadership

This chapter has presented statistics on the present-day educational participation of African Americans, Black males in the state of Michigan particularly. It has focused on the Black male achievement gaps that have been reported all along the educational pipeline. These findings and discussion have led to several conclusions. One of these is that it is incumbent upon our nation's schools, colleges, and departments of education to deliver teacher preparation programs that encompass both cultural competency training and professional development that can challenge the social constructions of bias, stereotyping, racism, and sexism that are manifested in schools across this land. Additionally, it is apparent that parent and teacher expectancy can produce self-fulfilling prophecies that counter student persistence; this is especially salient in terms of Black male student performance.

The role of African American parents, teachers, counselors, and administrators in the reform of the ineffective schooling typically provided an African American male is a crucial one. In Michigan, African American male students have lower educational outcomes than their female counterparts, but they fare as well as their gender, racial, and economic peers around the country. The critical nature of cultural factors such as racial identity and the social construction of race in the academic success of Black boys are often cited as factors behind this state-specific disparity, but very limited research specific to race and gender or poverty relative to identity development and academic success is available. Macro-reviews of research related to the educational achievement of African American males identify common structural and sociopolitical obstacles that are well supported by national and state data.

The policy and legislative landscape of access in Michigan has proven to be the litmus test for the engagement of more African Americans in the educational pipeline. The recent assaults on affirmative action place Michigan squarely in the middle of the national policy debate. The negative impact within Michigan of the proposed Civil Rights Initiative, which seeks to do away with affirmative action, could have detrimental effects on the state's people of color, most notably its African American males in higher education (Zamani-Gallaher, Green, Brown, & Stovall, 2009). Thus, the outstanding social justice issue for Michigan's—and the nation's—educators, administrators, and counselors is to alleviate unequal and discriminatory outcomes for African American males in K–12 and postsecondary education, and to promote access, equity, and the closing of the achievement gap between this group and other racial/gender groups. Educators and counselors alike must act and lead others to action in articulating future steps to remove structural, sociopolitical, and cultural barriers to Black male students' academic achievement.

The following list, which is by no means exhaustive, contains initiatives we consider critical for improving the educational outcomes and academic achievement of African American males:

1. The immediate establishment of a developmental teaching school to implement staffing, curriculum, and developmental programming that reflects sensitive and effective application of learning and developmental theories uniquely related to Black males.
2. Work with targeted low-income, urban districts, other programs, and national funding sources to implement specific program components as after-school, Saturday school, and rites of passage programs as data is compiled.
3. Collaborate with African American organizations to promote teaching as a career and to emphasize equity in accountability for student educational outcomes.
4. Work with state and national executive, legislative, and judicial branches to establish funding equity and close the per-pupil spending gap; target

low-income schools for interventions that measure educator competency and student achievement specifically related to the documented educational and achievement outcomes of African American males.

We believe that teachers and counselors alike must shoulder the responsibility in removing the systemic barriers that stifle the promise of African American males in our schools. These barriers in turn impede our collective progress. It is imperative that our nation move toward an educational system that not only promises but also operationalizes social justice through education for African Americans. Now more than ever, it is time to challenge the insidious status quo and eradicate the institutionalized racism and systemic discrimination that continues to jeopardize the ability of Black males to survive and thrive in American schools.

REFERENCES

Bailey, D. F. & Paisley, P. O. (2004). Developing and nurturing excellence in African American male adolescents. *Journal of Counseling and Development, 82,* 10–17.

Bandura, A. (1997). *Self-efficacy: The exercise of control.* New York: W. H. Freeman.

Becker, P. C. (Ed.). (2002). A *statistical report of the United States social conditions and trends.* Washington, DC: U.S. Department of Education, National Center for Educational Statistics.

Belgrave F. Z. & Allison, K. W. (2006). *African American psychology: From Africa to America.* Thousand Oaks, CA: Sage Publications.

Borman, Geoffrey & Overman, Laura T. (2004). Academic resilience in mathematics among poor and minority students. *Elementary School Journal, 104*(3), 177.

Brown, M. C., II & Davis, J. E. (2001). The historically Black college as social contract, social capital, and social equalizer. *Peabody Journal of Education, 76,* 31–49.

Burke, J. B. & Johnston, M. (2004). Students at the margins: Searching for the American dream in higher education. *Race, Gender & Class, 11*(3), 19–35.

Coulson, A. J. (2005, Feb. 2). *How ideology perpetuates the achievement gap.* Retrieved on July 4, 2009 from http://www.mackinac.org/article.aspx?ID=6974.

Day-Vines, N. L. & Day-Hairston, B. O. (2005). Culturally congruent strategies for addressing the behavioral needs of urban, African American male adolescents. *Professional School Counseling, 8*(3), 236–43.

Delpit, L. (1996). *Other people's children: Cultural conflict in the classroom.* New York: New Press.

Gibbs, J. T. (1988). Young Black males in America: Endangered, embittered and embattled. In J. T. Gibbs, A. F. Brunswick, M. E. Connor et al. (Eds.), *Young, Black and male in America: An endangered species,* 1–5. Dover, MA: Auburn House.

Great Schools, Inc. (2006). *Detroit public schools MEAP results.* Retrieved April 6, 2006, from http://www.greatschools.net/cgi-bin/mi/district_profile/346/.

Hoffman, K., Llagas, C., & Snyder, T. (2003). *Status and trends in the education of Blacks.* October 14. Washington, DC: National Center for Education Statistics.

Howard-Hamilton, M. F. (1997). Theory to practice: Applying developmental theories relevant to African American men. *New Directions for Student Services, 80,* 17–30.

Kids Count in Michigan. (2003). *2002 data book: County profiles of child and family well-being.* Lansing: Michigan Department of Education.

Lee, C. C. (1991). *Empowering young Black males.* December. ERIC Document Reproduction No. ED341887.

Luzzo, D. A. & McWhirter, E. H. (2001). Sex and ethnic differences in the perception of educational and career-related barriers and levels of coping efficacy. *Journal of Counseling & Development, 79,* 61–67.

Majors, R. & Billson, J. M. (1992). *Cool pose: The dilemmas of Black manhood in America.* New York: Lexington Books.

Noguera, P. A. (2003). The trouble with Black boys: The role and influence of environmental and cultural factors on the academic performance of African American males. *Urban Education, 38*(4), 431–59.

Ogbu, J. (1981). Origins of human competence: A cultural perspective. *Child Development, 52,* 413–29.

Ogbu, J. U. (1986). The consequences of the American caste system. In U. Neisser (Ed.), *The school achievement of minority children: New perspectives,* 19–56. Hillsdale, NJ: Lawrence Erlbaum Associates.

Osborne, J. W. (1999). Unraveling underachievement among African American boys from and identification with academics perspective. *Journal of Negro Education,* 68(4), 555–65.

Parham, T. A. & McDavis, R. J. (1987). Black men, an endangered species: Who's really pulling the trigger? *Journal of Counseling & Development,* 66(1), 24–27.

Rodriguez, J. (1997). At-risk: A measure of school failure in American education. March. ERIC Documents Reproduction No. ED412220.

Schott Foundation for Public Education (2005). *Public education and Black male students* (2nd ed.). Cambridge, MA: Schott Foundation for Public Education.

Steele, C. M. & Aronson, J. (1995). Stereotype threat and the intellectual test performance of African Americans. *Journal of Personality and Social Psychology,* 69(5), 797–811.

Taylor C. & Howard-Hamilton, M. F. (1995). Student involvement and racial identity attitudes among African American males. *Journal of College Student Development, 36,* 330–35.

Toppo, F. (2003). USA's teaching pool not diverse. *USA Today,* July 2.

U.S. Bureau of the Census. (2002). *Population division, population projections branch.* August. Washington, DC: U.S. Bureau of the Census.

U.S. Bureau of the Census. (2006). American community survey. Retrieved September 27, 2007, from http://factfinder.census.gov.

U.S. Department of Education. (2000). *College enrollment by racial and ethnic group, selected years, 1999.* Retrieved August 30, 2002, from http://www.ed.gov.

Varlas, L. (2005, August). *Bridging the widest gap: Raising the achievement of Black boys.* Alexandria, VA: Association for Supervision and Curriculum Development. Retrieved June 2, 2006, from http://www.bridges4kids. org/articles/8-05/Varlas8-05.html.

Warren, S. (2005). Resilience and refusal: African-Caribbean young men's agency, school exclusions, and school-based mentoring programmes. *Race, Ethnicity and Education, 8*(3), 243–59.

Zamani-Gallaher, E. M., Green, D. O, Brown, M. C., II, & Stovall, D. O. (2009). *The case for affirmative action on campus: Concepts of equity, considerations for practice.* Sterling, VA: Stylus.

The State of Public School Violence

A QUANDARY

ANTHONY TROY ADAMS

Aspate of shootings throughout the United States has permanently marred the public's perception about schools as safe and secure places where students learn and teachers teach. An example of this is the April 20, 1999, high school massacre that occurred in Littleton, Colorado. That incident of senseless killing left 12 students and one teacher dead and 21 other students directly injured by their assailants, Eric David Harris and Dylon Bennett Klebold. Another instance of youth violence occurred on the schoolyard March 24, 1998, in Jonesboro, Arkansas. Thirteen-year-old Mitchell Johnson and 11-year-old Andrew Golden opened fire on their classmates killing Natalie Brooks, Stephanie Johnson, Brittany Varner, Paige Ann Herring, and Shannon Wright, their teacher who was pregnant at the time. The gunshot blasts also seriously wounded one other teacher and ten students.

Despite these tragedies, violence in the nation's public schools appears to be on the wane. The Centers for Disease Control and Prevention reports that violence-related behaviors in school settings actually decreased during the 12-year period from 1991 to 2003. The 2007 CDC Youth Risk Behavior Surveillance report notes countrywide, 5.5% of students did not attend school on at least one day within 30 days because they felt unsafe going to and from school or unsafe at school. The findings of the survey indicated greater absenteeism from school among black (6.6%) and Hispanic (9.6%) than white (4%) students because of safety concerns. The fear of violence on school grounds is very prevalent as 18% of students had carried a weapon (e.g., a gun, knife, or club), with higher percentages of males (28.5%) than females (7.5%) students carrying weapons. Additionally, when examining the trends by gender and race/ethnicity, a higher percent of white males (30.3%) in contrast to black males (24.6%) or Hispanic males (28.2%) and larger numbers of black females (10%) and Hispanic females (9%) than white females (6.1%) (Centers for Disease Control and Prevention, 2008).

This chapter has a sixfold purpose: (1) to deconstruct school violence by examining popular conceptualizations of the phenomenon and incorporating a comprehensive view; (2) to present recent statistics on the prevalence of school violence in Michigan; (3) to explore indicators of factors linked to school violence; (4) to describe traditional theories of deviance related to school violence, critiquing them in terms of their utility for explaining school violence; (5) to examine how schools manage school violence, focusing on the relationship of school violence to exclusionary disciplinary techniques (i.e., suspension and expulsion), the medicalization of discipline, school uniform and zero-tolerance policies, and the deleterious effect of various managerial responses to violence and discipline; and (6) to describe the status of African American youth in Michigan. The last of these purposes is intended to elicit dialogue among parents, teachers and aspiring educators, administrators, researchers, policymakers, and concerned individuals. The chapter closes with several policy recommendations that can serve as a baseline for stimulating further conversation on the topic of school violence.

Deconstructing School Violence

School violence is often conceptualized as a generic or umbrella term. It includes many other social constructs. For example, school disturbance, indiscipline among youth, misbehavior, and asocial behavior are frequently associated with school violence (Adams, 2000; Crews & Counts, 1997). In recent years, however, the term has grown in popularity. This is partly due to the media frenzy that typically accompanies coverage of feature stories. The public's lack of a critical understanding about school violence exacerbates the oftentimes wild coverage in the news. I employ a two-pronged definition of school violence. First, school violence involves any act that harms or has the potential to harm students in or around school buildings. Such acts may include, but are not limited to, emotional and physical threats, bullying, assaults (including those of a domestic nature), rape, homicide, and possession of firearms or other deadly weapons.

Second, I widen the aperture on school violence by incorporating what Epp and Watkinson (1997) call *systemic violence*. Systemic violence is broad-based. It transcends victims and perpetrators; it considers school culture vis-à-vis the organization, leadership, and pedagogy. According to Epp and Watkinson, "Systemic violence is any institutionalized practice or procedure that adversely impacts on disadvantaged individuals or groups by burdening them psychologically, mentally, culturally, spiritually, economically, or physically. It is perpetrated by those with power, entitlement, and privilege against those with less" (1997, 5). This definition closely parallels Freire's (1970) philosophy of education, which asserts that any situation in which people are prevented from learning is one of violence.

PREVALENCE OF SCHOOL VIOLENCE IN MICHIGAN

Findings from the *School Safety Practices Report* (2001–2) include the following statistics about Michigan's public school districts:

- The rates of juvenile crime in Michigan's schools are drastically lower than the rates of juvenile crime within the state generally.
- Incidents involving physical assault, drugs or narcotics, and non-firearm-related incidents together accounted for 58 percent of all reported expulsions.
- Out of the approximately 1.7 million students enrolled in Michigan's public schools, 1,588 students (one-tenth of 1 percent) have a record of expulsion.
- Compared to other ethnic groups, African American students received a greater percentage of long-term (180 days or more) expulsions. African American students were expelled at higher rates than their prevalence in the general student population would predict.
- African American male expulsions represent 66.3 percent of all African American students expelled.
- African American students represent 19.5 percent of the Michigan public school student population but nearly two-fifths (39 percent) of all students expelled.

What Are the Indicators of Factors Linked to School Violence?

Minogue, Kingery, and Murphy (1999) list eight factors linked to school violence. These factors include (1) community characteristics, (2) family characteristics, (3) school climate, (4) substance abuse, (5) student engagement at school, (6) occurrences that instigate violence, (7) attitudes favoring violence, and (8) weapon possession at school or on campus grounds. The categories are not discrete. For instance, an act of violence may occur both because of school climate and because of family characteristics, making it difficult to disentangle a complex web of influences. As factor (1) indicates, community (structural features) factors are correlates of school violence as well (Adams, 1993; Cooley, Turner, & Beidel, 1995; Elliot, 1996; Farrell, Danish, & Howard, 1992; Farrell & Bruce, 1997; Gottfredson & Gottfredson, 1985; Hellman, 1986; National Institute of Education, 1978; Needleman et al., 1996). The effects of unemployment and underemployment of adults and youth, involvement of youth in violence, drug trafficking, gangs, and the proliferation of community blight (e.g., abandoned, boarded-up, and unoccupied dwelling units) may also affect the levels of violence occurring inside schools (Williams, Stiffman, & O'Neal, 1998). Schools tend to be mirror images of the neighborhoods and communities that engulf them. Community characteristics are also likely to affect the school organization in many unfavorable ways (e.g., unemployment, community-crime, normlessness, etc.).

Family risk and community factors may be linked to school violence (Bennett-Johnson, 2004). Family dynamics may also differentially affect school violence. For example, Dryfoos (1990) and Burton and Owen (1990) maintain that the absence of a parent, family poverty, parents' education, family approaches to handling conflict, parental and/or family involvement in their offspring's education, and parental substance abuse and past or present criminal activity can affect school violence. Family structure is a likely antecedent of school violence.

School climate is widely accepted as a correlate of school violence. The literature on the impact of school climate on violence in schools is comprehensive, spanning nearly three decades (Adams, 1993; Fitzpatrick & Boldizar, 1993; Gottfredson, 1986; Gottfredson & Gottfredson, 1985; Grossnickle, Bialk, & Panagiotaros, 1993; Hill, 1997; Jenkins, 1997; Moles, 1990; Toby, 1983; Walsh, 1995; Welsh, 2000). The availability school security and surveillance technology, whether consistent and fair application of school rules is practiced, the types of penalties, adherence to procedural due process, accurate reporting of school infractions, and sufficient training and staff have all been identified as potentially influencing school violence. Whether students perceive that academic excellence is encouraged, and that diversity is promoted and embraced, may also be related to the level of school violence (National Institute of Education, 1978).

Mounting evidence suggests that substance abuse in schools may intensify the level of school violence (Allen et al., 1997; Farrell, Danish, & Howard, 1992). Widespread substance abuse and corollary drug trafficking in the neighborhoods surrounding a school can increase the level of violence on schoolyards. Drug trafficking in schools and the local neighborhood environment may be associated with any number of drug-related permutations, including turf battles between gangs, competition for "customers," and physical violence both on and off campus. Substance abuse and drug trafficking are likely precursors to schools marred by violence.

A number of empirical studies suggest that student engagement, or lack thereof, contributes to school violence (Hanish & Guerra, 2000; Noonan, 2005; McNeely and Falci, 2004). Schools that promote academic excellence, have a diverse curriculum, and offer significant numbers of Advanced Placement courses have been found to experience less school violence than those schools that do not (Gottfredson & Gottfredson, 1985; McDermott, 1980). More broadly, this suggests that schools where unequal educational opportunities are prevalent; there is a greater likelihood for disobedience and violence (Lawrence, 1998; Polk, 1982; Jencks et al., 1972). Students that have greater "access" to educational opportunities in schools, including Advanced Placement courses, state-of-the-art facilities and equipment, extracurricular and extramural activities, and the resources to attract sought-after teachers and staff, may experience less school violence. An unexpected outcome, or latent function, of schools offering extensive extracurricular activities (e.g., band, sports, drama, and student government) is that fewer students are likely to feel alienated or disconnected. These activities can serve as social buffers. Extracurricular and extramural activities may discourage students from asocial behaviors and reduce the potential for school violence (Gottfredson & Gottfredson, 1985; Noonan, 2005).

The research on bullying has increased sharply. Students' experiences of being hassled, shoved, insulted, disrespected ("dissed"), annoyed, bullied, teased, bossed around, dared, talked about, called names, or disliked can also lead to school violence (Berman et al., 1996; Durant, Pendergrast, & Cadenhead, 1994; Espelage & Swearer, 2003). The extent to which students feel alienated, isolated, or polarized is an additional factor that can lead to school disorganization and school violence.

Some school cultures promote violence; other school cultures mitigate violence. A school's level of violence is, in part, a function of its uniqueness. We know that school cultures vary. No two school cultures are identical. School cultures differ according to the percentage of minority and nonminority students, socioeconomic status, and values and beliefs. Prevailing student attitudes can affect the level of school violence. Attitudinal factors that may be related to violence are students' admiration for peers who are well-versed at fighting and using weapons as well as their beliefs that students should defend themselves when confronted (and conversely that avoidance of conflict is cowardice). Fighting impresses some students. Some believe that instigation by others makes fighting inevitable. Such belief orientations, confounded by the influences of peers or intimate playgroups (reference groups), school culture, and family have an impact on the social organization of schools. These factors in turn heighten the potential for school violence. Social organizations and prevailing attitudes that glorify violence are almost certain to fuel emotions and spark violence.

Lastly, the availability of weapons in and around schools is another factor related to school violence. Potential weapons are ubiquitous. Knifes, guns, brass knuckles, clubs and bats, bricks and boards, scissors, explosives, razor blades, and school-related tools or equipment have been confiscated from students accused of assault on school campuses (Callahan & Rivara, 1992; Clough, 1994; Shapiro et al., 1998). The availability of makeshift weapons and the proliferation of firearms in public schools is a growing concern (Callahan & Rivara, 1992; Clough, 1994; Durant, Pendergrast, & Cadenhead, 1994; Durant et al., 1997). Although detection and surveillance equipment are widely used, more deliberate planning measures are called for. Careful thought must go into developing ways to identify and confiscate weapons before they can be brought into school buildings while guaranteeing students' right to privacy. Moreover, developing ways to deter students from using school-related tools or equipment (e.g., rulers, pencils, lab equipment, etc.) as weapons should be a reigning priority.

Traditional Theories Explaining School Violence

Three sociological theories of deviance are examined in this section. First, Merton's (1938) strain theory posits that a mismatch exists between culturally defined goals (e.g., material success, wealth, higher education, etc.) and culturally defined means for achieving those goals (e.g., quality schooling and education, Protestant work ethic, etc.). For instance, youths may embezzle, steal, sell illicit drugs, or cheat on examinations to achieve culturally prescribed goals of success (e.g., expensive watches, designer clothing, performing well in school, etc.). Strain theory predicts that some individuals will not conform to society's conventional goals, but instead they will achieve culturally defined goals by inventing ways to attain those goals. Students, for example, who break into school lockers and sell items to purchase trendy athletic apparel often do so to impress their peers. Expensive clothing provides some students with a modicum or "illusion" of success. Students on the fringes may feel equal to their middle-class schoolmates because they too have designer shoes, boots, and garments and accessories.

Behavioral theorist Edwin Sutherland's (1974) differential association theory posits that deviance is a by-product of social interaction. Sutherland asserts that delinquency and other misbehaviors are learned and reinforced through group acceptance and validation. Unacceptable forms of behavior may become the norm. Particularly for youth that internalize belief systems that run counter to socially acceptable forms of behavior, certain deviant acts become acceptable when youths are in the company of those who condone asocial behavior.

Hirschi's (1969) social control theory provides an alternative lens to examine school violence. According Hirschi, some deviance is tempting, but the risk of being caught, sanctioned, or punished keeps most people in check. For those with nothing to lose, however, deviance is attractive. They are more likely to violate rules. Social control theory is predicated upon the idea that *attachment, opportunity, involvement,* and *beliefs* determine the likelihood of deviance. Strong familial, work group, or organizational attachment coupled with strong beliefs in conventional morality and respect for authority figures encourages conformity. Moreover, it also creates situations that lead to access to legitimate opportunities.

WHAT ARE THE CRITICISMS OF TRADITIONAL THEORIES OF SCHOOL VIOLENCE?

Strain, differential association, and control theories have several limitations. The predictive power of strain theory is delimited. It assumes that youths, in general, and Black youth more specifically, live out their daily experiences concerned about their future and long-term aspirations. Moreover, strain theory assumes that students of color are cognizant of culturally defined goals. Youth aspirations are strongly influenced by parents, family, peers, schools, reference groups, media, and cultural (as well as subcultural) variation. Peer and media influences are like juggernauts. They represent a vexing problem for educators, and there is no clear causal connection between youth aspirations and school violence.

Differential association theory offers limited predictive power too. It predicts that deviance is the result of "negative" intimate social interaction among playmates. Notwithstanding the potential for peer influences, many factors provide social buffers and discourage student involvement in school violence. Social buffers, such as consistent adult supervision, extended family involvement, participation in extracurricular activities, and exposure to positive role models have been shown to reduce youths' propensity for violence. Some youths may join youth gangs regardless of the presence of these factors in their lives. They may participate in some illegal activities (e.g., smoking marijuana, drinking under the legal age) but abstain from others (e.g., criminal involvement, including auto theft, grand larceny, etc.).

Control theory is a distant cousin of strain theory. Control theory combines a number of the ideas about the causes of deviant behavior expressed in strain theory. For that reason it too has several limitations. First, control theory does not significantly enhance our understanding of deviant behavior beyond differential association theory's contribution. It is an amalgamation. Second, it operates from the presumption that weak attachment, limited access to legitimate opportunities and involvement, and lack of beliefs consistent with conventional morality are precursors to social deviance. Control theory thus fails to acknowledge the effects of familial, socioeconomic, cultural, and structural antecedents on deviance. The various concepts associated with control theory (e.g., attachment, opportunity, etc.) have been difficult to test empirically.

Public School Attempts to Manage Violence

This section explores several instruments of social control. Social control refers to any method used to regulate, suppress, subdue, or restrict group behavior. High school codes of conduct are an example. They spell out in detailed terms appropriate forms of deportment. Codes of conduct also articulate school norms and the penalties associated with rule violation (e.g., student-to-teacher insubordination results in a suspension of not more than five concurrent days). Public schools often have elaborate codes of conduct. Exclusionary techniques, including suspensions and expulsions, are two mechanisms public schools use to manage disruptive behavior.

Suspensions come in three forms. In-school, short-term, and long-term suspensions are used to deter and regulate student misbehavior. With in-school suspensions students are supervised by adults or certified staff, and a reasonable amount of instruction may take place. Importantly, students remain in school under the supervision of adults. Short-term suspensions (typically one to five days) and long-term suspensions (which vary in length according to school district and state laws) are used to reduce the number of nonthreatening behaviors (e.g., quarrelsome students, insubordination). Short-term suspensions are handled by principals and assistant principals. They may or may not require procedural due process proceedings. That depends on the gravity of the offense (e.g., whether there is a perceived threat or danger to other students).

Out-of-school suspensions are less desirable for several reasons. First, students who are disciplined using out-of-school suspensions are generally unsupervised by adults. This can increase their opportunity for delinquent behavior and crime (Adams, 1994). Second, suspended students may befriend youth who are predisposed to delinquent or criminal activity. Third, students may engage in risk-taking behaviors while suspended, including drug, alcohol, and substance abuse. Fourth, out-of-school suspension can derail students from the educative process, and increase the odds of dropping out (DeRidder, 1990). Finally, long-term suspension may undermine students' respect for authority, leading them to behave in ways that increase the chances of their removal from school. Concerns have been raised about over escalating rates of exclusionary disciplinary practices in America's schools (Adams, 2000, 144–46).

Expulsion is another social control apparatus used by schools. Only local school boards have the authority to expel students. Expulsion is the permanent denial and deprivation of schooling, typically for a period of not more than one year. African American and Hispanic male students are significantly more likely to be expelled and suspended from public schools (Skiba, Nardo, & Peterson, 2000).

The medicalization of discipline has become another mechanism through which schools manage violence. Over the last 50 years, the influence of psychiatry and medicine has led to the medicalization of discipline. Students' moral and legal deviance has been transformed from adolescent indiscretions into a medical predisposition (Macionis, 2006). As a result, youths are not blamed for misbehaving, nor are their parents accused of poor parenting skills. Instead, students misbehave because they have a "medical" problem. Attention Deficit Disorder (ADD) and Attention Deficit Hyperactive Disorder (ADHD) are two frequently diagnosed disorders among school-aged children. Both illnesses have medically recognizable symptoms (American Psychiatric Association, 1994). Methylphenidate and amphetamine stimulants have become the most widely used treatments for ADD and ADHD, which are characterized by some or all of the following symptoms:

- Difficulty with selective attention
- Poor impulse control
- Inability to maintain appropriate task-related activities
- Difficulty with organization of cognitive tasks
- Failure to recognize and respond to social cues
- Poor ability to follow directions or instructions
- Easy distraction by extraneous stimuli

Several dilemmas accompany the medicalization of discipline. First, African American and Hispanic males are more likely to be diagnosed as having either ADD or ADHD (MacMillian & Reschly, 1998). Students diagnosed with these conditions are often treated differently by their teachers (e.g., low expectations, increased disciplinary referrals). Second, because the diagnostics for assessing ADD and ADHD lack precision, many children are misdiagnosed. Overdiagnosis is a critical problem as well. The above-mentioned symptoms are ubiquitous in the general population. They can be easily masked by individual emotional and psychological duress, familial dysfunctions (e.g., physical abuse, inadequate childcare), and structural antecedents (e.g., poverty, nutritional deficiencies). To state the point alternatively, there is great potential for false-positive diagnoses.

According to Pfuhl and Henry (1993), the medicalization of discipline enhances public schools' administrative efficiency at the expense of due process. School administrators can do a tap dance around students' constitutional guarantees. They can recommend that disruptive students be seen by medical personnel. Subsequently these students are evaluated by school psychologists, social workers, or other professionals. These professionals have the legitimate authority to label disruptive students (e.g., ADD, ADHD, learning disabled, etc.). As a result of these labeling practices, students may be segregated or excluded from the educative process. "Medical discipline" is a clear example of how students can be deprived of fundamental guarantees of life and liberty, protected by the Fourteenth Amendment. Procedural due process is often ignored. It ensures that students have the right to *notification* (and official transcripts), access to *counsel,* and an opportunity to *confront their accuser.* Schools, in short, can control misbehaving youths by justifying therapeutic interventions while they deny students their constitutional rights.

The use of pharmaceutical treatments, including methylphenidate and amphetamine stimulants for attention disorders, has increased exponentially in recent decades. Two indicators provide evidence of this surge: the United States Drug Enforcement Agency's aggregate production quotas (APQ) for all Schedule I and II controlled substances, and the Food and Drug Administration's sales and inventory data on the amounts of these substances used for legitimate medical and research purposes. As Woodworth states:

> The methylphenidate quota has increased from 1,768 kilograms in 1990 at which time there were 2 bulk manufacturers and 4 dosage-form manufacturers. This year [1999], the APQ is 14,957 kilograms with 6 bulk manufacturers and 19 dosage form manufacturers. Prior to 1991, domestic sales reported by manufacturers of methylphenidate remained stable at approximately 2,000 kilograms per year. By 1999, domestic sales increased nearly 500 percent. (2000, 2)

Nationwide, the average methylphenidate quota was 3,082 grams per 100,000 people in 1999. Methylphenidate treatment for ADD and ADHD is widespread in the state of Michigan, which ranked third in its use of the drug, distributing 4,848 grams per 100,000 people. Table 1 offers a geographical perspective on the distribution of methylphenidate nationwide. It provides a list of the top 10 methylphenidate-using states for 1999 (U.S. Drug Enforcement Administration, 2000).

The increase in the production and use of methylphenidate is more compelling when compared to worldwide usage. According to a report of the United Nations International Narcotics Control Board (1999), the United States produces and consumes about 85% of the world's production of methylphenidate. The vast majority of all U.S. prescriptions for methylphenidate are written for children diagnosed with ADHD. More than 50% of those prescriptions are written by pediatricians. Boys are four times more likely to be prescribed stimulant medication.

TABLE 1. TOP TEN STATES FOR METHYLPHENIDATE USE, 1999

RANK	STATE	GRAMS PER 100K
1	New Hampshire	5,524
2	Vermont	5,005
3	**Michigan**	**4,848**
4	Iowa	4,638
5	Delaware	4,439
6	Massachusetts	4,318
7	South Dakota	4,235
8	Virginia	4,207
9	Minnesota	3,941
10	Maryland	3,935

SOURCE: U.S. Drug Enforcement Administration, 2000.

Given the disturbingly high levels of methylphenidate production in the United States and the many lingering questions surrounding its use, one wonders how many African American students are being senselessly subjected to stimulant treatment for ADD and ADHD. Worse still, how many are suffering from methylphenidate's noted side effects, including stomach pains, appetite loss, seizures, severe headaches, agitation, aggression, and possible carcinogenic exposure? Children by their very nature are energetic, hyperactive, reactive to stimuli, and impulsive. When and why did we as a society decide that they needed to be "medicated" to be educated?

Public school uniform policies are another managerial approach aimed at reducing school violence. The first districtwide public school uniform policy was implemented in the Long Beach (California) Unified School District (LBUSD) in 1994. The LBUSD policy was institutionalized to reduce peer competition and strife associated with students' wearing or lacking name-brand clothing. It was pegged as a "cure-all" for many of the problems plaguing public schools. In the 10 years following the first implementation of the LBUSD policy, approximately one-quarter of the nation's public schools—mostly elementary schools and disproportionately those schools serving poor and minority students—were enforcing some kind of standardized school uniform policy (Brunsma, 2006). Are school uniform policies inversely correlated with school violence?

The empirical evidence linking school uniform policies and school violence is inconclusive. A great deal of media attention and public debate surrounded the publication of Stanley's (1996) study on the impact of the Long Beach Unified School District's school uniform policy. Although inconclusive, the study maintained that students' behavioral problems and gang-related activities decreased following implementation of the standardized uniform policy; however, very few published accounts since have tested theories, used rigorous methodologies, or collected sound empirical evidence to test the worth of Stanley's assertion. Indeed, the literature on school uniform policies is fraught with methodological problems.

Much of the discussion about such policies stems from anecdotal statements, news articles, and policy reports; while the bulk of the research examining the relationship between school uniform policies and school violence emanates from doctoral dissertations. From 1994 to 2004, twenty-five dissertations examined the issue of school uniforms. Brunsma (2006) contends that these dissertations vary widely in quality and depth. Some are largely descriptive; others use multivariate approaches to account for "between-group" variation linking the effects of school uniform policies to attendance, disciplinary referrals, and classroom environments (Burke, 1993; Hughes, 2006). Many of the dissertations relied upon small and nonrandomized samples. Sampling errors are plentiful with small samples, and many of the studies were cross-sectional. To confound matters, many of these studies were not subjected to the scrutiny of the peer review process. More research on the impact of school uniform policies on school violence is needed. The school uniforms literature has failed to develop and test theories, impose strict methodological adherence, and feed further discourse.

The literature on school uniform policy and its outcomes also suffers from conceptual and methodological problems. First, the very notion of conceptualizing school uniforms is a murky proposition. Researchers have not reached consensus on what exactly constitutes a school "uniform," and for this reason conceptual clarity remains tentative. School uniform policies can be placed on a continuum. They can range from uniforms that require polo shirts, navy pants, and solid-colored shoes to the more restrictive policies that require sport jackets adorned with iconic symbols. These uniforms are reminiscent of those worn by students attending elite boarding schools. In fact, Fossen (2002) distinguishes between distinctive uniforms that identify the wearer as a group member (e.g., uniforms bearing school-specific iconography) and uniforms that are nonrestrictive dress (e.g., not bearing school-specific iconography); he latter he called common or standard dress. Hughes (2006) uses a bifurcated framework to distinguish uniform types, describing casual uniform policies as *modes of dress.* He labels as *formal* those dress policies that require students to purchase uniforms from uniform companies.

Another method that educators employ in curbing school violence is zero-tolerance policies. These stringent conduct codes have been adopted by urban school districts as a means to manage and deter violence. Historically, zero-tolerance policies evolved from federal drug enforcement terminology in the 1980s. The intent of school districts that deploy zero-tolerance policies is to send a message. This school response makes it loud and clear that certain behaviors will not be tolerated. Zero-tolerance policies are fraught with problems. For instance, there is no causal link between zero-tolerance policies and violence reduction (Skiba & Peterson, 1999). Second, numerous civil rights controversies have arisen because of the broadness of many zero-tolerance policies (Skiba & Peterson, 1999). Third, significant numbers of African American and Hispanic students have been suspended or expelled from school for relatively minor offenses. Fourth, low-income students are overrepresented in suspension and expulsion statistics. Racial disproportionality persists, even after controlling for social class. It is the author's opinion that zero-tolerance policies have the deleterious effect of derailing large numbers of already marginalized students from the educational process. This further undermines students' respect for authority figures and deprives them of education they so desperately need. Zero-tolerance approaches have also been shown to lead to the indiscriminate use of suspension and expulsion (Essex, 2001; Skiba and Leone, 2001; Skiba & Peterson, 1999; Civil Rights Project & Advancement Project, 2000), and no evidence confirms that suspension and expulsion change students' behaviors or have additional school safety benefits.

THE STATUS OF AFRICAN AMERICAN MALES NATIONALLY AND IN MICHIGAN

- Nationally for the past 25 years, African American and Hispanic students have been suspended, expelled, and subjected to corporal punishment out of proportion to their percentages in the schools. (Children's Defense Fund, 1975)
- In 2000, 65% of Black male high school dropouts in their twenties were jobless—that is, unable to find work, not seeking work, incarcerated, or otherwise incapacitated. By 2004, that level catapulted to 72%, compared to 34% of Whites and 19% of Hispanic dropouts. (Holzer, Edleman, & Offner, 2006)
- Rates of incarceration for African American males skyrocketed in the 1990s: In

1995, 16% of Black men in their twenties who did not attend college were in jail or prison; by 2004, 21% were incarcerated. (Holzer, Edleman, & Offner, 2006)
- In the nation's inner cities, more than half of all Black men do not finish high school. (Holzer, Edleman, & Offner, 2006)
- In Michigan, African American students received a greater percentage of long-term (180-day) expulsions than students of other ethnic groups. The percentage of African Americans expelled was disproportionate relative to their percentage in the general student population. (*School Safety Practices Report*, 2001–2)
- 39% of expelled students in Michigan, but just 19.5% of the student population, were African American. African American males represent 66.3% of African American expulsions.

Implications for Policy and Practice

In sum, to reverse the disturbing trend of African American male school violence both in Michigan and nationally, I suggest the following policy recommendations:

1. Increase training and augment preparation of teachers to deal effectively with diverse student populations, thus enabling them to address social, cultural, economic and social class differences and how these differences affect educational outcomes (e.g., in-service training that targets students' various communication styles)
2. Increase programs designed to educate and assist African American male students (e.g., mentoring and after-school programs, and individualized educational plans)
3. Increase monitoring of African American males' educational, extracurricular, and behavioral outcomes (e.g., greater oversight and scrutiny of African American male students' academic records, disciplinary referral patterns, and involvement in social clubs and athletic teams)
4. Increase counseling and other appropriate interventions that target at-risk youths (e.g., drug counseling)
5. Concentrate efforts on violence reduction to target boys
6. Increase the number of university-community partnerships aimed at violence reduction

REFERENCES

Adams, A. T. (1993). Violence in public secondary schools: The contributions of community structure and school factors. *Journal of Applied Sociology, 10,* 75–98.

Adams, A. T. (1994). The economic determinants of high school punishments: A travesty of justice. Paper presented at the annual meeting of the Eastern Sociological Society, Baltimore, March.

Adams, A. T. (2000). The status of school discipline and violence. *Annals of the Academy of Political and Social Science, 567,* 140–56.

Allen, T. J., Moller, F. G., Rhodes, H. M., & Cherek, D. R. (1997). Subjects with a history of drug dependence are more aggressive than subjects with no drug use history. *Drug and Alcohol Dependence, 46,* 95–103.

American Psychiatric Association. (1994). Diagnostic criteria from DSM-IV. Washington, D.C.: The Association.

Bennett-Johnson, E. (2004). The root of school violence: Causes and recommendations for a plan of action. *College Student Journal, 38*(2). Retrieved September 7, 2008 from http://findarticles.com/p/articles/mi_moFCR/is_2_38/ai_n6130139.

Berman, S., Kurtines, W. M., Silverman, W., & Serafini, L. (1996). The impact of exposure to crime and violence on urban youth. *American Journal of Orthopsychiatry, 66*(3), 329–36.

Breuer, N., Lowry, R., Barrios, L., Simon, T., and Eaton D. (2005). Violence-related behaviors among high school students—United States, 1991–2003. *Journal of School Health, 75*(3), 81–85.

Brunsma, D. L. (2006). *Uniforms in public schools: A decade of research and debate.* Lanham, MD: Rowman & Littlefield Education.

Burke, N. D. (1993). *Restructuring gang clothing in the public schools. Education Law Report,* 513 (April), 391–404. Laramie: University of Wyoming College of Law.

Burton, D. L. & Owen, S. M. (1990). The relationship between trauma, family dysfunction, and the psychopathology in male juvenile offenders. Doctoral dissertation, Fuller Theological Seminary, Pasadena, CA.

Callahan, C. M. & Rivara, F. P. (1992). Urban high school youth and handguns: A school-based survey. *Journal of the American Medical Association,*

267(22), 3038–42.

Centers for Disease Control and Prevention (2008, June 6). *Youth risk behavior surveillance—United States, 2007*. Atlanta, GA: Centers for Disease Control and Prevention (CDC), U.S. Department of Health and Human Services.

Children's Defense Fund. (1975). *School suspensions: Are they helping children?* Cambridge, MA: Washington Research Project.

Civil Rights Project & Advancement Project. (2000). *Opportunities suspended: The devastating consequences of zero tolerance and school discipline policies.* Cambridge: Civil Rights Project, Harvard University.

Clough, J. B. (1994). Attitudes toward guns and violence. In L. L. Dahlberg, S. B. Toal, & C. B. Behrens (Eds.), *Measuring violence-related attitudes, beliefs, and behaviors among youths: A compendium of assessment tools,* 40–43. Atlanta: Centers for Disease Control and Prevention.

Cooley, M. R., Turner, S. M., & Beidel, D. C. (1995). Assessing community violence: The children's report of exposure to violence. *Journal of the American Academy of Child and Adolescent Psychiatry, 34*(2), 201–8.

Crews, G. A. & Counts, M. R. (1997). *The evolution of school disturbance in America: Colonial times to modern day.* Westport, CT: Praeger.

DeRidder, L. M. (1990). How suspension and expulsion contribute to dropping out. *Educational Horizons,* 153–57.

Dryfoos, J. (1990). *Adolescents at risk: Prevalence and prevention.* New York: Oxford University Press.

Durant, R. H. (1996). Intentions to use violence among young adolescents. *Pediatrics, 98*(6), 1104–8.

Durant, R. H., Kahn, J., Beckford, P. H., & Woods, E. R. (1997). The association of weapon carrying and fighting on school property and other health risk and problem behaviors among high school students. *Archives of Pediatric Adolescent Medicine, 151,* 360–66.

Durant, R. H., Pendergrast, R. A., & Cadenhead, C. (1994). Exposure to violence and victimization and fighting behavior by urban Black adolescents. *Journal of Adolescent Health, 15,* 311–18.

Elliot, D. S. (1996). The effects of neighborhood disadvantage on adolescent development. *Journal of Research in Crime and Delinquency, 33*(4), 389–426.

Epp, J. R. & Watkinson, A. M. (1997). *Systemic violence in education: Promise broken.* Albany: State University of New York Press.

Espelage, D. L. & Swearer, S. M. (2003). Research on school bullying and victimization: What have we learned and where do we go from here? *School Psychology Review, 32*(3), 365–83.

Essex, N. L. (2001). The limits of zero tolerance. *Principal Leadership, 1*(8), 5–7.

Farrell, A. & Bruce, S. E. (1997). Impact of exposure to community violence on violent behavior and emotional distress among urban adolescents. *Journal of Clinical Psychology, 26*(1), 2–14.

Farrell, A., Danish, S. J., and Howard, C. W. (1992). Risk factors for drug use in urban adolescents: Identification and cross-validation. *American Journal of Community Psychology, 20*(3), 263–86.

Fitzpatrick, K. M. & Boldizar, J. P. (1993). The prevalence and consequences of exposure to violence among African American youth. *Journal of the American Academy of Child and Adolescent Psychiatry, 32*(2), 424–30.

Fossen, L. L. A. (2002). School uniforms and sense of school as a community: Perceptions of belonging, safety, and caring relationships in urban school settings. Doctoral dissertation, University of Houston.

Freire, P. (M. B. Ramos, transl.). (1970). *Pedagogy of the oppressed.* New York: Seabury Press.

Gottfredson, D. C. (1986). An empirical test of school-based environmental and individual interventions to reduce the risk of delinquent behavior. *Criminology, 24,* 705–31.

Gottfredson, G. & Gottfredson, D. (1985). *Victimization in schools.* New York: Plenum Press.

Grossnickle, D. R., Bialk, T. J., & and Panagiotaros, B. C. (1993). The school discipline climate survey: Toward a safe, orderly learning environment. *NASSP Bulletin, 77,* 60–69.

Hanish, L. D. & Guerra, N. G. (2000). Children who get victimized at school: What is known? what can be done? *Professional School Counseling, 4*(2), 113–19.

Hellman, D. A. (1986). The pattern of violence in urban public schools: The influence of school and community. *Journal of Research in Crime and Delinquency, 23,* 102–27.

Hill, S. C. (1997). School-related violence: A secondary analysis of the youth risk behavior survey data (1993 and 1995). Doctoral dissertation, Southern Illinois University at Carbondale.

Hirschi, T. (1969). *Causes of delinquency.* Berkeley: University of California Press.

Holzer, H. J., Edelman, P., & Offner, P. (2006). *Reconnecting disadvantaged young men.* Washington, DC: Urban Institute Press.

Hughes, E. (2006). Effects of mandated school uniforms on student attendance, discipline referrals, and classroom environment. In D. L. Brunsma (Ed.), *Uniforms in public schools: A decade of research and debate.* Lanham, MD: Rowman & Littlefield Education.

Jencks, C., Smith, M., Acland, H., Bane, M. J., Cohen, D., Ginits, M., Heyns, B., and Michelson, S. (1972). *Inequality: A reassessment of the effect of family and schooling in America.* New York: Basic Books.

Jenkins, P. H. (1997). School delinquency and the school social bond. *Journal of Research in Crime and Delinquency, 34,* 337–67.

Lawrence, R. (1998). *School crime and juvenile justice.* New York: Oxford University Press.

Macionis, J. J. (2006). *Society: The basics.* Upper Saddle River, NJ: Pearson Prentice Hall.

MacMillian, D. L. & Reschly, D. J. (1998). Overrepresentation of minority students: The case for greater specificity or reconsideration of the variables examined. *Journal of Special Education, 32*(1), 15–24.

McDermott, J. (1980). High anxiety: Fear of crime in secondary schools. *Contemporary Education, 52,* 3–8.

McNeely, C. & Falci, C. (2004). School connectedness and the transition into and out of health-risk behavior among adolescents: A comparison of social belonging and teacher support. *Journal of School Health, 74*(7), 284–92.

Merton, R. (1938). Social structure and anomie. *American Sociological Review, 3*(6), 672–82.

Minogue, N., Kingery, P., & Murphy, L. (1999). *Approaches to assessing violence among youth.* Washington, DC: Hamilton Fish National Institute on School and Community Violence.

Moles, O. C. (1990). *Student discipline strategies.* Albany: State University of New York Press.

National Institute of Education. (1978). *Violent schools—safe schools: The safe school study report to Congress.* Washington, DC: U.S. Government Printing Office.

Needleman, H. L., Riess, J. A., Tobin, M. J., Biesecker, G. E., & Greenhouse, J. B.

(1996). Bone lead levels and delinquent behavior. *Journal of the American Academy of Medicine, 275*(5), 363–69.

Noonan, J. (2005). School climate and the safe school: Seven contributing factors. Safety in the schools. *Educational Horizons, 83*(1), 61–65.

Pfuhl, E. H. & Henry, S. (1993). *The deviance process.* New York: Aldine de Gruyter.

Polk, K. (1982). Curriculum tracking and delinquency: Some observations. *American Sociological Review, 47,* 282–84.

School safety practices report. (2001–2). Lansing: Michigan Department of Education.

Shapiro, J. P., Dorman, R. L., Welker, C., & Clough, J. B. (1998). Youth attitudes towards guns and violence: Relations with sex, age, ethnic group, and firearm exposure. *Journal of Clinical Child Psychology, 27*(1), 98–108.

Skiba, R. J. & Leone, P. (2001). Zero tolerance and school security measures: a failed experiment. In T.J. Johnson, J.E. Boyden, & W. Pittz (Eds), *Racial profiling and punishment in U.S. schools,* 34–38. Oakland, CA: Applied Research Center.

Skiba, R. J., Nardo, A. C., & Peterson, R. (2000). *The color of discipline: Source of racial and gender disproportionality in school punishment.* Bloomington: Indiana Education Policy Center.

Skiba, R. J. & Peterson, R. (1999). The dark side of zero-tolerance: Can punishment lead to safe schools? *Phi Delta Kappan, 80*(5), 372–82.

Stanley, M. S. (1996). School uniforms and safety. *Education and Urban Society, 28*(4), 424–35.

Sutherland, E. H. (1974). *Criminology* (9th ed.). Philadelphia: Lippincott.

Toby, J. (1983). Violence in school. In M. Tonry & N. Morris (Eds.), *Crime and justice: An annual review of research,* vol. 4, 1–47. Chicago: University of Chicago Press.

United Nations International Narcotics Control Board. (1999), *Narcotics control board releases report on worldwide use of controlled drugs.* INCB Annual Report Embargo, February, Release No. 2.

U.S. Drug Enforcement Administration (2000). Www.house.gov/ed_workforce/hearings/106th/ecyf/ritalin51600/woodworth.htm.

Walsh, M. (1995). The relationship of exposure to community violence with posttraumatic stress disorder and expression of anger in adolescents. Doctoral dissertation, Fordham University.

Welsh, W. N. (2000). The effects of school climate on school disorder. *Annals of the American Academy of Political and Social Science*, (January), 88–107.

Williams, J. H., Stiffman, A. R., & O'Neal, J. L. (1998). Violence among urban African American youths: An analysis of environmental and behavioral risk factors. *Social Work Research, 22*, 3–13.

Woodworth, T. (2000). *Statement of Terrance Woodworth, Deputy Director Office of Diversion Control, Drug Enforcement Administration, before the Committee on Education and the Workforce Subcommittee on Early Childhood, Youth Families.* http://www.house.gov/ed_worforcehearings/106th/ecyf/ritalin51600/woodworth.htm.

Uneasy Ties

RACE, GENDER IDENTITY, AND URBAN EDUCATION
REFORM FOR AFRICAN AMERICAN MALES

JAMES EARL DAVIS

To be African American and male in America's urban schools, many would argue, places one at risk for a variety of negative consequences including school failure, special education assignment, suspension, expulsion, and violence (Brown & Davis, 2000; Roderick, 2003). Much of the cause for the high rates of school attrition, substandard academic performance, and decreasing college enrollment and persistence reported for urban African American males has been attributed to these students' inability or disinclination to fulfill their roles as conventional learners in school settings (Davis, 2001). Little is known, however, about how school context affects African American males' educational and social experiences.

In many urban communities in the United States today, schooling is a predominantly or exclusively African American experience. Given that the nation's urban schools have been racially resegregated largely due to residential patterns, concerns about inner-city African American males being disadvantaged because of the racial makeup of their schools have been silenced (Nembhard, 2005). A focus on gender identity issues as a means of increasing these students' opportunities to learn, and of addressing their achievement and performance lags, is increasingly drawing the attention of administrators, teachers, and policymakers who work and advocate on their behalf. The actions, inactions, or half-hearted reactions taken by federal, state, and local education departments to address African American males' gender-identity issues have largely failed to allay fears or increase optimism about educational equity and quality schooling for this group of students. The resulting inertia has compounded the long-standing tensions surrounding the role public schools should assume in the racial and gender development of students.

The uneasy ties between race and gender are illuminated by the current status of African American males in urban schools. Nevertheless, education is a more significant area of concern and hope for improving the life chances of African American boys and men than ever before. The connections between race and gender are steeped in uneasiness; what is the role of race versus gender identity in efforts to reform urban education? Thus, understanding how they play out in educational research, policy, and practice related to improving the educational status of African American boys and men in the nation's largest cities is critical.

This chapter locates education reform at the nexus of race and gender identity in an effort to provide both a sensitive and a discerning examination of the problems, potentials, and possibilities of educating African American males in urban school contexts and to provide some direction for improving their schooling experiences and outcomes. After exploring how African American males are positioned at the intersection of race and gender identity, it addresses (1) the ways African American males challenge urban schools and reform efforts, particularly with regard to achievement outcomes; (2) the shifting meanings of racial and gender identity for African Americans and how research and practice in this area complicate efforts at urban school reform; (3) school-based gender-identity interventions for urban African American males; (4) early schooling of urban African American males as potentially viable research and policy directions; and (5) the roles of teachers and curricula in the racial and gendered school lives of urban African American male students.

Centering African American Males in the Race and Gender Debates

As an educational researcher, I have a keen interest in the experiences and outcomes of schooling. Specifically, my research and teaching agenda during the better part of my career has focused on how schools shape gender identity and behavior, particularly among males. As a product of racially segregated schools during my elementary years in the South, I have some firsthand knowledge of segregated education that was legally sanctioned according to racial categories. The curriculum, teachers, family, and peers within the African American community in which I lived, unsurprisingly, informed my racial identity and awareness. My primary interest in gender, however, developed later as a way in my personal and intellectual journey to better explain the experience of race at school.

Although research on the schooling experiences of African Americans has a long history, recent discussions, particularly those presented by popular media about the unique plight of urban African American males, have captured the interest of many. Previously, the discourse surrounding the educational status of these males and the nature of their precarious educational position were infused with compelling phrases such as "endangered species," "epidemic of failure" and "conspiracy to destroy African American boys" (Gibbs, 1988; Kunjufu, 1983; Madhubuti, 1990). From these metaphors emerged an urgency to address the educational problems of African American males in urban areas. It seems ironic that previous warnings have now been replaced by more compelling data regarding these males being "left behind" and "pushed out" of the mainstream of society (Mincy, 2006). Still, little is known about the most effective programmatic and policy directions for educating this group of students.

During the past two decades, journal articles, reports, and scholarly and popular books have detailed the precarious nature of African American males in urban schools and society. Recent publications have recaptured the attention of the nation that often chooses to turn its head away from difficult problems (Edelman, Holzer, & Offner, 2006). This recent work highlights concerns about the growing number of urban African American males who are disconnected from the social and economic mainstream of American society. Though their plight is the focus of this work, their marginalized social location is not a new phenomenon. What is new is consideration of their realities within the context of a new global economic order, which presents new challenges for a group that historically has been vulnerable to economic shifts.

From a research perspective, considerable attention has been directed toward understanding gender identity in education (Weaver-Hightower, 2003). Central to this effort has been the investigation of the effects of gender on schooling experiences and achievement (Adler, Kless, & Adler, 1992; Kessler et al., 1985; Wexler, 1988). In most of this work, gender is viewed from a social constructivist perspective, in which qualities of masculinity and femininity are culturally attributed and defined (Connell, 1995). Schooling contexts are often cited as important sources for gender construction and development (Thorne, 1986). Likewise, school experiences and opportunities are also circumscribed by race and ethnicity, but the intersection between gender and race in these contexts is often overlooked in educational research. In particular, the current plight of young African American males in urban schools demands much more focus, both in theory and in practice.

More recent attention to the racial and gendered conditions of urban African American male youth is ripe for new insights into race and culture. Although social, cultural, and economic conditions have been noted in the larger narrative about the precarious condition of these males (Canada, 1998; Noguera, 2003; Winbush, 2001), the opportunities now exist for encouraging and demanding nuanced portraits. Authors who are part of this Black-gender-revisionist scholarship movement are not shying away from the complexities of the actual lives of urban African American males, but are trying instead to meet that challenge head-on (Brown & Davis, 2000; Sewell, 1997; Young, 2003).

Challenging Urban Education Reform

African American males challenge urban education reform in many ways. Perhaps the single most important challenge that has garnered recent attention in research reports, policy documents, and public commentary has been the increasing disparity in the educational achievement of urban African American males relative to their peers. Indeed, the achievement gap is probably one the most critical "edu-political" problems facing this group of students. Although other issues such as the need to develop programs that promote school readiness, to improve teacher education and the quality of teachers assigned to urban schools, and to provide resources to meet increasing academic standards are important, the implications for achievement differentials are even more far-reaching.

A few assumptions undergird my analyses. First, I assume that African American males in urban settings need to be cared for and nurtured in responsive schools. Second, I assume that teachers must be supported in meeting the needs of all students, including African American males. My third assumption is that a critical component of this support includes increasing the ability of urban schools, via human and economic resources, to contribute to African American males' social, cognitive, gender, and academic development.

High rates of school attrition and special education assignment, along with relatively poor academic performance and college enrollment and persistence, are seen by some as result of the unwillingness of African American males to embrace the roles as conventional learners in urban school settings (Davis, 2001; Ferguson, 2000). Conversely, these students' negative school experiences and outcomes are also viewed as products of structural factors—that is, the results of maladaptations to systemic pressures of being marginalized and stereotyped at school (Harry & Anderson, 1999).

Although African American males as well as African American females have been shown to be negatively affected by the schooling they receive in American schools, some research suggests that the problems facing urban African American boys and young men are more chronic and extreme and therefore deserving of special policy and programmatic attention. Others cite the negative cultural messages about African American males that are perpetuated in the media today and describe the construction of these messages and how they are perceived in everyday life. They contend that contemporary images portray the African American male as violent, disrespectful, unintelligent, hypersexualized, and threatening (Young, 2003). These cultural messages, without a doubt, carry over into schools and negatively influence the ways urban African American male students are treated, positioned, and provided opportunities to learn. For instance, their demeanors and dispositions are often misunderstood by most teachers and seen as defiant, aggressive, and intimidating (Neal et al., 2003).

Federal educational reform efforts include millions of dollars to cover the cost of developing annual state assessments of students' reading and mathematical skills. States typically are responsible for selecting and designing their own assessments (e.g., the Michigan Education Assessment Program or MEAP). Clearly, by all current measures and assessment of school attainment and achievement, urban African American males are on the path for academic failure. In addition to their lags in test score performance and grades (Davis, 2003), these students are referred for special education placement at a much higher rate than are all other groups, and they are much more likely to be suspended or expelled from school. Without a doubt, new state assessments, like old wine in new bottles, will continue to show achievement and performance gaps between urban African American males and their peers of other racial and gender groups. Unlike the wine in old bottles, however, high-stakes consequences for achievement lags today take on even more urgency for urban African American males, with potentially far more dire consequences.

SHIFTING MEANINGS OF IDENTITY AND URBAN EDUCATIONAL REFORM

Educational policymakers, school districts, educators, researchers, and communities continue to grapple with the ghosts of racially segregated schools—ghosts that haunt modern attempts at school reform to address the educational disparities of students of color and low-income students in urban areas. The resegregation (and reconcentration) of African American students, particularly those in low-income inner-city communities, clearly troubles the equal educational opportunity cause championed in federal legislation. The most important evidence to date centers on issues of racial identity and the meaning children give to race in America.

The racial identity "wars" unearthed by social science research of the past few decades are critical to an understanding of the reasons for changing meanings in identity and development among African Americans. The current attention to racial identity, specifically its meaning and ramifications for African American children, though steady, has been captured by a "new" political and social reality: rather than viewing African American children as being severely disadvantaged by a school's racial makeup, segregated and resegregated schools are seen as the source of new thinking about the racial identity "problem." Many scholars continue to stress the importance of African American culture in the education of Black children (Boykin, 1994; Foster, 1997). Though evidence suggests that African American students value their culture, concern persists about the lack of Afrocentric curricula and of pedagogy that reflects Afrocentric dispositions (Diller, 1999; Ginwright, 2004).

In most urban areas, African American students are too often trapped in or relegated to underresourced and low-performing schools that are racially segregated and isolated. Although the realities of unequal education revealed in the data on racially segregated schools are in the main both disturbing and controversial, the educational policy context of desegregation remains critical. This is particularly true for American cities where substantial demographic shifts have occurred. In such settings, given meanings of race, gender, and class that are acutely informed by popular youth culture and consumerism, issues of identity are more complex. What is at stake for urban students, however—and revealed in most contemporary research—is too critical to go unchallenged.

Two important cultural shifts in collective identity development among African Americans students have occurred. One is the movement toward inclusion of multiple-identity perspectives and positions. This new politicized multiple-identity formation that has emerged focuses on salient references to gender and class. The second cultural shift is that urban African American students, less concerned and interested in the desegregated social environments, have in many ways retreated inward to embrace and nurture a collective or shared sense of identity in exclusive African American environments. Their new ideas about racial identity are being supported by research that argues that oppositional behavior is a means of reifying identity—that is, their racial or ethnic identity and identity formation occurs primarily in the oppositional context of "we" versus "them" (Ginwright, 2004). Compelling evidence highlights the significance and meaning that urban African American males place on racial identity and how that relates to important outcomes in educational achievement and mental health (Dimitriadis, 2003). These studies suggest that racial identity appears to be both a predictor of outcomes as well as a protective factor for urban African Americans, particularly males, against the psychological impact of discrimination, adversity, and other negative life experiences.

The political reality and positioning of African Americans today is vastly different than that found in the United States of the 1950s and 1960s, but in many urban communities, today as in the past, it is a given that the schools will be predominantly or exclusively African American. However, in contemporary urban educational contexts, where many schools are racially segregated, the concern that students are being disadvantaged because of their school's racial makeup is not as apparent or as vigorously voiced as during the previous generation. Thus, other strategies and educational reforms to increase urban African American students' opportunities to learn and to address their achievement lags are being proposed.

Gender is increasingly drawing the attention of many administrators, teachers, and policymakers who work and advocate for students in urban schools and communities today. Support for separate male and female academies in urban school districts has increased, and many urban communities are buying into these schooling alternatives. For example, in some urban school districts in Michigan, including Detroit, parents and communities have embraced a gender reform model that specifically targets low-performing African American students. The focus of this approach is to explore how gendered education settings enhance achievement opportunities for these students.

The creation of African American male and female classes and academies challenges the traditional education reform models (Hudley, 1995). For schools to consider race and gender in their attempts to address the needs of urban African American students complicates the reform landscape, but the potential for success is enough for many parents and communities who have grown tired of failures of other reform strategies. Nevertheless, the unprecedented growth of single-sex schools for African American males in urban areas across the country requires close monitoring and analysis. How this gender reform model is being "sold" to urban communities with low-performing schools and predominantly African American student populations must also be studied.

School-Based Gender Identity Intervention and Reforms

In recent years, public concern about the status of urban African American youth, particularly male youth, has increased. Reports of violence, sexual exploits, and declining rates of college entry and literacy have spawned a public discussion that insists that something is terribly awry with these young men and boys (Edelman, Holzer, & Offner, 2006; Dellums Commission, 2006). At the same time, competing notions of masculinity are circulating within a national discourse on the urban African American male's educational "crisis" (Hunter & Davis, 1994). Each of these conceptions has the potential to influence educational reform and social policy dramatically.

Some have used these discussions to blame gender-equity efforts for giving greater attention to the educational and social needs of girls while leaving boys dazed, confused, and ignored (Ginsberg, Shapiro, & Brown, 2004). These researchers, educators, and public figures frequently call for a renewed focus on young males, often with an emphasis on efforts to teach them to be "real men." To the extent that such efforts blame females for male failures and fail to adequately define or understand what is meant by "real" manhood, this discourse has dangerous potential to reinforce dominant notions of masculinity and to silence discussions about gender equity (hooks, 2004). Other researchers and reformers frame the African

American male educational crisis as evidence that popular notions of masculinity must be examined, challenged, and redefined as a critical next step in developing interventions that increase the educational and life expectancies of these young men (Harper, 1996; Hunter & Davis, 1994).

Much current thinking suggests that urban schools are not meeting the particular social and developmental needs of African American males and that gender-exclusive school environments are necessary to reverse these students' disproportionate rates of school failure (Davis, 2001; Grahams & Hudley, 2005). Hudley (1997) suggests that the involvement of consistent and positive males in urban educational settings provides essential models for young African American males to emulate. These positive role models are believed to counter inappropriate sex role socialization and maladaptive masculine identity, and to develop conceptions of masculinity that are not antithetical to expected behaviors, roles, and expectations in school settings (Cunningham & Meunier, 2004).

Other researchers see broader sociological and economic forces as undermining both the development and the appropriate expressions of masculinity among African American males, particularly those among the nation's inner-city poor. According to Poynting, Noble, and Tabar (1999), for these males, the meaning of masculinity and schooling objectives are incongruent and often diametrically opposed. One reason for the alienation and poor academic performance of some African American males, Poynting et al. maintain, is that they perceive most educational activities as feminine and irrelevant to their masculine identity and development. Furthermore, schools—and teachers in particular—are viewed as imposing a feminine culture on African American males that induces their oppositional behaviors. Given such school contexts and gender expectations, urban African American males are both victims and participants in their own educational demise. As Majors & Billson (1992) contend, African American males' negative school experiences and outcomes, to varying degrees, are products of structural factors and results of cultural adaptations to systemic pressures and maladaptive notions of masculinity.

What has emerged from the recent focus on the educational problems of urban African American males is an ideal of masculine behavior that Hunter and Davis (1994) contend buckles under the weight of racism, economic marginality, and cultural pathology. Masculinity is an important consideration, they concur, but it is not one-dimensional; nor is it implicitly universal. Thus, they reject frameworks that obscure the diversity and complexity of the myriad constructions of masculinity for

African American males in urban schools. They contend instead that perspectives on African American masculinity and male role performance that are steeped in the hegemony of traditional conceptions of masculinity fail to incorporate variations in the meaning of masculinity. They further note that urban African American males' own constructions of masculinity are sorely missing in the discussions and research, an omission that can only be remedied by efforts to capture the complexity of meaning and variations in the experiences of urban African American males concerning issues of schooling and educational achievement.

Adler, Kless, and Adler (1992) stress that students develop a stratified social order in schooling environments that is determined by their interactions with peers, teachers, and parents. Knowledge of social position is influenced by students' conceptions of status, or what Weber (1946) refers to as prestige or social honor. Though most researchers agree that peers are especially influential with regard to the school-related behaviors of urban African American males, little attention has been paid to explaining these students' personal conceptions of masculinity and behavior in relation to other influences in school settings. Understanding the role of peers, in addition to teachers and families, in these students' social construction of masculinity would constitute a major effort in addressing peers' influences.

Related to this concern, an array of strategies has captured the attention of school administrators, local communities, and parents as possible solutions to the problems associated with African American males in urban schools. These programs are of two primary types: assistive/supportive and reconstructive. The assistive programs aim to augment and support current school structures by providing the positive presence of adult African American men in school settings. Mentoring programs that assign professional African American men as role models for young boys, typically in elementary and middle schools, have been established in many school districts, both urban and suburban. In such settings, African American men serve as teacher's aides, tutors, and reading partners for African American boys in need of academic support and guidance. The justification for these initiatives points to the need for consistent and positive African American men in educational settings who can provide models for young urban African American males to emulate (Canada, 1998). These programs attempt to counter negative, peer-driven, gender-role socialization that might lead to maladaptive masculine identity formation (Cunningham, 1993). Their primary objective is the development of conceptions and expressions of masculinity that are not adversative to expected behaviors, roles, and attitudes in school settings. Reconstructive strategies, on the other hand, such as those promoted by all-male schools and classrooms, take a more radical approach to current schooling conditions. Given the severity of problems associated with African American males in urban schools, advocates for gender-exclusive schooling defend these strategies, whose goal is to reconstruct the gendered nature of schools and classrooms, as the most appropriate recourse (Watson & Smitherman, 1991).

Both these intervention strategies highlight the potential role schooling plays in a broader social narrative about urban African American males being left behind. As a way of countering the purported crisis facing these males in public school education, assistive/supportive and reconstructive approaches are grounded in the assumption that public schooling and its alleged feminizing culture disproportionately victimize this population. As such, these intervention strategies are proffered as compensatory measures aimed at restoring a normative masculinity to the center of urban African American boys' and young men's schooling experiences. They further assert that the feminine standards of behavioral expectations imposed upon these male students by female teachers lead to oppositional behaviors in academic attitude and engagement. Afrocentric models of masculinity also have been proposed as alternatives to traditional views of masculinity (Akbar, 1991; Ginwright, 2004; Jeff, 1994). These models call for a rejection of Western ideas of male socialization and for the reenvisioning of the African American male experience within a new cultural awareness.

Urban African American Boys and the Promise of Early Schooling

Growing evidence suggests that urban African American males' disengagement with schooling develops in the early grades and continues to intensify as they progress through school (Ferguson, 2000). By all assessment indicators, African American males generally lag behind other students in early grade performance while leading their peers in school infractions and other negative outcomes. Slaughter-Defoe and Richards (1994) suggest that as early as kindergarten, African American males are treated differently than other male and females students. Throughout elementary and middle school, Rong (1996) notes, African American boys consistently receive lower ratings by teachers for social behavior and academic expectations. New educational reforms potentially will increase the use of ability grouping and academic tracking, which will surely have even negative consequences for the achievement levels of African American males in urban elementary schools. Though large amounts of data specifically aggregated by race and gender are not readily available today, some studies already are pointing in this direction (Entwisle, Alexander, & Olson 2007). Other school reorganization efforts such as magnet schools, charter schools, after-school programming, block scheduling, looping, and extended and year-round schooling are important areas for study to determine if specific achievement effects in mathematics and reading are related to the implementation of these strategies for urban African American males.

Starting in the early grades, African American males are overenrolled in lower-level courses. For example, in one study of a prominent metropolitan school district, African American males were found to perform as well as their peers on district-wide assessments in reading and mathematics until the third grade (Simmons & Grady, 1992). Beginning in the fourth grade, however, these students experienced a sharp decline in their test scores. Indeed, the percentage of African American males in the top reading group dropped from 23% in grades 1 and 4 to 12% in grade 6. These declines correspond with findings revealing that African American males are disproportionately consigned to ability groups in which they only have access to lower-level, lower-content standard courses and materials (Watkins & Kurtz, 2001). When urban African American males have unequal access to the curriculum at the elementary school levels, achievement inequalities in the later grades are not surprising.

The need for early school-based intervention for urban African American males who are placed at-risk for underachievement is supported by findings from research on schooling (Davis, 2003). Although early intervention strategies for these students are important, this research shows that they are not always sufficient; the effects of early interventions alone generally have been found to fade over time, particularly for cognitive outcomes. Thus, more research on early and sustained interventions, particularly whole-school reform initiatives, especially in urban school districts is needed to map achievement accurately over time for African American males. Some whole-school reform interventions, where implementation generally begins in grades K–3 or PK–3 and then continues up to grades 4 and 5, appear appropriate and effective (Entwisle, Alexander, & Olson, 1997). Though evidence suggests that substantial reading effects typically occur in the first year of implementing such programs (usually at kindergarten and first grade), some large effects have been found in the second and third grades after the initial year of implementation. To ensure academic success for urban African American males, curriculum improvement, instruction, and support for teachers should begin in preschool and earlier—before these students begin to underachieve. Research continues to show that program interventions are less effective if they are implemented after these students have fallen too far behind (Entwisle, Alexander, & Olson, 2007).

Teachers' Roles in Identity-Development Reform

The role of teachers in increasing the achievement levels of urban African American males should not be minimized. Teacher accountability is certainly a dominant theme in the urban education reform literature. Much of this concern for accountability centers on student learning and achievement outcomes, but should urban teachers be held responsible for the academic and social outcomes of African American males? These teachers undoubtedly play a significant role in the school lives of their students. Since most of the latter's school day is spent in classrooms under the supervision and guidance of the former, the influence of teachers on African American males should never be taken for granted. Though teachers often are blamed for many of the problems African American males face in urban schools, most of the reform solutions aimed at remedying the educational plight of these students ironically have excluded teachers' perspectives. The rationale for this exclusion is that teachers are responsible for students' poor levels of academic performance and engagement, and consequently should not be part of the solution (Davis, 2001). Nonetheless, the influence of teachers on urban African American male students is too important for them not to be included in critical policy and practice discussions about the education of African American males.

The current political context of instructional accountability and student achievement has increased the urgency of efforts to improve the problem-solving and reasoning skills of all students. Methods for accomplishing these objectives are not as apparent as the consequences for failing to do so; but the need to engage students, particularly urban African American male students, in curriculum activities is rather obvious. The infusion of culturally relevant learning activities into classroom practice is an area that holds much promise for keeping these students excited about learning (Ladson-Billings, 1994). This connection of cultural relevance and student achievement potentially can offer a ray of hope for schools, teachers, parents, and communities responsible for raising the test scores of underachieving urban students.

Recognizing the influence of teaching strategies in the creation of classrooms that link culture with learning outcomes is essential to facilitate learning among urban African American males (Foster, 1997; Lee, 2005). As Lee maintains, to be effective, culture must be both connected to content and based on African American male students' prior knowledge and shared history. She posits that this alignment of culture and context encourages the modeling of classroom practices that make explicit the linkages between cultural knowledge and expectations of content learning. Another benefit of this cultural and context alignment is that it helps African American male students learn how to create narratives that reflect their shared history and culture. Combined, Lee suggests, the social interactions of urban African American males with each other, the incorporation of culturally based materials into the curriculum, and effective pedagogical practices can motivate these students to learn in classrooms they often find boring and irrelevant.

Teachers' social and personal characteristics are also important to consider. As a recent study by the Urban Institute concludes, holding teacher quality constant, positive educational effects can be obtained when African American students have African American teachers (Tatum, 2005). Additional evidence reveals that gender congruency of teachers is an important factor in urban African American males' academic and social development (Patterson, 2005). Studies additionally point out that many of these students feel they are misunderstood and wrongly judged because of who they are and how they look and act; as well, they typically desire a more personal and community connection with teachers (Neal et al., 2003).

Teachers bear a disproportionate role in monitoring social relationships, not only in their classrooms but also in other social settings at the school (Lewis, 2006). Traditionally, teachers have felt that their students' social networks and relationships were off-limits to them. As educational reform initiatives increasingly hold teachers more accountable for structuring student's learning opportunities, so urban teachers must take a more active role, when necessary, in providing their African American male students with social lessons that cultivate these students' appreciation for the importance of school and achievement. However, the recent educational reform mandates' emphasis on teacher quality, measured almost exclusively in assessment terms, misses the mark by failing to endorse what is becoming ever more apparent to educators: the social and cultural dimensions that connect to the experiences and realities of their students.

Future Directions and Considerations

Dismal, compelling statistics that reveal myriad achievement disparities and behavioral problems aside, understanding the "urban African American male student achievement problem" calls for a broad solutions-oriented research and policy agenda. This agenda must include a focus on the active role these males play in creating their school experiences and opportunities for achievement. To be certain, many urban African American male students bring to the schools many of the skills, dispositions, and behaviors that marginalize them. This is not to say, however, that the ways in which urban schools structure students' opportunities to learn is not important. Inequalities in schooling have potentially lifelong consequences for urban African American male educational attainment, employment, and family relations. Access to quality academic programs, curricula, and teachers are thus extremely important for these students. To cast them as victims strips them of any agency in how they make meaning of who they are at school and how they determine what schooling and success mean for them.

New projects in the schooling of African Americans are needed, particularly projects that seek to capture and optimize the complexity and variations in the voices and experiences of urban African American males at school. Understanding the role of peers, in addition to teachers and families, in the social construction of academic success would constitute a major step forward in resolving these students' disengagement and underachievement. How urban African American males link these constructions to academic achievement, motivation, and performance is also important to understand.

Though increased research attention has focused on the relatively poor academic performance of urban African American males on statewide assessments (Holzman, 2006), the this attention is clearly not enough. Much of this work is not really about understanding the achievement disparities among these students and their peers. Rather, it appears more concerned with documenting urban African American male students' poor school performance and achievement deficits for accountability purposes, and less concerned with potential successful strategies and interventions available to address that performance. As a result, insights about effective ways of countering these students' challenges go wanting. Sadly enough, the potential consequence of most urban educational reform is that African American males will continue to be left behind.

Support for innovations aimed at increasing urban African American male academic achievement—innovations such as gender-exclusive schooling (at the building or class level) and the infusion of stable, positive adult African American male role models in educational settings—is becoming more common. However, application of the standards of scientifically based research to prove the legitimacy of these approaches creates additional burdens of accountability and perceptions of usefulness. It is not sufficient to have a good idea about improving achievement and school engagement; privileged evidence must also be produced.

Research- and practice-based work on gender issues in education is important, not only for its timeliness, but also for its potential contributions to the improvement of schools and student outcomes. At the core of this work is an interest in capturing the complexity of, and potentially redressing, the intersection of gender and race in education. If research and practice can be moved to a nuanced understandings of this intersection, then the uneasy ties between racial and gender identity that influence urban African American males' school experiences and outcomes may be effectively addressed.

African American males challenge urban schools and society in a variety of ways. Like the canary that foresees and forecasts the impending danger of poisonous gases for miners burrowing deep below the earth's surface, the urban African American male is emblematic of the most vulnerable in the present social order. Not only do the educational challenges facing this group call our nation's attention to what is wrong with schooling and society, they also hold the key to what is potentially effective in improving the educational and life chances of all Americans.

REFERENCES

Adler, P. A., Kless, S. J., & Adler, P. (1992). Socialization to gender roles: Popularity among elementary school boys and girls. *Sociology of Education, 65*, 169–87.

Akbar, N. (1991). *Visions of Black men.* Nashville, TN: Winston-Derek Publications.

Boykin, A. W. (1994). Reformulating educational reform: Toward the proactive schooling of African American children. In R. J. Rossi (Ed.), *Educational reforms and students at risk*. New York: Teachers College Press.

Brown, M. C., II & Davis, J. E. (2000). *Black sons to mothers: Compliments, critiques, and challenges for cultural workers in education*. New York: Peter Lang.

Canada, G. (1998). *Reaching up for manhood: Transforming the lives of boys in America*. Boston: Beacon Press.

Connell, R. W. (1995). *Masculinities*. Berkeley: University of California Press.

Cunningham, M. (1993). Sex role influence on African American males. *Journal of African American Males Studies, 1*, 30–37.

Cunningham, M. & Meunier, L. N. (2004). The influence of peer experiences on bravado among African American males. In N. Way & J. Chu (Eds.), *Adolescents boys in context: Exploring diverse cultures of boyhood*, 219–34. New York: New York University Press.

Davis, J. E. (2001). Black boys at school: Negotiating masculinities and race. In R. Majors (Ed.), *Educating Our Black Children: New Directions and Radical Approaches*, 169–82. London: Routledge-Falmer.

Davis, J. E. (2003). Early school and academic achievement of African American males. *Urban Education, 38*(5), 515–37.

Dellums Commission. (2006). *A Way Out: Creating Partners for our Nation's Prosperity by Expanding Life Paths of Youth Men of Color:* Final Report. Washington, D.C.: Joint Center for Political and Economic Studies.

Diller, D. (1999). Opening the dialogue: Using culture as a tool in teaching young African American children. *Reading Teacher, 52* (May), 820–27.

Dimitriadis, G. (2003). *Friendship, cliques, and gangs: Young Black men coming of age in urban America*. New York: Teachers College Press.

Edelman, P., Holzer, H. J., & Offner, P. (2006). *Reconnecting disadvantaged young men*. Washington, DC: Urban Institute Press.

Entwisle, D. R., Alexander, K. L., & Olson, L. S. (1997). *Children, schools, and inequality*. Boulder, CO: Westview Press.

Entwisle, D. R., Alexander, K. L., & Olson, L. S. (2007). Early Schooling: The Handicap of Being Poor and Male. *Sociology of Education, 80*, 114–38.

Ferguson, A. A. (2000). *Bad boys: Public schools and the making of Black masculinity (law meaning and violence)*. Ann Arbor: University of Michigan Press.

Foster, M. (1997). *Black teachers on teaching*. New York: New Press.

Gibbs, J. (1988). *Young, Black, and male in America: An endangered species.* Dover, MA: Auburn House.

Ginsberg, A. E., Shapiro, J. P., & Brown, S. P. (2004). *Gender in urban education: Strategies for student achievement.* Portsmouth, NH: Heinemann.

Ginwright, S. A. (2004). *Black in school: Afrocentric reform, urban youth, and the promise of hip-hop culture.* New York: Teachers College Press.

Graham, S. & Hudley, C. (2005). Race and ethnicity in the study of motivation and competence. In C. Dwick and A. Elliott (Eds.), *Handbook of motivation and competence*, 392–413. New York: Guilford Press.

Harper, P. M. (1996). *Are we not men? Masculine anxiety and the problem of African American Identity.* New York: Oxford University Press.

Harry, B. & Anderson, M. G. (1999). The social construction of high-incidence disabilities: The effects on African American males. In V. C. Polite & J. E. Davis (Eds.), *African American males in school and society: Policy and practice for effective education*, 34–50. New York: Teachers College Press.

Holzman, M. (2006). *Public Education and Black Male Students: The 2006 State Report Card.* Cambridge, MA: Schott Foundation for Public Education.

hooks, b. (2004). *We real cool: Black men and masculinity.* New York: Routledge.

Hudley, C. A. (1995). Assessing the impact of separate schooling for African American male adolescents. *Journal of Early Adolescence, 15*, 38–57.

Hudley, C. A. (1997). Teacher practices and student motivation in middle school program for African American males. *Urban Education, 32*, 304–19.

Hunter, A. G. & Davis, J. E. (1994). Hidden voices of Black men: The meaning, structure and complexity of Black manhood. *Journal of Black Studies, 25*(1), 20–40.

Jeff, M. F. X. (1994). Afrocentrism and African-American male youth. In R. Mincy (Ed.) *Nurturing young Black males: Challenges to agencies, programs and social policy*, 99–118. Washington, DC: Urban Institute Press.

Kessler, S., Ashenden, D. J., Connell, R. W., & Dowsett, G. W. (1985). Gender relation in secondary schooling. *Sociology of Education, 58*, 34–48.

Kunjufu, J. (1983). *Countering the conspiracy to destroy Black boys.* Chicago: African-American Images.

Ladson-Billings, G. J. (1994). *The dreamkeepers: Successful teachers of African American Children.* San Francisco: Jossey-Bass.

Lee, C. A. (2005). Taking culture into account: Intervention research based on current view of cognition and learning. In J. King (Ed.), *Black Education*, 73–114. Mahwah, NJ: Lawrence Erlbaum.

Lewis, C. W. (2006). African American teachers in public schools: An examination of three urban districts. *Teachers College Record, 108*(2), 224–45.

Madhubuti, H. (1990). *Black men: Obsolete, single, dangerous?* Chicago: Third World Press.

Majors, R. G. & Billson, J. M. (1992). *Cool pose: The dilemmas of Black manhood in America.* New York: Lexington.

Mincy, R. B. (Ed.) (2006). *Black males left behind.* Washington, DC: Urban Institute Press.

Neal, L. I., McCray, A. D., Webb-Johnson, G. G., & Bridgest, S. T. (2003). Effects of African American movement styles on teachers' perceptions and reactions. *Journal of Special Education, 31*(1), 49–57.

Nembhard, G. J. (2005). On the road to democratic economic participation: Educating African American youth in the postindustrial global economy. In J. King (Ed.), *Black education: A transformative research and action agenda for the new century*, 225–40. Mahwah, NJ: Lawrence Erlbaum.

Noguera, P. (2003). The trouble with Black boys: The role and influence of environment and cultural status on the academic performance of African American males. *Urban Education, 38*, 431–59.

Patterson, K. B. (2005). Increasing positive outcomes for African American males in special education with the use of guided notes. *Journal of Negro Education, 74*(4), 311–20.

Poynting, S., Noble, G., & Tabar, P. (1999). "Intersections" of masculinity and ethnicity: A study of male Lebanese immigrant youth. *Race Ethnicity and Education, 2*(1), 59–77.

Roderick, M. (2003). What's happening to the boys? Early high school experience and school outcomes among African American male adolescents in Chicago. *Urban Education, 38*, 538–607.

Rong, X. L. (1996). Effects of race and gender on teachers' perception of the social behavior of elementary students. *Urban Education, 31*, 261–90.

Sewell, T. (1997). *Black masculinities and schooling: How Black boys survive modern schooling.* Stoke-on-Trent: Trentham.

Simmons, W. & Grady, M (1992). *Black male achievement: From peril to promise.* Report of the Superintendent's Advisory Committee on Black Male

Achievement. Prince George's County Public Schools, Upper Marlboro, MD.

Slaughter-Defoe, D. T. & Richards, H. (1994). Literacy as empowerment: The case for African American males. In V. L. Gadsden & D. A. Wagner (Eds.), *Literacy among African American youth: Issues in learning, teaching, and schooling*, 125–47. Cresskill, NJ: Hampton Press.

Tatum, A. (2005). *Teaching reading to Black adolescent males: Closing the achievement gap*. Portland, ME: Stenhouse Publishers.

Thorne, B. (1986). Girls and boys together, but mostly apart: Gender arrangements in elementary schools. In W. Hartup & Z. Rubin (Eds.), *Relationships and Development*, 176–84. Hillsdale, NJ: Lawrence Erlbaum.

Watkins, A. & Kurtz, D. P. (2001). Using solution focused intervention to address African-American male overrepresentation in special education: A case study. *Children and Schools, 23*(4), 223–35.

Watson, C. & Smitherman, G. (1991). Educational equity and Detroit's male academies. *Equity and Excellence, 25*, 90–105.

Weaver-Hightower, M. (2003). The "boy turn" in research on gender and education. *Review of Educational Research, 73*(4), 471–98.

Weber, M. (1946). Class, status, and party. In H. Gerth & C. W. Mills (Eds.), *From Max Weber*. New York: Oxford University Press.

Wexler, P. (1988). Symbolic economy of identity and denial of labor: Studies in high school. In L. Weis (Ed.), *Class, race and gender in American education*, 302–16. Albany: State University of New York Press.

Winbush, R. A. (2001). *The warrior method: A program for rearing healthy Black boys*. New York: Amistad.

Young, A. (2003). *The minds of marginalized Black men: Making sense of mobility, opportunity, and future life chances*. Princeton, NJ: Princeton University Press.

Coming Out of the HIV/AIDS Closet

THE DISPARATE IMPACT OF HIV/AIDS
ON AFRICAN AMERICAN MEN

DERRICK L. ANDERSON *and* ROBERT W. SIMMONS III

T he between-the-legs spin move and the behind-the-back pass characterized the basketball wizardry of a childhood idol. The revelation that he had tested positive for the human immunodeficiency virus (HIV) would later come to characterize that same champion athlete: Earvin "Magic" Johnson. Growing up in Detroit, Michigan, allowed us to witness the triumphs of that great Michigan-born hero. Whether watching Magic drop no-look passes to James Worthy en route to beating our beloved Pistons or the hated Boston Celtics, efforts to emulate him led to practicing junior basketball moves until the wee hours of the morning.

For many, efforts to emulate Magic's moves on the basketball court were pushed aside when he revealed that he was HIV-positive in 1991. In the Black community, a chord was struck; Magic's disclosure would not only raise my consciousness about HIV/AIDS but also, some would conjecture, the consciousness of the entire African American population of the United States. When he told the world about his HIV status, one could almost hear a collective gasp of disbelief issuing from within the Black community. This gasp revealed a growing crisis within the Black community, and more importantly, it exposed the deadly silence that had existed for too long around the issue of HIV/AIDS (HIV infection with or without AIDS, or acquired immune deficiency syndrome) and African Americans.

Prior to Magic's shocking revelation in 1991, HIV/AIDS within the Black community seemed to take a backseat to the host of other grave health, economic, and social matters facing Blacks in the United States. And Magic's condition was not the first in the Black community—not by a long jump shot—nor would it be the last. To be sure, 1987 was a seminal moment in the Black community's battle against HIV/AIDS. In 1987, African American AIDS activism seemed to explode onto the scene with the establishment of the National Black Leadership Commission on AIDS and the National Minority AIDS Council (Wright, 2006). Despite these and other groups', agencies', and individuals' valiant efforts, far too many lives would continue to be lost to this surging medical predicament.

The HIV/AIDS crisis in the African American community is part of a much larger challenge facing Black America—namely, that of basic health care. African Americans have borne a disproportionate share of many health care and medical problems in the United States. Such problems as a higher-than-average infant death rate and higher death rates from cancer as well as disproportionate rates of diabetes have made the overall Black-White health disparity one of the most challenging civil rights issues of the twenty-first century (Washington, 2006). Certainly, infant mortality, cancer, diabetes, and other conditions are contributing factors to what can only be described as a health crisis in the Black community; however, the HIV/AIDS epidemic has added a bold signature to the wide range of health care disparities affecting African Americans.

HIV/AIDS has had a major impact on the Black community in the United States. Though African Americans represent only 12% of the U.S. population, they comprise 51% of all the nation's HIV/AIDS patients (Wright, 2006). Further investigation into these numbers reveals that African American women are 25 times more likely than White American women to be diagnosed with HIV/AIDS, and Black men are 10 times more likely than White men in this nation to be stricken with the disease (Washington, 2006). Even more shocking are the childhood HIV/AIDS statistics for Whites and non-Whites in America. Eighty-three percent of all U.S. children with HIV/AIDS are Black or Hispanic (Washington, 2006). With so many young African Americans contracting HIV/AIDS, it is imperative that the nation's educational institutions become involved in the struggle to fight this deadly disease.

African American males are 10 times more likely to be diagnosed with HIV/

AIDS. The impact of HIV/AIDS on these men and boys has added another dimension to the struggles and challenges they face. Like the disproportionate number of Black males suspended from school and the overrepresentation of Black men in the U.S. penal system, the HIV/AIDS crisis places Black men at risk for "a variety of negative consequences" (Polite & Davis, 1999, 1).

Central to this chapter is an exploration of the size and scope of the HIV/AIDS crisis in the African American community, both nationally and statewide in Michigan, and of the reasons why the HIV/AIDS infection rates are significantly higher within this population (although relatively stable over time). Examination of one of the more troubling aspects of this issue, its socioenvironmental context, requires that specific attention be given to how socioenvironmental influences within the African American community, in concert with other cultural influences and perceptual attitudes, leave many Black men vulnerable to being exposed to HIV. This chapter also demonstrates how the convergence of these factors informs the development of HIV/AIDS public policy and public health care and disease prevention practices. Last, before presenting a solid educational strategy to combat the numbing statistics that accompany discussions of African Americans and HIV/AIDS, the chapter provides background information on the educational fight that has been waged against the disease, looking specifically at educational programs from the United States and Africa that have been effective in developing a solid knowledge base among young people and at the role to be played by service learning.

HIV/AIDS in the African American Community

In 2003, an estimated 1.2 million persons in the United States were living with HIV infection, 47% of whom were non-Hispanic Blacks. In a report released by the Centers for Disease Control (CDC) (2005b) based on data from 2001 to 2004, racial/ethnic disparities in diagnoses of HIV/AIDS are evident. Of the estimated 157,252 diagnoses of HIV infection during that same period, the number of cases and diagnosis rates among African Americans was higher (51%) than those for all other racial/ethnic populations combined (Hispanic, Asian, and Native American). Based on the previously mentioned report from the Centers for Disease Control, among males, Blacks had the largest or second-largest percentage of cases in every transmission category. Among females, Blacks had the largest percentage of cases in all transmission categories. Moreover, among both males and females, Blacks represented the largest percentage of HIV/AIDS diagnoses in every age group.

The adult transmission of HIV/AIDS can be classified into the following hierarchy of transmission categories: (1) male-to-male sexual contact (i.e., that between men who have sex with men [MSM]); (2) injection drug use (IDU); (3) both male-to-male sexual contact and injection-drug use (MSM/IDU); (4) high-risk heterosexual (HRH) contact (i.e., with a person of the opposite sex known to have HIV/AIDS or a risk factor [e.g., MSM or IDU] for HIV/AIDS); and (5) all other risk factors combined. Pediatric cases can be classified as either perinatal transmission or all other transmission categories combined.

African American Men and HIV/AIDS: The National Picture

Although African Americans accounted for approximately 13% of the population of the 33 states included in a report from the Centers for Disease Control (Alabama, Alaska, Arizona, Arkansas, Colorado, Florida, Idaho, Indiana, Iowa, Kansas, Louisiana, Michigan, Minnesota, Mississippi, Missouri, Nebraska, Nevada, New Jersey, New Mexico, New York, North Carolina, North Dakota, Ohio, Oklahoma, South Carolina, South Dakota, Tennessee, Texas, Utah, Virginia, West Virginia, Wisconsin, and Wyoming) looking at data from 2001 to 2004, Blacks accounted for the majority (80,187 or 51%) of HIV/AIDS diagnoses (2005b). While this report does not contain information from all 50 states, the CDC gathered data from states with reporting systems that allow for confidential name-based reporting.

The CDC report points out that the average annual rates of HIV diagnoses for specific transmission categories were calculated using race/ethnicity and age-specific census data as the denominators. For example, the rate of cases among Black men with male-to-male sexual contact represents the number of cases per 100,000 Black males from 2001 to 2004. Black men had the highest average rates for all MSM transmission categories—69.0 per 100,000—compared to 13.9 for White males, 37.8 for Hispanic males, 8.2 for Asian/Pacific Islander (A/PI) males, and 12.1 for American Indian/Alaska Native (AI/AN) males. For cases among males reporting IDU, the rate for Blacks was 26.9 per 100,000 compared to 1.7 for Whites, 12.0 for Hispanics, 1.6 for A/PIs, and 2.7 for AI/ANs. For cases among HRH males, the rate for Blacks was 35.5 per 100,000 compared to 1.1 for Whites, 10.9 for Hispanics, 2.3

for A/PIs, and 2.4 for AI/ANs. Among all these at-risk groups, Black men were far more likely to be infected with HIV than were any other population group.

The estimated annual percentage change (EAPC) was used as a measure of the change in HIV diagnosis rates from 2001 to 2004. At one level, these results are encouraging: the number of new cases diagnosed over this three-year period declined slightly for both Black and Hispanic males. That decline was modest, however, and A/PI males HIV/AIDS rates increased. As shown in the previously mentioned report from the CDC (2005b) the EAPC for Blacks was −4.4%, for Whites +1.4%, for Hispanics −4.7%, for A/PIs +8.1%, and for AI/ANs +2.4%. Although the annual percentage decrease in HIV diagnosis rates among Blacks overall was statistically significant ($p < 0.05$), the annual HIV diagnosis rates among Black males remained higher than the rates for all males of other racial/ethnic populations. In 2004, among males, the rate of HIV/AIDS diagnosis for Blacks (131.6 per 100,000) was 7.0 times higher than that for Whites (18.7 per 100,000), 2.2 times higher than that for Hispanics (60.2 per 100,000), 9.5 times higher than that for A/PIs (13.9 per 100,000), and 6.3 times higher than that for AI/ANs (20.8 per 100,000). The problem is not becoming self-correcting. African American males remain most at risk for HIV infection. By region Blacks accounted for the majority of diagnoses in the South (47,497 [54%]) and Northeast (23,674 [53%]) (CDC, 2005b). Black males accounted for more HIV/AIDS diagnoses than males of any other racial/ethnic population in the South (29,532 [48%]) and the Northeast (14,104 [47%]).

HIV/AIDS in the State of Michigan

By the year 2006, a total of 16,200 Michigan residents were living with HIV infection or AIDS (Michigan Department of Community Health [MDCH], 2006). This estimate includes 11,981 persons reported confidentially and 1,516 persons reported anonymously.

HIV-RELATED DEATHS IN MICHIGAN

After the introduction of more effective treatment regimens, HIV-related deaths declined sharply among all groups between 1995 and 1997, and then again, though less sharply, between 1998 and 2000. The MDCH (2006) data show a decline in

HIV-related deaths between 1995 and 2001 among Black men (65%), White men (79%), and women (47%). Moreover, the years 2001 to 2003 saw a continuing decline in deaths among Black men (of 37%), while HIV-related death rates among White males and all females remained level during this period. Few HIV-related deaths were reported for other race/sex groups. Thus, one could surmise that the HIV/AIDS problem in the state of Michigan is being solved; however, we do not believe this to be the case. Rather, as HIV-infected people live longer, the number of persons living with HIV/AIDS continues to rise, and this creates several more problems. One is the growing need for treatment drugs and medical services. Of equal importance, the growing numbers of people living with HIV/AIDS in the African American community increases the potential risk that HIV infection will spread still more widely within the populations that are most vulnerable to exposure—namely, MSM and injection drug users (IDUs).

Trends in New Diagnoses of HIV Infection in Michigan, 1999–2003

To evaluate trends over time, MDCH (2006) researchers estimated the number of persons newly diagnosed with HIV infection each year to determine if any statistically significant changes occurred in that regard from 1999 through 2003. This number was estimated by adjusting the number of reported cases for people diagnosed between 1999 and 2003 against those cases that may not have been reported to the health department by January 1, 2005. The 2006 report marks the second time this adjustment was based solely on Michigan reporting patterns; previously, adjustments were made using multistate regional data. Although the date of new HIV diagnosis does not indicate when persons were first infected because their HIV diagnosis may have taken place months or years earlier, these figures represent the best current measure of how fast the epidemic is spreading among different populations in the state. The No Identifiable Risk (NIR) cases reported during this period were also redistributed to other risk categories based on past patterns of NIR reclassification.

Overall, the number of newly diagnosed Michigan residents with HIV each year increased by about 200 cases between 1999 and 2003, from 725 to 922 new cases each year. However, this upward trend was due entirely to the low number recorded in 1999, which, based on MDCH speculations, is related to reporting patterns and not reflective of true changes in the epidemic. For this reason, the 1999 data were excluded from the MDCH analysis and only the trends from 2000 to 2003 were reported. This provided a more accurate reflection of the current trends in HIV diagnoses in Michigan, which include the number of persons who learned of their HIV infection status after developing symptoms of AIDS. Thus, for each of the four years examined, the data reveal that the number of Michigan deaths from AIDS surpasses the new diagnoses of HIV infection; furthermore, they show that the reported number of persons living with HIV/AIDS in the state is increasing rather than decreasing.

Risk Behaviors for HIV Infection in Michigan, 2000–2003

For the purposes of HIV prevention service provision, a high-risk heterosexual (HRH) is an individual who is at increased risk for HIV infection by virtue of opposite-gender sexual contact. HRHs include female sex partners of MSM, sex partners of IDUs, sex partners of HIV-positive individuals with a sexually transmitted disease, commercial sex workers (CSW), and those who provide sex for money or drugs. The proportion of HRHs in Michigan diagnosed with HIV infection between 2000 and 2003 decreased significantly, from 16% to 8% (140 to 76 cases) (MDCH, 2006). The proportion of HIV diagnoses for another group, presumed heterosexuals (PHs), increased significantly, from 20% to 25% (179 to 231 cases). Presumed heterosexuals are persons for whom their only risk is heterosexual sex with a partner whose risk and HIV status are unknown. When these two heterosexual groups are combined, the infection trend is steady. The proportion of new diagnoses remained level in all the other risk groups as well. These other risks groups include those infected with HIV via transmission from blood products and perinatal exposures. Less than 1% of diagnoses were among persons who first acquired infection from blood products received either before 1985 in the United States or in other countries. Less than 1% of diagnoses were among infants born to HIV-infected mothers.

The 922 new Michigan HIV diagnoses reported in 2003 include the following:

- MSM: 425 new cases (46%)
- PHs: 231 (25%)
- NIRs: 88 (10%)

- HRHs: 76 (8%)
- IDUs: 76 (8%)
- MSM/IDUs: 18 (2%)
- Other Risk Categories: 8 (1%) (MDCH, 2006)

Race and Gender Disparities in Michigan HIV/AIDS Diagnoses, 2000–2003

In Michigan, the proportion of African American females among those diagnosed with HIV infection between 2000 and 2003 decreased from 22% to 17% (196 to 156 cases). In all other race/sex groups, the trend was level (MDCH, 2006). In 2003, a total of 401 (43%) Black males were diagnosed as HIV-infected compared to 282 (31%) White males, 156 (17%) Black females, 51 (6%) non-White/non-Black males, 32 (3%) White females, and 0 (0%) non-White/non-Black females. Although the trend in new HIV diagnoses among Black males was found to be level during that period and on the decline among Black females, Black males and females, who, combined, comprise 14% of Michigan's general population, were disproportionately affected by HIV/AIDS, comprising 58% of persons living with the virus and/or the disease in the state (MDCH, 2006).

CONCURRENT HIV AND AIDS DIAGNOSIS IN MICHIGAN, 2000–2003

Among persons who were diagnosed with HIV infection between 2000 and 2003, the percentages that were diagnosed concurrently with AIDS remained stable at 25% (219 cases) (MDCH, 2006). The proportion of concurrent diagnoses also did not change significantly for any of the race/gender groups. In 2003, the MHCD reported 105 (26%) concurrent diagnoses for Black males, 76 (27%) for White males, 41 (26%) for Black females, 13 (25%) for non-White/non-Black males, 7 (22%) for White females, and 0 (0%) cases for non-White/non-Black females. Every concurrent diagnosis represents a failure to diagnose HIV infection early as well as to start treatment early.

AFRICAN AMERICAN MEN AND HIV/AIDS IN MICHIGAN

African American men in Michigan represented 9,450 cases of HIV prevalence in the MDCH (2006) report. Of the 6,072 individuals diagnosed as living with AIDS in Michigan, African American males represented 3,532 or 58% of these cases. Their primary mode of HIV transmission was male-to-male sex, with African American men representing 2,489 (50%) of the total number (5,531 or 60%) of cases who acquired HIV infection through this mode of transmission.

African American men who identify as IDUs represented 742 (15%) of HIV infections. MSM who were also IDUs represented 317 (6%) of Michigan's HIV infection rate, and heterosexual African American men represented 331 (7%). Among other methods of HIV infection reported by African American men during the study period were blood recipients, 18 (0%); those infected perinatally, 59 (1%); and those whose infection mode was undeterminable, 976 (20%). Looking carefully at this data, one sees that African American men in Michigan who have sex with men account not only for 60% of HIV-infection cases among MSM but also for 60% of all cases of HIV infection found among African American men. The sexual practices of fully 20% of African American men in Michigan reported with HIV were unknown.

Michigan's HIV/AIDS Prevention Priority Populations

MEN WHO HAVE SEX WITH MEN (MSM)

In health surveys related to men with HIV/AIDS, men who self-report having sex with men (MSM) make up about 1.5% of Michigan's population and account for over 8,240 reported cases of people living with HIV/AIDS (Michigan HIV/AIDS Council [MHAC], 2006). The surveys further reveal that large numbers of Michigan's MSM population do not believe they are at risk for HIV infection, even though they are engaging in unprotected sex. Furthermore, survey data indicate that 25% of this population have never been tested for HIV, 43% do not discuss or disclose their status to partners, 54% had not used a condom during their last sexual encounter, 76% never use condoms for oral sex, and 30% never used condoms for anal sex. Additionally, as the Michigan HIV/AIDS Council indicates, many MSM are not asking their partners about their HIV status either.

Prevention needs for MSM fall into four categories: knowledge, persuasion, supportive norms, and skills. The MHAC recommended six strategies to address this group's prevention needs. These include counseling, testing and referral services, skills building workshops, structural interventions, health communications, and outreach and community building.

INJECTION DRUG USERS (IDUS)

According to a 2004 MDCH report on HIV/AIDS and health-related needs among IDUs in Michigan, 30% of the state's IDUs reported using dirty needles and other injection paraphernalia (or *works*) within the past year. At last injection, 25% had not used a new or clean needle, and over 60% did not use clean works. Furthermore the Michigan Department of Community Health (2004) indicates that almost none of those who reported cleaning needles used the cleaning technique recommended by the CDC. IDUs also reported facing difficulties in acquiring clean works, particularly from pharmacies. Needle Exchange Programs (NEP) were noted as essential to helping IDUs reduce their HIV/AIDS risk, but were not readily available in most areas of the state (MHAC, 2006). Condom use with primary sexual partners was low (about 4% among female IDUs) and only 22% of male IDUs reported using condoms with nonprimary partners every time. Forty-two percent of respondents indicated that they had at one time exchanged sex for money or drugs.

These risk behaviors reveal that IDUs are placing themselves at risk through both sexual and drug-using practices. Less than one-third of those interviewed listed HIV infection as a primary health concern, and many stated that they believe they will not get HIV/AIDS. When asked about routes of transmission most respondents were knowledgeable, but this did not translate into strategies that successfully reduced their risk.

HIGH-RISK HETEROSEXUALS (HRHS) AND PRESUMED HETEROSEXUALS (PHS)

Data are limited for this population because many HRH do not know the sexual and drug-use habits of their partners, nor are they typically aware of their serostatus. Seventeen percent of reported HIV cases and 13% of AIDS cases in Michigan involve presumed heterosexuals. These findings are especially frustrating for the MHAC (2006), which claims that it cannot confidently include HRHs and PHs in its priority-setting process because of the difficulty of identifying which risk groups actually fall into the presumed heterosexual category. The MHAC's HIV testing survey and assessment of the needs of commercial sex workers (CSWs) suggest that most HRHs do not use condoms with their primary partners (MHAC, 2006). Thus it appears that the prevention needs of HRHs are overwhelmingly those of persuasion, skills, and supportive community norms. Five intervention models have been matched to these needs: individual-level prevention counseling, testing and referral services, health communications, skills-building workshops, and structural interventions (MHAC, 2006).

Michigan's HIV/AIDS Surveillance and Research Needs

The MHAC (2006) report identifies a number of gaps in knowledge and information related to the HIV prevention needs of Michigan's residents. To address these gaps, it offers the following observations and recommendations:

- Future needs assessment activities should strive to obtain data that will enable MHAC to better characterize the HIV/AIDS prevention needs of racial/ethnic minorities within each of the four populations identified.
- Additional research on interventions for HIV-positive Michigan residents is urgently needed.
- Future research on MSM should address a larger and more diverse population, particularly those in rural communities, African American MSM, and young MSM.
- More information is needed about IDUs, expressly how many have access to clean needles, through what mechanisms, and where. The MHAC should work with the federal Office of Drug Control Policy to obtain better data about substance abuse treatment admissions and clients.
- The only data on HRHs that was available to the MHAC came from its survey of CSWs and from the limited information provided by the HIV Testing Survey.
- The MHAC should place a priority on conducting needs assessments targeted to the partners of persons living with HIV/AIDS. Local public health departments providing STD treatment and services may serve as sources of additional information about this group.

Going forward, the Needs Assessment Committee of the MHAC plans to ensure the generation of more and higher-quality data. Focus groups and key informant interviews will be conducted to help give voice to the subjective experiences of those most affected by the HIV/AIDS epidemic. These methodologies are also important in identifying the specific prevention needs and priorities of individuals at risk for HIV/AIDS. Although epidemiological and other quantitative data are essential to the planning process, they do not adequately address the contexts within which individuals act and make decisions. This information is critical to ensuring that prevention interventions and strategies will be effective as well as culturally competent.

Socioenvironmental Issues Affecting Black Men with HIV/AIDS

Regardless of gender or race/ethnicity, HIV/AIDS is stigmatizing. The intersection of HIV/AIDS with issues of sexuality, particularly among African American men, creates a powerful dynamic. African American MSM must navigate many cultural, social, spiritual, sexual, racial, and economic issues that alone may appear to be similar to those affecting other populations; however, when combined, these issues pose a unique set of challenges. Among these challenges are the following:

- The powerful role of the Black church in establishing sexual norms
- The connection between African American masculinity and the expression of sexuality
- External and internalized prejudice
- The impact of violence and substance abuse
- High rates of incarceration among young African American men
- The lack of culturally competent providers and access to quality health care, treatment, and information

Data released by the CDC (2005a) at the 2005 National HIV Prevention Conference in Atlanta, Georgia, confirmed the HIV epidemic's disproportionate impact on Black MSM. These data were obtained from a study of MSM conducted in five U.S. cities (Baltimore, Los Angeles, Miami, New York City, and San Francisco) from June 2004 to April 2005. The CDC findings follow several previous studies documenting high rates of HIV prevalence among this group: 46% of Black MSM tested were HIV-positive, and 67% of those men were unaware of their status.

BLACK MEN, INCARCERATION, AND HIV/AIDS

More than 1 in 10 African American men in their 20s and 30s are incarcerated in U.S. prisons and jails, where inmates are at high risk for HIV infection. According to the U.S. Department of Justice (2005), among male inmates, Blacks were nearly twice as likely as Whites to be HIV-positive, and the rate of HIV infection among White female inmates was nearly half that of Black female inmates. Additionally, Black inmates were twice as likely as Hispanics and 2.5 times as likely as Whites to die from AIDS-related causes. In 2002, AIDS-related deaths among Black inmates accounted for two-thirds of all AIDS-related deaths. Co-infection of HIV and the hepatitis C virus, another issue of concern that has been well documented among high-risk populations such as African American IDUs and the incarcerated, makes addressing HIV/AIDS in African American communities even more complex.

Policies and programs addressing HIV infection within African American communities must consider the profound impact of incarceration on the health of African Americans. Organizations such as the Association of State and Territorial Health Officials work with state public health officials and corrections officials to encourage collaboration, influence sound HIV/AIDS prevention policy in correctional facilities, and promote transitional planning programs for HIV-positive inmates reentering the community (Association of State and Territorial Health Officials, 2005). Collaboration among a variety of stakeholders is critical to meeting the HIV/AIDS prevention, care, and treatment needs of the incarcerated.

INTERSECTION OF CULTURAL AND SOCIOENVIRONMENTAL INFLUENCES AND HIV/AIDS

Some institutions and organizations within the African American community, even those with historic foundations in the fight for equitable human rights, are greatly hampered by traditional, conservative belief systems that promote conflict between them and the people they need to serve. The structural homophobia of many such groups is so embedded and polarizing that these entities are unable to provide a humane response to the largest intracommunity subpopulation that is so disproportionately affected by HIV disease: Black MSM. They are likewise resistant to accepting diverse elements within the African American community (i.e., homosexuals and IDUs). Their denial pervasively contributes to the burden of HIV/AIDS cases that currently weighs disproportionately on the shoulders of the African American population.

The many organizations that have been created to address the disproportionate impact of a wide-ranging spectrum of health care issues, including HIV/AIDS, on African Americans generally and Black males specifically suffer other types of shortcomings. The most common is inadequate cross-communication and networking among these stake holding providers regarding the common-ground issue of African American male health. As an AIDS activist, I believe this failing has at its core the often-intense competition in which these groups perceive they must engage for governmental and private funding. This perception creates and seeds "turfism" and distrust; it also impairs the ability to organize in good faith a cross-representational coalition focused on eliminating health care disparities within the African American community.

The political climate in the United States has degenerated to a point where the efforts of a small but powerful arbiter of political power, the extreme fundamentalist/conservative Right, blur the boundaries of the constitutionally mandated separation between church and state. This noninclusive, judgmental merger of politics and dogma has in turn crippled concrete, scientifically based HIV/AIDS prevention efforts. It has blinded the drafters and implementers of public policy, who now forego both scientific evidence and the development of inclusive public health policy that seeks to heal the human condition. Instead, their policies and practices blame and also victimize those who already are disproportionately affected by health care problems due to embedded structural racism, heterosexism, and faith-based beliefs.

Additionally, the stigma of HIV/AIDS within the African American community has rendered silent many African American heterosexuals who are living with HIV disease, who try to put as much distance as possible between themselves and "those others" who are at high risk of HIV/AIDS—namely, homosexuals, commercial street workers, and injection drug users. Their fear is valid, for within the African American community HIV infection exposes one to a slew of widely held negative assumptions, including those which contend that anyone with HIV/AIDS *deserves* to be infected. Such conclusions are the end result of preconceived stereotypes about the kinds of behaviors in which a person engages to become infected. One can only wonder if the present reality is a result of broad, deliberately misinformed prevention campaigns conducted by governmental and other AIDS service organizations? Regardless of the disconnect between policy, those infected with HIV/AIDS, and community organizations within the Black community, education remains the strongest method to engage African Americans in reflection and dialogue about this crisis.

The Role of Education in HIV/AIDS Prevention

The number of African Americans who have been affected by HIV/AIDS has added an additional chapter to the health care crisis within the Black community. The AIDS crisis has challenged many different parts of that community—its members, social welfare agencies, spiritual organizations, and educational institutions. A most disturbing layer of this well-developed calamity is the impact that HIV/AIDS has had on young African Americans.

As noted earlier, 83% of all HIV/AIDS cases among children in the United States are situated within Black and Hispanic communities. This unfortunate development locates schools as an important partner in fighting this epidemic. The need to place schools at the front lines of the fight against HIV/AIDS is attributable to their daily contact with children and the role of teachers as great influences on the lives of students (Mannah, 2002). To provide African American children and youth with the types of educational measures that can help combat the spread of HIV/AIDS in their communities, one must connect with what is going on in that regard in Africa, which has a lengthy history of addressing the HIV/AIDS crisis.

WHAT CAN AFRICA TEACH US ABOUT HIV/AIDS?

We African Americans would be well served to heed the lessons our kinfolk on the African continent have learned about HIV/AIDS. The ravaging effect of the AIDS virus and disease on the African continent has been well documented. Though the number of cases of HIV/AIDS seems to be decreasing in Europe and North America, the HIV/AIDS crisis in sub-Saharan Africa has reached an almost pandemic level (Okibgo et al., 2002). Of all of the HIV/AIDS cases reported in the world, over 60% of the cases are in sub-Saharan Africa (Okibgo et al., 2002).

South Africa has become the epicenter of the increase in HIV/AIDS cases in Africa. With that increase has come the realization, apparent to some, that the long-term impact of the HIV/AIDS crisis is far-reaching. As the rise in the number of South African cases has reached epidemic proportions, so too have the number of children affected. Mannah (2002) indicates that the number of children enrolling in South African schools is on the decline. This is because the parents of those children are dying much younger, leaving their older children behind to care for younger siblings or leaving them orphaned or impoverished. Furthermore, the growing number of South Africa's Black teachers affected by the disease has the potential to limit the number of adults who will be capable of delivering the most powerful weapon against the spread of HIV/AIDS: education. Despite the jarring impact that HIV/AIDS is having on the children who attend its schools and the teachers who can deliver a quality education, however, South Africa and several other African nations have developed extensive HIV/AIDS educational programs.

Indeed, one of the most important lessons that can be learned by African Americans from the African example is that of the centrality of K–12 (kindergarten through twelfth grade) education in the South African fight against HIV/AIDS. According to Mannah, the World Health Organization's (WHO) Health Promoting Schools (HPS) initiative "sees the school as a vehicle to improve the health of students, school personnel, families, and members of the community" (2002, 159). The HPS curriculum, developed by WHO and teachers from 14 African countries as well as Haiti, provides teachers with lesson plans, activities, and information on valuable community resources that can assist them in their teaching. While the impact of this program, in terms of numbers of deaths or lives saved, has yet to be determined, the educational impact is evident as several new groups have become more involved in the fight against HIV/AIDS and, more importantly, the fight to educate the young people of South Africa. Mannah (2002) indicates several specific results from this program that could serve as models for educational policy and practice in the United States:

1. The teachers union has become more involved in the effort to educate the students, as well as supporting the teacher's development and implementation of HIV/AIDS curriculum.
2. The Department of Education has been more vocal in its support of HIV/ AIDS education.

3. International organizations have become more involved in the educational process.

In the country of Tanzania in East Africa, a program designed for sixth- and seventh-graders has had a resounding impact on the attitudes of students toward persons living with HIV/AIDS as well as on students' general attitudes about behaviors that can lead to HIV infection (Stigler et al., 2006). The program, called *Ngao*, means "shield" in Swahili, Tanzania's national language. It provides teachers with a handbook of developed lessons and a similar handbook for students to take home. Grounded in educational best practice, the program offers the following types of lessons:

1. Teacher collaborations with health workers to lecture on HIV/AIDS
2. Small-group dialogue (peer-led) about student experience with HIV/AIDS
3. Student-developed plays related to HIV/AIDS in their community
4. The development of posters, songs, poems, and other materials designed to educate others in the school community about HIV/AIDS
5. Structured interviews with parents, community members, and friends, with some aspect(s) of HIV/AIDS as the topic
6. Panel discussions among community elders, parents, and religious leaders on HIV/AIDS-related matters
7. Single-gender-group discussions about the impact of sexual behavior on young people's chances to contract HIV/AIDS

Stigler et al.'s (2006) analysis of the results of the program found an increase in student awareness about HIV/AIDS, a reduction in discriminatory attitudes and behavior toward those with HIV/AIDS, and an increase in students' ability to advocate for others who are infected with the virus. The programs in South Africa and Tanzania are just two examples of possible educational developments that might be implemented in American schools. One critical component of each program was that of collaboration between school personnel and community organizations, community members, and nongovernmental organizations. The "tool" used to develop this collaboration was service learning.

THE ROLE OF SERVICE LEARNING IN AFRICAN HIV/AIDS EDUCATION

Service learning is well suited to engage African American youth in meaningful discussions about HIV/AIDS. Furthermore, the implementation of high-quality service-learning programs in U.S. schools serving large numbers of African American students would not only empower the students but also allow others in the communities surrounding these schools to become engaged in substantial dialogue about this major health crisis confronting them today.

Inserting service learning into this discussion requires a definition of service learning. Although there are many definitions from which to choose, for the purposes of this chapter, service learning will be framed from within the context of the community—in other words, community-based service learning will be the focus here. Price (2006) offers a six-part definition of service learning, particularly that targeting African American students:

1. Service learning is a form of experiential learning in which students learn through hands-on service projects.
2. Service learning is integrated into the core curriculum so that students learn the "real life" application of the academic curriculum.
3. Service learning uses higher-order, critical thinking skills where students use reflection to pose critical questions and to solve "real" problems.
4. Service learning is about addressing authentic community needs.
5. Service learning is designed to help students, teachers, and community members create partnerships through which their service can help solve the authentic community need.
6. Service learning is a proven paradigm and educational reform known for building character, leadership skills, and developmental assets in students.

Given the numbing statistics on African Americans and HIV/AIDS, service learning centering on HIV/AIDS as a community issue and as the basis of student service projects clearly fits into this paradigm. The statistics related to youth infection rates in the African American community are alone enough to jolt Black students into action.

Kaye (2004) list several statistics as prompts to begin such discussions with African American youth:

- More than 2,000 children are infected with HIV each day worldwide.
- In the United States, it is estimated that two adolescents are infected with HIV each hour.
- More than 6,000 young people between the ages of 15 and 24 become infected with HIV every day—that is, about four young people every minute.
- Approximately 11 million children in Africa have been orphaned by AIDS.

High-quality service learning is not just about dialogue and data, it is also about action. The actions that students can take once they have obtained the data they need to hold informed discussions about HIV/AIDS can yield remarkable results. One example of a successful service-learning project focusing on HIV/AIDS is reflected in the experience of a group of seventh- and eighth-grade students in an urban middle school in New York City (O'Donnell et al., 1999). That project coupled community involvement with quality health instruction to yield a positive impact on the students' attitudes and ideas related to sexual activities that predispose youth to contracting HIV/AIDS. The students in the study worked with several community organizations as a part of their service component, including local nursing homes, a neighborhood full-service health clinic, a senior citizen center, and child day care centers. Their teachers used the Reach for Health curriculum, which focuses on drug and alcohol use, violence, and sexual behaviors that can lead to contracting HIV to guide their students to translate what they observed in their community partnerships into classroom practices.

Student reflection, both during and after, is critical to all high-quality service-learning projects. Moreover, as Price (2006) contends, it is always important to ensure that community service-learning projects are tied into the curriculum. The O'Donnell et al. study provided evidence of both these aspects being incorporated. Curriculum-only (health) efforts to engage students in dialogue about HIV/AIDS were found to be somewhat successful in helping them rethink their sexual decisions. However, analysis of student data at the conclusion of the project revealed a much higher correlation between service-learning experiences (service, curriculum, and reflection) and change in attitudes about sexual activities.

The impact of service learning on the students in Brooklyn (O'Donnell et al., 1999) is not the only example of high-quality service learning related to HIV/AIDS. The National Youth Leadership Council (NYLC) has developed a multifaceted program to address the HIV/AIDS crisis by empowering young people. As one of the leading service-learning organizations in the United States, NYLC's Y-Rise Project (Youths Replicating Innovative Strategies and Excellence in HIV/AIDS) is training young people to lead the fight against HIV/AIDS. Through the development of a body of research by collaborating with researchers, field testing service-learning tools and curricula, and training young people as peer educators, Y-RISE is a great example of an innovative service-learning program helping fight HIV/AIDS in the Black community (NYLC, 2005).

The development of the Y-Rise Project serves as a great model for the development of large-scale service-learning initiatives within the HIV/AIDS arena. Nonetheless, through the leadership of Dr. Verna Price and her innovative program Girls in Action (Minneapolis, MN), African American girls on the north side of Minneapolis were able to put many of the Y-Rise principles into action. With its roots firmly planted in the African American community in Minneapolis, Girls in Action is designed to reduce violence and increase the academic achievement and leadership skills of girls at Minneapolis North Community High School. While Minneapolis serves as a model city representing all aspects of racial, ethnic, and cultural diversity, North Minneapolis is home to the largest population of African Americans in the Twin Cities. As is the case with high-quality service learning, the students determined that there was a need to engage in dialogue about the HIV/AIDS crisis in North Minneapolis. In order to address the issue, the girls researched the topic, paying particular attention to community organizations that were already dealing with the issue. Upon completion of the research the young women partnered with the Freemont Clinic, which provides free HIV/AIDS testing to teenagers. Never ones to not practice what they preach, not only did the girls carry their message of being tested to all schools in Minneapolis, they were all tested themselves. Because of this partnership with the Freemont Clinic, the students created an educational video that is still in use throughout the Minneapolis community. Because of the success of the many programs contained with the Girls in Action initiative, the Inkster Public Schools (Inkster, MI) are currently piloting the Girls in Action curriculum.

Implications and Conclusions

Although every subpopulation within the African American community is experiencing disproportionate rates of HIV/AIDs, the needs of two cohorts—men who have sex with men (MSM) and injection drug users (IDUs)—are particularly critical and demand special attention. As national and Michigan epidemiological data makes clear, these groups are in dire need of innovative HIV/AIDS prevention programming. They further need a new kind of community HIV/AIDS service-provider assessment—one that evaluates who and what organizations and agencies can best provide HIV/AIDS prevention services to these subpopulations as well as support from local schools.

In Michigan, efforts to empower African American MSM and IDUs to protect themselves, and those with whom they associate, from the spread of HIV/AIDS and to get more effective treatment for them if they are already infected have been hampered by a variety of challenges. One such challenge is the outreach approach of some faith-based organizations in Michigan's African American communities. These organizations couch their approach toward MSM and IDUs living with HIV/AIDS in a "hate the sin, love the sinner" perspective, a focus on attempting to provide supportive services to the "innocent victims" of HIV/AIDS (heterosexuals of both genders and children), approaches that leave many MSM and IDUs feeling distrustful, rejected, and on the defensive. It also renders them less able to accept any health advice these groups may provide. Compounding the problem, the single agency responsible for most of the HIV-prevention services for MSM in Detroit, Michigan's largest city, was recently closed because of financial irregularities and other problems. The closure of this agency has created an even greater dearth in Michigan's ability to provide a safe atmosphere in which MSM of color can receive HIV/AIDS prevention services. To make matters worse, needle exchange programs are prohibited in the state of Michigan, and federal funding for that purpose is also disallowed. Detroit, Grand Rapids, and cities within Washtenaw County, however, have obtained waivers to distribute clean needles to IDUs. Nonetheless, a significant number of the organizations that attempt to provide services to those IDUs in the state's African American community who are most vulnerable to (or living with) HIV infection have exhibited some apprehension about being associated with certain groups of HIV/AIDS patients, which severely limits their effectiveness. A thorough and ongoing appraisal of what organizations or agencies work most effectively with African American MSM and IDUs, and what methods they employ, is needed.

The literature on African Americans and HIV/AIDS is unified in recommending community organizing among providers/stakeholders along with encouraging schools to take a more active role in educating young people, as the most viable way to develop methods that can reduce the disproportionate impact of HIV/AIDS on the African American community. However, entrusted and identified leaders/institutions within the African American community must conduct an objective, thorough, internal assessment of any biases, institutional or personal, that prevent them from recognizing the diversity and the interdependence of that community. Failure to do so will inhibit the development of sincere and humane responses to HIV/AIDS.

Empowering the MSM subpopulation of African American men to act in ways that protect themselves and others is critical to making headway in reducing the disproportionate burden of HIV/AIDS cases among African Americans. Critical to the development of empowerment programming are three activities: the identification of internalized homophobia; programs that challenge culturally informed and narrowly defined gender roles for Black men; and cultural competence programming that explores the historical context that has brought Black men (and the overall African American community) to a place where multiple health care problems thrive and flourish. This subpopulation especially needs skills-building education that helps them challenge and confront institutional and community biases that limit their access to informed, innovative health care.

We challenge Black institutions and those African Americans who view themselves as leaders and agents of social change to make a conscious effort to become acutely aware of what motivates them to get involved in HIV/AIDS work in our Black communities. We call them to strive to make a difference not just for those living with HIV/AIDS with whom they can easily identify or with whom they are not uncomfortable. I implore them: Are you willing to risk being uncomfortable? Can you make an effort to discover and discard organizational and personally held biases? Are you willing to work for inclusive social justice within the African American community?

The Black community in the United States at large, and Michigan in particular, can and must courageously "come out of the closet" to address these challenges so that our HIV/AIDS prevention gains will not continue to be overshadowed by the sheer volume of African American men living with and dying from HIV/AIDS. Our community's history of survival in the face of extreme adversity demonstrates that we have the ability to do better. We can, and we must.

We wish to acknowledge the following organizations and individuals for their support in helping to develop this chapter: Linda Draper, MSLS, Detroit Community AIDS Library; Max Heirich, Ph.D.; Laura Hughes, MPH; Renee McCoy, MSW; Eve Mokotoff, MPH; Robin Orsborn, MPH; Melissa Reznar, MPH; David Rupprecht, MSPH; Barbara Wood, Editor, MI HIV and STD Report; Michigan Department of Community Health, Bureau of Epidemiology, Division of Health, Wellness and Disease Control; and Michigan HIV/AIDS Council.

REFERENCES

Association of State and Territorial Health Officials (2005). *The use of HIV/AIDS surveillance data for prevention, care, policy, research, and evaluation: A focus on Florida, Washington, Alabama, and Washington.* January. Retrieved August 23, 2007, from http://www.astho.org/pubs/HIVSurveillance2005.pdf.

Centers for Disease Control and Prevention. (2002). *HIV/AIDS surveillance report: HIV testing survey, 2002.* Atlanta: Centers for Disease Control and Prevention. Also available at http://www.cdc.gov/hiv/topics/surveillance/resources/reports/2004spec_no5/pdf/HIV-Test-Survey2002.pdf.

Centers for Disease Control and Prevention. (2005a). *HIV/AIDS surveillance report, 2004* (Vol.16). Atlanta: Centers for Disease Control and Prevention. Also available at http://www.cdc.gov/hiv/topics/surveillance/resources/reports/2004report/default.htm.

Centers for Disease Control and Prevention. (2005b). Trends in HIV/AIDS diagnoses, 33 states, 2001–2004. *Morbidity and Mortality Weekly Report, 54*(45), 1149–53.

Kaye, M. (2004). *The complete guide to service learning: Proven, practical ways to engage students in civic responsibility, academic curriculum, & social action.* Minneapolis: Free Spirit Publishing.

Mannah, S. (2002). South Africa: The complex role of teaching about HIV/AIDS in schools. *Prospects, 32*(2), 156–70.

Michigan Department of Community Health. (2004). *HIV/AIDS health-related needs among injecting drug users in Michigan.* January. Retrieved January 20, 2006, from http://www.mihivnews.com/mhac/IDU%20Report.pdf.

Michigan Department of Community Health. (2006). *Quarterly HIV/AIDS analysis.* January. Retrieved January 23, 2006, from http://michigan.gov/documents/Jan_2006_147752_7.pdf.

Michigan HIV/AIDS Council. (2006). *Michigan's comprehensive plan for HIV prevention.* March. Retrieved January 20, 2006, from http://www.mihivnews.com/hapis/p_rfp/prevention_plan_2006.pdf.

National Youth Leadership Council (2005). *Y-Rise: The service-learning and HIV/AIDS initiative.* December. Retrieved August 9, 2007, from www.nylc.org/y-rise.

O'Donnell, L., Stueve, A., San Doval, A., Duran, R., Haber, D., Atnafou, R., Johnson, N., Grant, U., Murray, H., Juhn, G., Tang, J., & Piessens, P. (1999). The effectiveness of the Reach for Health Community Youth Service Learning Program in reducing early and unprotected sex among urban middle school students. *American Journal of Public Health, 89*(2), 176–81.

Okibgo, C., Okibgo, C., Hall, W., & Ziegler, D. (2002). The HIV/AIDS epidemic in African American communities: Learning from UNAIDS and Africa. *Journal of Black Studies, 32*(6), 615–53.

Polite, V. & Davis, J. E. (1999). Introduction. In V. Polite & J. E. Davis (Eds.), *African American males in school and society,* 1–7. New York: Teachers College Press.

Price, V. (2006). How can service-learning increase the academic achievement of urban African American students? In J. Landsman & C. Lewis (Eds.), *White teachers/diverse classrooms: A guide to building inclusive schools, promoting high expectations, and eliminating racism,* 265–85. Sterling, VA: Stylus.

Stigler, M., Kugler, K., Komro, K., Leshabari, M., & Klepp, K. (2006). AIDS education for Tanzanian youth: A mediation analysis. *Health Education Research: Theory and Practice, 21*(4), 441–51.

U.S. Department of Justice. (2005). *Bureau of Justice Statistics Bulletin.* Retrieved January 19, 2006, from http://www.ojp.usdoj.gov/bjs/pub/pdf/hivp03.pdf.

Washington, H. (2006). *Medical apartheid: The dark history of medical experimentation on Black Americans from colonial times to the present.* New York: Doubleday.

Wright, K. (2006). *AIDS in blackface: 25 years of an epidemic.* Retrieved July 9, 2007, from http://www.blackaids.org/image_uploads/article_202/.pdf.

A Serious Dialogue

THE INFLUENCE OF HIP-HOP CULTURE
ON THE STATUS OF YOUNG AFRICAN
AMERICAN MALES

MARWIN J. SPILLER *and* RODERIC R. LAND

A few points should be made at the outset of this chapter: We are both Black male Chicago natives and graduates of the University of Illinois who love hip-hop. We are also profoundly concerned about the status of African American young men today and their future well-being. It is this concern that prompted a series of conversations between the two of us regarding hip-hop culture and the plight of young Black males in the United States. Those conversations resulted in the chapter you are now reading.

At issue for us are the depressed levels of educational attainment, the persistent joblessness, and the high rates of idleness experienced by African American males in urban communities. These challenges are coupled with excessive levels of Black-on-Black crime and an exploding Black male incarceration rate on one hand; and a popular brand of hip-hop culture that extols "gangsta-ism," conspicuous consumption, immediate gratification, and an oppositional, confrontation-oriented attitude on the other hand. Although we both have strong personal opinions about the relationship between hip-hop culture and the plight of young Black males, we are careful not to assert a cause-and-effect influence of one of these realities on the other. We wonder, however, what effect, if any, hip-hop culture has had on young African American males' education, employment, and incarceration levels. More specifically, do the dominant image of Black males within hip-hop culture—and the messages accompanying that image—have any impact on their educational aspirations, labor-force experiences, attitudes about race, and overall feelings of personal well-being?

It is not the intent of this chapter to offer a definitive answer to this question. Rather, it will offer both reflection and exploration in the form of a dialogue mapping our separate interpretations of the state of young African American males today and the role that hip-hop culture has and continues to play in shaping the Black male experience in post-civil rights America. Given the similarities in our backgrounds and intellectual interests, one could easily assume that we would espouse homogeneity of thought. To the contrary, our interpretations of the relationship between hip-hop culture and the plight of African American young males differ radically.

For Roderic R. Land, this interpretation takes the form of a discussion grounded in critical race theory coupled with an exploration of theories of power. Within this framework, he argues that the dire situation faced by so many young African American men today is largely the product of a set of prevailing racialized forces (i.e., racial ideologies, attitudes, beliefs, etc.) working in concert to construct Black males in dehumanizing ways. Not withstanding generations of violent oppression, he posits that more covert forces of White hegemonic power have socialized African Americans, particularly African American males, to have grave disregard for themselves and others. He focuses on the controlling nature of the mass media in general and of the music industry, in particular to conclude that hip-hop has thus been embodied with the capacity and power to construct and dictate pejorative messages and images to and about African Americans, particularly young Black males.

Marwin J. Spiller takes a different approach. His understanding of the African American male predicament is couched in a Marxian analysis that emphasizes class exploitation and the unscrupulous drive for capital accumulation as the most important activity in American life. Using this framework, he asserts that Black males are viewed as both the victims and the perpetrators of capitalism and its product, hip-hop culture. He argues that within the confines of hip-hop culture violent, misogynist, and wanton images of young Black men are the product that is being manipulated, manufactured, and sold, often with the cooperation and blessings of young Black men. It is within this context that Spiller asserts that young Black men must accept some responsibility for the creation and perpetuation of harmful, problematic images of and messages about themselves. The quest and intense desire for capital accumulation, Spiller maintains, not only engenders a sense of "false consciousness" among Black males but also provides a context for them to participate in their own oppression. This uncritical embrace of capitalism has led many members of the hip-hop generation to believe that their social, economic, and political interests are consistent with those of the capitalist class, rather than poor and working-class people of all races. A market mentality, then, is believed to have effectively pushed race, as a salient dimension of Black male identity, to the margins, replacing it with a class identity, albeit a false one.

Different approaches aside, we two authors agree on several fronts. For both of us, any interpretation of the plight of today's young African American males must include an analysis of macroeconomic changes, shifts in race relations, and changes in the priorities, choices, and actions of Black males themselves. It must also include an analysis of hip-hop culture.

This chapter is written as a public dialogue presenting a series of conversations between two African American college professors who have spent a considerable amount of time studying hip-hop culture and interacting with young Black males. Grounded in our respective disciplines, we discuss (and at times debate) the various tendencies of hip-hop culture and their implications for young African American men. However, the diversity of opinions expressed in the following dialogue and the range of ideas touched upon should not be seen as a shortcoming or point of concern; rather it should be viewed as testimony to just how complex and nuanced the issues are for African American males. Taken together, our discussions represent an authentic contribution to the "courageous conversation" about the state of African American males upon which the editors of this volume commissioned us to embark.

Hip-Hop Culture and Its Social and Economic Underpinnings

Although little agreement exists on how best to define hip-hop culture, few scholars or practitioners dispute the time and place of hip-hop's origins. By all accounts, hip-hop arrived on the urban landscape in the late 1970s and early 1980s (George,

1998; Rose, 1994). As a post-civil rights/postindustrial cultural phenomenon, the attitudes, styles, and expressions of members of the hip-hop generation are largely informed by the fading promises of civil rights legislative victories on the one hand and the harsh realities of urban blight and social disorganization on the other hand. Like the generation before them, African American young people today inherited a community with a number of social and economic problems. However, unlike the group who came of age during the 1960s and 1970s, members of the hip-hop generation seem to lack the political organization or cultural resources to put the necessary pressure on government to bring about important changes. With many of the traditional civil rights leaders dead, in jail, or battle-worn, and Black institutions and organizations bankrupt or without middle-class support, persistent kinds of racial inequality during the post–civil rights years were not only intractable but also, by comparison to problems involving civil rights, insurmountable.

Blatant class differences within the Black community spawned, in part, by the successes of the civil rights movement further exacerbated conditions for the Black poor, and even more so for poor Black men. Prior to the late 1970s and early 1980s, for example, race-based residential segregation confined most Black people to all-Black communities regardless of their social and economic status. The passage of fair housing legislation in 1968, however, enabled working- and middle-class African American individuals and families to move out of traditionally Black communities, leaving behind a group of the poorest of the poor.

Compounding the realities of the concentration of Black poverty were broad economic changes. The shifting job market was characterized by the destruction of working-class occupations on the one hand and the relocation of blue-collar manufacturing jobs out of central cities on the other hand. These factors conspired to drive down labor force participation for working-class people in general and Black males in particular. We see, then, that while hip-hop was largely a by-product of other African American cultural traditions such as the blues, jazz, and bebop, its content and aesthetic is largely a reflection of a growing tide of discontent, impatience, and hopelessness festering among working- and lower-class young men of color. In this regard, hip-hop as a cultural phenomenon can be broadly understood as a creative response to the experiences of marginalization, limited opportunity, and social isolation.

The socioeconomic context that gave rise to hip-hop culture in the late 1970s and early 1980s was extremely racialized and gendered. Unemployed, residentially segregated, politically disenfranchised, and idle young Black (and Latino) men channeled their creative energies into music, break dancing, graffiti, and deejaying. They subsequently transformed their play into work and their poverty into style. Likewise, denied a voice in electoral politics or mainstream media outlets, they spoke out in their music, telling aggressive stories of the harsh realities of life in postindustrial, urban America. In their communities, extreme poverty, pervasive unemployment, social disorganization, gang violence, frustration, welfare dependency, and other social problems ruled the day. These aspects became recurring themes in the music that would catapult hip-hop culture to commercial success. Socially conscious hip-hop artists often spoke out in their music and art, against societal ills such as institutional racism, Black-on-Black crime, and government neglect of needy populations, while encouraging community activism and social responsibility.

This all changed, however, with the commercialization of hip-hop and the ascendancy of "gangsta" rap music. Major record labels, seeking to capitalize on a new sound and aesthetic, figured it important to lift hip-hop from its local origin and cleanse it of its social and political critique, so as to offend no one and appeal to everyone. Once hip-hop got repackaged as a reflection of "American" culture, large profits were available to anyone who was savvy and unconscionable enough to position themselves to sell Americanized, culturally based fears and anxieties regarding race, class, and gender. Indeed, given the economic agendas of the major records labels and the absence of a defined set of strategic goals related to the ongoing struggle of African Americans, hip-hop changed; now, partying and edifying storytelling that extolled violence and hypersexuality are esteemed above the more serious themes involving collective responsibility and organization.

The Dialogue

If one accepts the argument that hip-hop is now (as it was originally) the primary cultural outlet for young Black males to be heard and seen, then one must ask oneself several questions. First, what are most mainstream hip-hop artists rapping about? Second, how are the vast majority of them portrayed in their music? Third, what are the predominant themes and issues driving mainstream hip-hop culture? Forth, is hip-hop today—and by association, African American males—less critical of the social ills that plague Black America than it was 10 to 20 years ago? Lastly, would the answers to these questions tell us anything about the capacity of young African American males to assess their situation objectively and improve their life-chances? Our dialogue begins.

Marwin J. Spiller: Regarding the last question, I would say, "Yes." Hip-hop culture underwent a major transformation from 1980 to 1990 to 2000, and with each change the music, the language, and the attitude became less and less political. Coming off the heels of the civil rights and Black power movement, hip-hop in the 1980s had more of a Black Nationalist, group-consciousness appeal, as symbolized by then-popular tracks like "Fight the Power" by Public Enemy, "Self-Destruction" by the Stop the Violence All-Stars, and "The Message" by Grandmaster Flash and the Furious Five, just to name a few. Consistent with the music, hip-hop fads, styles, and fashions also reflected the resistance politics of the day. Reagonomics and the backlash against affirmative action, coupled with double-digit unemployment rates, cuts in social service and urban development programs, as well as the social unrest that was taking place in South Africa with the imprisonment of Nelson Mandela, all conspired to politically engage and invigorate young Black people during the 1980s. Their widespread concern for social and economic redress and for the liberation of African people everywhere was perhaps most symbolically expressed by the hip-hop community's widespread adoption of the red, black, green, and later yellow or gold colors represented on pan-African flags. Combinations of these colors were found on the trendiest articles of clothing and headgear worn by hip-hop artists and fans alike. Similarly, fashion-conscious Black youth in the 1980s could also be seen wearing leather medallions bearing images of the African continent as a show of support for ending apartheid in South Africa.

In contrast to the 1980s, hip-hop in the 1990s was dominated by themes of gang warfare, police brutality and claims of Black authenticity. Tracks like "F—— the Police" by NWA, "Murder Was the Case" by Snoop Dog, and "All Eyes on Me" by Tu Pac Shakur were very popular. Young Black males' creative energy seemed to have turned from a critique of the conditions in Black America to a celebration of the self-absorbed, individualistic, macho figure—the "pimp," the "thug," and the "gangsta," as ironically epitomized in the phrase, "keeping it real." Accordingly, "real niggas" are Black men who can successfully negotiate violence, are hyper-confrontational, disrespect and hurt other men without remorse, or have spent time in prison. One's realness could also be established by rejecting mainstream values, norms and cultural practices such as, dropping out of school, getting poor grades, shunning the formal economy in favor of hustling on the street or evading one's parental responsibilities, just to name a few.

By the year 2000, the situation shifted again, but this time in the direction of vulgar materialism. Much of the music coming out during that time was about money, cars, jewelry, and women. A case in point, Jay-Z and Jermaine Dupri boasted in their (1998) hit single that "Money Ain't a Thang." Likewise, Nelly's (2003) "Tip Drill" and the Cash Money Millionaire's (1999) track "Bling Bling" followed similar themes of extolling misogyny and material excess. In addition, perhaps most notorious were 50 Cent's (2003) "P.I.M.P.," Jay-Z's (1999) "Big Pimpin'," and Ludacris's (2005) "Pimping All Over the World"? As can be seen, within a 20-year span, hip-hop went from "Fight the Power" to "It's Hard Out Here for a Pimp" to "Laffy Taffy."

Additionally, just about every influential Black man in hip-hop had his own clothing line, complete with a full-scale marketing campaign targeting low-income, young Black males encouraging them to buy $32 T-shirts, $70 jeans, $100 tennis shoes, and $300 coats. Indeed, hip-hop artists have come a long way from the days of encouraging activism and social responsibility to that of heralding wanton consumerism or what bell hooks calls "class warfare" (2000, 11). Of course, there were numerous exceptions, hip-hop artists and representatives who maintained their political and critical edge. However, few can deny that the product being sold as hip-hop today has little relevance to the ongoing struggle of African Americans.

Roderic R. Land: I can agree with this to an extent. Yes, a lot of the music that is broadcast across the airwaves on most of our major radio stations is not "political," and that, I argue, is no accident. However, the piece that is not present today and rarely talked about is the reason why this affinity with such status symbols and culture has developed and evolved over the years.

Generations of exploitation of Black people and of denial of their entrée and entry into particular enclaves, knowledge, wealth, and resources (i.e., education, landownership, voting rights, etc.) are not being talked about, not to mention the reality that a good number of young Black males as well as many hip-hop artists do not come from well-to-do backgrounds. Is it because Black people for so long have been kept out of the loop and met with virulent and vitriolic resistance when they try to make an honest living? Or is it due to White people's racial antipathy for Black people or White people's beliefs about Black people's ability and intellectual competency? If you bought into the "American Dream" and that dream became a nightmare riddled with constant rejection, lack of respect, and falsified opportunities, how do you expect one to respond? Though I do not condone the maladaptive behaviors being promoted as a means of attaining this elusive dream, I *over-stand* them.

On the other side, our young Black males need to take a more positive approach to how they handle their responsibility for the conditions in which they find themselves. Now, don't get it twisted, many have taken responsibility, they just may not have taken the moral and ethical path one might have preferred, but they have taken ownership of their thoughts and actions. The task and question at hand then becomes: What can we as a society, as a community, as a family, and as two Black, male professors do to aid in changing the negatives into positives? What is our role and commitment aside from just pontificating about the issue? What effective strategies can we present to provide alternatives to the maladaptive behaviors that hip-hop has engendered and nourished? I strongly believe young Black males need to take more responsibility, but we would be highly disillusioned to think that we, as well as the rest of society, have no responsibility to aid in their transformation. I guess it boils down to the timeless question, "Am I my brothers' keeper?"

On the other hand, hip-hop has been given a bad rap (no pun intended) for conditions that were present and brewing well before its emergence onto the global stage. Again, I am in no way saying that I agree with the misogynistic messages found in so much of the music, videos, and art of hip-hop or with its prevailing glorification of violence, sex, and drugs, but the mistreatment of women, the rampant abuse of drugs, and the violence reflected in hip-hop were prevalent well before it came into being. Yes, these messages are common in the music; but yes, they are also a very real part of our society. Thus, I would push you to view this music more as a form of social commentary that describes *lived* experiences, things witnessed, or fantasies than as the staple of hip-hop culture. Again, not discounting the agency of the artists who create the music and the images of hip-hop, one cannot negate the important role of the music industry, the media, as well as the consumers of this music. As Jay-Z so eloquently stated, hip-hop is "just the shit I'm sprinklin' to keep the registers ringin'." All I am encouraging here is that one should not contribute to the character assassination of the Black male or hip-hop by failing to look at the complete picture or consider all the nuances involved.

MJS: It is certainly not my intent to demonize young Black males or the culture that appears to inform the thoughts, actions, and perspectives of a number of them. Hence, I make no claims of a relationship between the messages, images, and other aspects of hip-hop culture and the life chances and/or sociopolitical outlooks of young Black males. I do wonder, however—as I observe young Black males frequent use of the "N" word, their embracement of the pimp and the hustler, their apparent lack of regard for each other's lives, and their willingness to internalize negative stereotypical images—what happened to the social critique that gave birth to hip-hop culture in the first place? For me, the answer lies in what appears to be an absence of a sophisticated analysis of racism.

Indeed, I am always amazed when I talk and interact with young African American men about their experiences and various current events at how little emphasis they place on the salience of race as a factor in American life. I have often gotten the sense that this group of males, which statistically is not fairing well by any measure, believes wholeheartedly that American society has changed to the extent that race is no longer a major determinant of their life chances. Though I would be the first to concede that the effect of race has been weakened somewhat by social class, I would not go as far as *The Game*, who in his 2008 track "My Life" with Lil Wayne said, "f—k Jesse Jackson cause it ain't about race now." For sure, 30 to 40 years ago a young Black man would not be able to speak of owning an expensive car with 24-inch spinning rims, so yes the economic conditions for African Americans have improved. However, well-being measures still show Black Americans lagging behind their White counterparts on everything from access to fair lending practices to grocery stores that sell fresh fruits and vegetables. The refusal or inability of young Black men to see the world through racialized lenses in a society that still distributes most of its valued resources along lines of race is dangerous and hip-hop's endorsement of this false consciousness is even more problematic.

That said, I am clearly aware that the relationship between abstract social forces and concrete thoughts is complex so I do not blame hip-hop culture for fashioning an apolitical mind-set among young Black males or for introducing violence, misogyny, and materialism to their lives. I agree with you that these things were prevalent in the culture long before hip-hop. Nonetheless, I wonder about the long-term implications of the constant bombardment of multimedia, multicontextual apolitical, violent, and misogynist messages and images. What impact will these have on how young African American males think about themselves, how others think about them, and how they think about the predicament they are in and what they can realistically do about it?

RRL: Interesting enough, I cannot completely disagree with all your sentiments. Unfortunately, a number of African American students with whom I interact in my classes lack some sense of racial history. This is not to say that their lived experiences are devoid of racialized encounters, because I do not believe that. Rather, I suspect these students lack a clear understanding of the role race has played in the way this country was developed and the way it is organized, as well as of the conditions in which many folks of color find themselves today, and of the opportunities—or lack thereof—afforded them presently. To some extent, I attribute my Black students' lack of understanding of America's racial history to the fact that they are living in a post-civil rights environment in which racism, racial oppression, discrimination, and prejudice are supposed to have been remedied. My students today see the problem as more of a class issue.

Unlike my colleague, however, I am not ready to cast blame upon young Black people or to hold hip-hop solely responsible for their, and Black males' in particular, failure to be cognizant of this racial history. Nor am I willing to convict the world of hip-hop alone for producing an "instant-gratification generation." Over the span of its 30-plus-year history, hip-hop has undergone major transformations and has grown beyond anything one could ever fathom. Depending on one's understanding of this cultural juggernaut, it can easily be argued that hip-hop has gone from what Harold Cruse (1968) calls a "cultural revolution" to a cultural de-evolution that has destroyed the moral fabric of our supposedly pristine society. Furthermore, I contend that hip-hop has done more for the visibility of urban Black and Latino(a) youth than any other movement and that it has consistently maintained its platform to give voice to historically silenced and marginalized groups of people. The problem facing hip-hop is the images and messages that are being portrayed, glamorized, and glorified in its name throughout the popular media.

MJS: I agree that at its best, hip-hop culture has been an extremely empowering force in the lives of young Black males. Certainly, no other genre of music, bundle of tastes, or cultural aesthetic has commanded such a worldwide audience. The crossover appeal of the music and style of young Black urban males has made them global cultural icons responsible for a billion-dollar industry. But what is the product being sold? And what image of Black males is being projected? How much are Black males actually benefiting from hip-hop's worldwide exposure and mass marketing appeal? More pointedly, are Black males as a group victims or beneficiaries of hip-hop culture?

RRL: I would say that Black males are victims, beneficiaries, and co-producers of hip-hop culture. From a psychosocial stance, this venue benefits Black males because it provides a space for a voice that historically has been silenced, marginalized, and missing from mainstream society. Having the ability and platform to name, shed light on, and be heard with regard to one's position is an empowering and liberating experience. Furthermore, being able to talk through the pains, frustrations, and stressors that everyday life brings can often times be therapeutic.

The overarching and undergirding theme I wish to emphasize here is this notion or concept of voice. Delgado (1989) draws upon three key factors that are essential to critical race theory (CRT) insofar as assertions about the viewpoints of people of color—in this case, Black males—are concerned: (1) reality is socially constructed; (2) narratives provide members of marginalized groups a method for mental self-preservation; and (3) the discussion between teller and listener can aid in overcoming ethnocentrism and the dysconscious way that many people view the world. My point in mentioning these racialized discourses and ethnic epistemologies is not simply to "color" this dialogue but to expose and challenge the hegemonic structures that maintain and perpetuate injustice and inequities. Another aspect that must be explored is that of how Black people take on the role of their oppressors. As noted by Macedo (1994), once one has adapted to the status quo and has been rewarded by it, it becomes increasingly easier for one to live within a lie and ignore true reality, thus becoming a keeper of one's own oppressor.

MJS: I also agree that Black males are both victims and beneficiaries simultaneously. What gets muddled for me, however, is when we attempt to rationalize or sympathize with the pathologies of Black male youth (i.e., hip-hop) culture rather than hold these individuals and the culture accountable. Now before you cast me over to the Republican Party, let me explain: It is my understanding that for every Chris Brown, Jay-Z, 50 Cent, P. Diddy, and Damon Dash who benefit from the imagery of hip-hop culture, there are millions of impressionable, everyday young Black men caught up in the criminal justice system, opting to reject formal education, see women only as objects of pleasure, shun delayed gratification, and place the highest value on consumption by any means necessary—all in the name of the hip-hop adage of "keeping it real." Now, certainly hip-hop culture does not hold a monopoly on cultural decay, as incarceration and high-school dropout rates are on the rise for all groups and the debt-to-income ratio has ballooned across the board, suggesting that most Americans are consuming far beyond their ability to pay. Nonetheless, one has to wonder about the effects of the blatant promotion and glamorization of these trends and cultural practices on an already marginalized and oppressed group.

By definition, social institutions are stable, resilient, and designed to maintain the status quo. Thus, if the education and criminal justice systems of this society are not going to change and adapt to the shifting attitudes and worldviews of young Black men, then it behooves these males to change in order to live and prosper in society. That said, the construction of Black male identity as thugs, pimps, hustlers, and super-athletes in a milieu that offers few other images is destructive and highly problematic, particularly when those images are being produced, promoted, and capitalized on by other Black men.

Essentially then, with the exception of perhaps Barack Obama, much of what the world in general and White Americans in particular know about Black males is largely the commoditized creations of P. Diddy, Damon Dash, Russell Simmons, Hype Williams, the NBA, and the NFL. If it were not for the fact that so few Americans have meaningful interactions with people who are different from themselves with regard to race, class or region this situation would not be so bad. However, as Barbara Diggs-Brown and Leonard Steinhorn (2000) point out in their book, *By the Color of Our Skin: The Illusion of Integration and the Reality of Race*, the vast majority of Americans live in racially segregated communities, attend racially segregated churches, socialize in racially segregated settings, and send their children to racially segregated schools. Therefore, though I do not blame Black males or hip-hop culture, I am neither ready to absolve them of their social and personal responsibilities nor willing to say or believe that Black males have no agency in their demise. I am just not sure how much agency.

As a Black man in America it would be misguided and foolish of me to assert that systemic forms of racism and discrimination, both historical and contemporary, do not affect my life chances in ways that I am neither aware of nor have control over. I live and work in one of the least diverse places in the country, so I understand firsthand how racialized assumptions can and do play out in ways that even the mentally strongest individuals would find difficulty mustering up the intestinal fortitude to ward off. I also know how difficult it is to shield off the psychic burden of feelings of inferiority engendered by subtle and not-so-subtle racial slights, put-downs, and insults. The question is, then, do those experiences give me a free pass to wallow in mediocrity, to level my aspirations, or to expect members of the dominant group to lower the bar for me as compensation for years of racial discrimination? I say, "No." Even if such accommodations could be made, I would challenge those young Black males steeped in hip-hop culture for wanting to have it both ways. I take further issue with folks who play the "race card" in order to acquire a license, if you will, to call another Black man by the "N" word, yet in the same breath pledge their allegiance to a type of capitalism that ignores race, community, and brotherhood in exchange for getting paid.

Today's hip-hop culture, like mainstream culture, promotes the individual rather than the group. To use Cornel West's (West & Hewlett, 1998) phrase, it further pushes "non-market values" such as love, care, linked fate, group consciousness, and historical memory to the margins because they have no commercial value. Within such a context, only "market values" are promoted and celebrated because they can be traded and sold. Contemporary hip-hop culture praises the value of making money by any means necessary, as symbolized in the title of 50 Cent's 2003 album *Get Rich or Die Tryin.* The overarching assumption of many of today's hip-hop artists is that the market only rewards talent and hard work, and that in such an equation no one cares if you are Black or White. That is, if you got game, you will "get paid."

I contend that it is precisely this false notion of equality of opportunity promoted by hip-hop culture that is most detrimental to the status of young Black males. It is this errant interpretation that dulls their critical senses and enables so many to buy into the hype, thus creating a context that allows a very few to exploit and profit off so many. Hip-hop culture permits Black males to call each other by the "N" word because it provides them with no racialized analysis of the word's historical meaning. It posits instead that Black people have progressed so much that any of us who are willing to "get rich or die tryin'" can make it and be seen on an equal footing with members of the dominant group. Thus, the power of the "N" word is reduced.

On a different but related note, perhaps the greatest tragedy of capitalism as it is played out in hip-hop culture is its attack on education. This attack tends to be carried out in one of two ways. First, there is the impatience factor. The process of schooling requires a person to invest a substantial amount of time and effort at one point in time so that he or she may receive a return on that investment at some later designated time. This notion of delayed gratification, however, goes against the grain of modern hip-hop culture, which places an extremely high premium on fast money, hustling, and "blowing up" or achieving immediate success. Accordingly, if LeBron James can come out of high school and get a $90 million contract to play in the NBA, then I can too.

Then there is the relevance factor. Having pursued a postsecondary education, most of us assume that a healthy relationship between number of years of schooling and modest success will ensue. This notion of education as a means to an end places formal schooling at odds with the dictates of hip-hop culture, which values a predatory style of capitalism as both means and end. Put differently, if one's objective is to make enough money to satisfy his or her appetite for material possessions, then the long route of formal schooling is definitely not the way to go. This dilemma becomes particularly relevant when one considers the extremely high materialistic bar that hip-hop sets for its generally low-income participants and followers.

The pressure to have the designer clothes, the expensive jewelry, and the cars with the custom rims leads many young Black men to reject education as a relevant route to material success. In this light, the drug trade, hip-hop, the NFL, and the NBA appear to be options that are far more viable. School thus becomes irrelevant. As hip-hop artist Kanye West alludes to in one of the many problematic skits on his 2004 CD *The College Dropout,* "All those degrees are not going to keep you warm," implying that even after four years of college many Black men will still find themselves poor. Add to this 50 Cent, who in his 2003 track "If I Can't" boasts about being "the dropout who made more money than those teachers," and the cultural shift from a racial analysis to a class analysis or from an emphasis on the group to that of the individual becomes abundantly clear.

RRL: You make some interesting comments, but I do not believe you can necessarily discount the race factor because it was racialized struggle that made possible the context in which many hip-hip artists operate. You cannot discount historic and present-day systemic racism that limits the opportunity for Black males to better their life chances for upward social mobility. As a result of racism, Black males had to be creative in their efforts to achieve the American Dream, whether through legal or illegal means.

Well, you may ask, what about the "Eminem factor" or the fact that White hip-hop artists have risen to the top of the hip-hop world? I contend that this speaks to the same class issue. Although there is no reason to discount the talents of these artists, one must contextualize their success in the cauldron out of which hip-hop emerged. Hip-hop was born out of the necessity for young Black and Latino males to gain voice and speak to the disparate—that is, class-based—conditions in which many of them lived, which, I believe, was and is a direct result of race rather than class. Now does race carry all the weight? I would say, "No." I am sure that other factors such as motivation, willingness, ability, and so forth were also viable, but if you were to run a regression analysis to determine which factor had the most influence, I guarantee you that the race variable would account for most of their experience.

Given this very racialized discourse, White hip-hop artists of today, much like other White musician/performers of the past, have found that something within them resonates with "Black" music, and they have very successfully adopted it to their advantage. So, yes, it may appear to be "a class thing" because you have this White male, Eminem, "representing" from 8 Mile, a tough area of Detroit. However, even Mr. Mathers (Marshall Mathers, aka Eminem) realizes the benefits of his White skin. In his *joint* (or single), "White America," he raps,

> Let's do the math, if I was Black I would of sold half. I didn't have to graduate from Lincoln High School to know that. Sittin' back, look at this shit—Wow, I'm like, my skin is startin' to work for my benefit now.

Don't be fooled, my brotha'! The national lens through which White hegemonic forces have pushed for class to be at the front of the debate in order to mask the racial oppression seated at the core of the inequities experienced by Black males is real. George Lipsitz (1998) describes this as a possessive investment in Whiteness. Similarly, Cheryl Harris (1993) speaks to the very notion of Whiteness as property. Even in these economic- and class-driven theories, race is still center stage.

Regarding the Kanye West piece, it is interesting that you mention that particular quote, which is inaccurate because he actually states that the degrees *will* keep you warm. It is a cynical play on the fact that the father of Lil' Jimmy, the subject of West's rap, had gotten too many degrees and was a lifelong learner who had never achieved gainful employment. However, a good majority of the other tracks on this joint are extremely thought provoking and offer great social critique. They also bring to the forefront the disparate conditions that spark the quest for fortune and fame via different means than going to college. I agree with your agency piece and believe we should hold hip-hop performers accountable to some degree; however, I think Jay-Z states it best on his *Black Album* in the track entitled "Moment of Clarity":

> Music whizzes hate me because the industry ain't make me. Hustlers and booz-ers embrace me and the music I be makin' I dumb down for my audience and doubled my dollars. They criticize me for it, yet they all yell, holla! If skillz sold, truth be told, I'd probably be lyrically Talib Kweli. Truthfully, I wanna rhyme like Common Sense, but I did five mill. I ain't been rhyming like Common since. When your sense got that much in common and you been hustling since your inception, f—k perception, go with what make sense. Since I know what we up against, we as rappers must decide what's most important. I can't help the part if I one of them. So I got rich and gave back to me, that's the win-win.

Here Jay-Z speaks directly to your agency piece and states that he made a conscious decision to get paid and give back. This is his moment of clarity.

Jay-Z is about more, however, than just himself. He makes the music to which common, everyday folk can relate because he realizes that being too political would be professional suicide, negatively affecting him economically. He claims that he takes some of his earnings from the music and gives back by creating various jobs in his community and donating to various charities. And for the record, Jay-Z, aka Shawn Carter, is not the only rapper who has had this "moment" of clarity.

MJS: I agree that race remains a powerful determinant of Black life and was a major impetus behind the origins of hip-hop music and its oppositional stance. However, I am not convinced that race factors largely in how the average members of the hip-hop community think about themselves and their relationship to the group. So when I say that race is irrelevant to young Black males, I am speaking to their willingness (or lack thereof) to think of themselves as part of a deprived group and feel politically accountable to that group in the same way that Arthur Miller and his colleagues (1981) spoke about group consciousness and political participation.

To pursue the American Dream as a Black man, without any regard for the health and welfare of the Black community, is not only socially irresponsible but also seems to be particular to the hip-hop generation. True, the vast majority of young Black men who came of age during the 1960s and 1970s did not participate in the civil rights activity, but popular youth culture during that time period did not seem to promote and celebrate crass individualism, or "gettin' mines," at the expense of the larger community.

The culture of narcissism often exhibited today is not unique to young Black people, as selfishness can be found in all communities; however, it is more destructive for African Americans, particularly given, as you indicate, the persistence of systemic racism that limits the opportunity for Black males to better their life chances. It is here where I take issue with Kanye West, whose primary message appears to be that school is not for everyone. In his view, if the American Dream is what you are seeking, then school is definitely not the route you want to take because, he asserts, the only thing four years of college will get you is a drug habit from all the partying you are bound to do and a $25,000-a-year job working for someone who did not even go to college. Granted, dropping out of college worked for Kanye West, but neither hip-hop, nor professional sports, will ever be a realistic or viable alternative to getting an education. But these are the images and messages to which young Black men are exposed daily. Rarely are they shown, on television or in print media, Black men as anything other than athletes, entertainers, or drug dealers. Thus, for me, any effort to address the bleak realities of an expanding population of young Black men who are seriously disconnected from the mainstream society must first address the culture of narcissism that hip-hop culture glamorizes and promotes.

RRL: Could you explain what you mean by "young Black men who are seriously disconnected from the mainstream society"? I have an idea of what you mean, which I am okay with, but I also have another idea that might possibly speak to the notion that these young men *are* well connected to the mainstream via pop culture, which has taken the imagery of young Black males and capitalized on it. So when you say they are seriously disconnected, one could easily argue that they are indeed the very foundation of the economic, political, and cultural components of mainstream society. Economically this is so because even without essentializing it, the money made from hip-hop and its imagery—that which the prison industry makes from the incarceration of Black males who emulate the gangsta lifestyle and from the cheap labor provided by all those incarcerated Black males—is "large." Second, the political system continues to carry some of the same ideology inherent in Chief Justice Tanney's ruling in the 1856 *Dred Scott v. Sandford* case—that Blacks have no rights that Whites are bound to respect.

Various policies have been created that have bureaucratically and systemically prohibited Black people's attainment of education, stifled their opportunities for social mobility, and garnisheed their equal protection under the law, but they have each been dismantled. Finally, Black men are at the core culturally because there is no other unique or original American art form other than jazz, which we can also claim that has had the type of impact, nationally and globally, hip-hop has had. These are just a couple of thoughts.

MJS: I follow your interpretation, but either I disagree or we are talking about two different things—which is not necessarily a bad thing. When I say that young Black men are seriously disconnected from the mainstream I am speaking more to dire social and economic situations in which so many young Black men find themselves, circumstances that set them distinctly apart from other Black people, irrespective of social class, as well as from White people and even young Latino males. Yes, I would agree that hip-hop has successfully positioned the Black male image to make it extremely marketable, as it has definitely been embraced worldwide. However, I must make a distinction between the Black male cultural icon and the adulation of Black male bodies and the realities of Black life in America as experienced by the average Black male.

Basketball player LeBron James maybe viewed and loved by many as "King James," but I suspect that the public's love does not extend to the vast majority of Black males who are experiencing extreme levels of joblessness, statistical discrimination, residential and social isolation, incarceration, and so forth. And we need not even discuss such racist and exploitative practices as those that encourage highly talented Black high school basketball players to skip college while sending the not-so-best-and-brightest White players to Ivy League schools like Duke, Stanford, and the like.

I contend that young Black males *are* disconnected from the societal opportunity structure and thereby rendered disproportionately unable to participate in and benefit from that structure. Without a formal education beyond high school, coupled with time spent in jail or prison, a sizable number of young Black men lack the human and cultural capital to secure a job that pays a livable wage. Even more, with very little money to contribute to a household, they are less attractive as potential mates. I could go on, with the point being that the experiences of this group are vastly different from those of others in American society and hence seriously disconnected from the mainstream. But if you call exploitation participation, then yes, I agree that Black males are very much a part of the mainstream. On a different note, I think your concerns could also be framed in the context of a "progress or the lack thereof" analysis. Young Black men as the engines that make the prison industry turn, is that progress or a setback?

The preceding discussion above about the status of today's young Black males and their alleged disconnection from mainstream society focused almost exclusively on hip-hop culture, but we easily could have highlighted the role of poor schools, the breakdown of families, racism, residential segregation, and the erosion of blue-collar jobs as factors that negatively influence young Black males' life chances. This is not to suggest that our discussion is incomplete, but rather that hip-hop culture—its images and messages—are part of a plethora of issues that must be addressed if one wishes to gain a full understanding of the plight of young Black males today and to begin to turn around the bleak prospects faced by so many of them.

An Exploratory Study of the Influence of Hip-Hop on Black Males

Up to this point, our discussion of the images and messages associated with hip-hop culture and their suspected influence on the plight of young Black males has been largely theoretical. In this section, we assess more concretely the particular social, economic, and personal experiences of young Black males during the 30-plus years of the hip-hop era and compare them to the experiences of young Black women and White men. Consistent with our earlier discussion, we expect young Black men's education, employment, marriage, and general happiness statistics not only to change over time but also to be significantly different from the statistics given for Black women and White men. To test this assumption, we focused our analysis on a sample of Black men, Black women, and White men ranging in age from 18 to 35 years old drawn from the General Social Science Surveys (GSS) cumulative data file, which spans from 1972 to 2004. This time period is approximately the same time frame of the hip-hop era under investigation. The GSS is a national survey designed to monitor social trends relevant to public policy. This cumulative data file merges 25 surveys into a single file, with each year or survey acting as a subfile. Items in the cumulative data file have appeared in previous national surveys.

To assess the particular social, economic, and personal experiences of young Black males during the hip-hop era and compare them to the experiences of Black women and White men, we considered 12 indicators. For purposes of analysis, we divided these indicators into three categories: socioeconomic and sociodemographic status (SES/SDS), personal and financial well-being, and racial attitudes and group affect. The SES/SDS indicators included educational attainment, work status, income, occupational prestige, and marital status. Personal and financial well-being were measured using the items that assessed general happiness and financial satisfaction. Racial attitudes and group affect are somewhat broader concepts and were assessed by the following items: "Blacks shouldn't push for equal rights"; "Have conditions for Blacks improved?"; "How close do you feel to Black people?"; "How close do you feel to White people?" and "Are group differences due to discrimination?"

We estimated trends over time for each indicator by gender and race as well as compared the mean scores for Black men against the mean scores for Black women and White men. Our goal was to explore how much of the current social and economic conditions faced by young Black men are particular to them and how much is influenced by broad social and economic trends prevalent during the time period when hip-hop culture first emerged and later established itself as a viable and influential artistic expression. We assumed that within-group comparisons of the social, economic, and personal experiences of young Black men over time would yield a very different picture than between-group comparisons involving young Black women and White men. More specifically, we expected young Black males' educational attainment, income, occupational status, feelings of general happiness, and overall sense of racial affinity to be lower today than they were in years past. We further anticipated that compared to young Black women and White men, young Black males would rank significantly lower on these measures.

We began this chapter with a dialogue about the images and messages associated with hip-hop culture and their suspected influence on the plight of young Black males. In that dialogue, Land, on one side, asserted that the dire situation faced by so many young African American men today is largely the product of a set of prevailing racialized forces working in concert to construct Black males in very dehumanizing ways. More specifically, he focused on the controlling nature of the mass media in general and of the music industry in particular to conclude that hip-hop images and messages related to young Black males are merely social constructions endemic of their subordinate status. Spiller, on the other side of the debate, contended that Black males are both the victims and the perpetrators of capitalism and its product, hip-hop culture. He argues that within the confines of hip-hop culture violent, misogynist and wanton images of young Black men are the product that is being manipulated, manufactured, and sold, often with the cooperation and blessings of young Black men. It is within this context that Spiller asserts that young Black men must accept some responsibility for the creation and perpetuation of harmful, problematic images of and messages about themselves.

It was beyond the scope of our dialogue to settle this issue; however, the findings of our analysis of the GSS data provide us with some context for framing the debate. Accordingly, the data revealed that when comparing the experiences of young Black males today to those of young Black males 20 to 30 years ago, some support exists for Land's position, as this comparison suggests that social and economic progress has been made by young Black males despite the omnipresent force of hip-hop culture. However, when comparing the social and economic experiences of young Black males to those of young Black females and White males, a much more troubling reality emerges: one that supports Spiller's position. The race-gender comparisons indicate persistent and in some instances growing inequities between Black men and the comparison groups, suggesting that something particular is happening to young Black men in the hip-hop era, as their social and economic experiences appear to be vastly different from those of young Black women and White men.

Table 1 presents the mean differences over time for young Black males across several measures of SES/SDS, personal and financial well-being, and racial attitudes and group affect factors. Overall, the table shows that young Black males have made steady progress in terms of their social and economic well-being from 1972 to 2004. The young Black males surveyed as part of the GSS study between 2000 and 2004 not only reported significantly higher levels of educational attainment

TABLE 1. MEANS FOR KEY VARIABLES FOR YOUNG BLACK MALES:
GENERAL SOCIAL SCIENCE SURVEY, 1972–2004

VARIABLE	1972–78	1980–89	1990–98	2000–04	T-TEST
Socioeconomic and Socio-demographic Status					
Educational Attainment	11.79	12.65	12.93	13.09	−6.13*
	(2.85)	(2.29)	(2.13)	(2.32)	
Work Status (1 = Full-Time)	0.646	0.669	0.711	0.707	−1.63
	(0.478)	(0.470)	(0.453)	(0.455)	
Income	6.56	8.26	9.85	10.19	-17.86*
	(3.03)	(3.35)	(2.81)	(2.93)	
Occupational Prestige	33.58	33.63	37.86	42.12	−16.12*
	(12.34)	(12.70)	(15.47)	(15.52)	
Marital Status (1 = Married)	0.529	0.339	0.342	0.355	4.35*
	(0.499)	(0.490)	(0.475)	(0.479)	
Personal and Financial Well-Being					
General Happiness	1.88	1.95	2.00	1.32	7.55*
	(0.674)	(0.606)	(0.636)	(1.11)	
Satisfied with Financial Situation	1.75	1.65	1.67	1.10	8.93*
	(0.746)	(0.688)	(0.705)	(0.986)	
Racial Attitudes and Group Affect					
Blacks Shouldn't Push for Equal Rights?	—	3.12	3.08	3.16	0.279
		(1.06)	(1.12)	(1.10)	
Have Conditions for Blacks Improved?	—	—	1.83	2.21	—
			(0.868)	(0.929)	
How Close Do You Feel to Black People?	—	—	1.63	3.43	—
			(3.21)	(4.06)	
Groups Differences Due to Discrimination?	—	0.812	0.737	0.633	2.64*
		(0.392)	(0.441)	(0.484)	

*$p\_0.01$ ($p < 0.05$ unless otherwise noted).

NOTE: Numbers in parentheses are standard deviations. *N* values for particular items vary because of nonresponses in particular years. Numbers in the *t*-test column are the results of tests of mean differences for Black males surveyed between 1972 and 1978 and between 2000 and 2004.

(X = 13.08) than their 1972–78 counterparts (X = 11.79) but were also significantly more likely to have higher incomes ($X_{2000–04}$ = 10.19 compared to $X_{1972–78}$ = 6.56) and higher occupational status ($X_{2000–04}$ = 42.12 compared to $X_{1972–78}$ = 33.58).

With regard to marital status and personal and financial well-being measures, table 1 illustrates sharp declines. That is, among the sample of young Black males surveyed between 1972 and 2004, the subgroup surveyed between 2000 and 2004 was least likely to be married and feel generally happy or satisfied with their financial situation. Further, young Black males surveyed between 1980 and 2004 appear to have grown increasingly weary of claims of discrimination as a cause for group differences in levels of economic success. Their mean score in this area dropped significantly during this time period, going from .812 in the 1980s to .737 in the 1990s to .633 in the 2000s. Taken together, these data reveal that although young Black males in 2004 were better educated, earned higher incomes, were employed in much more prestigious occupations, and were less inclined to attribute group differences to discrimination, they were paradoxically less likely to be married, generally less happy, and more discontented with their financial situation than were young Black males in the 1970s. These findings lend some support to Land's position, as most of the social and economic statistics for young Black males improved significantly over the past four decades. The findings further suggest that despite hip-hop culture's unfettered promotion and celebration of the pimp, thug, and hustler image throughout the 1990s and 2000s, young Black males gained significant ground in the areas of education, income, and occupational prestige during this time period.

It thus goes without saying that young Black males today are materially better off than young Black males in years past. What is not so clear, however, is just how much progress this group has made. Simple comparisons of young Black male's social and economic experiences to those of young Black females and White males reveal a more dire situation than that stemming from the within-group comparisons presented in table 1.

Tables 2 through 5 presents mean scores for young Black males, Black females, and White males by decade across a number of key SES/SDS variables, personal and financial well-being measures, and racial attitude and group affect. Compared to the social and economic status of the comparison groups, young Black men have not faired very well during the hip-hop era years from 1980 to 2004. Rather, they lagged consistently behind young Black women and White men, socially, economically, and personally.

Table 2 presents the mean differences in SES/SDS and personal and financial well-being by race and gender for individuals surveyed between 1972 and 1978. These data show that, on average, young Black men in the 1970s were not as highly educated as their female counterparts (X_{male} = 11.79 compared to X_{female} = 12.30), but they were significantly more likely to work full-time and earn a higher income than were young Black women (X_{male} = 6.56 compared to X_{female} = 4.69). Nevertheless, young Black men reportedly worked in occupations that were significantly lower

TABLE 2. MEANS FOR KEY VARIABLES BY RACE AND GENDER:
GENERAL SOCIAL SCIENCE SURVEY, 1972–1978

VARIABLES	BLACK MALES	BLACK FEMALES	WHITE MALES	T-TEST[1]	T-TEST[2]
Socioeconomic and Socio-demographic Status					
Educational Attainment	11.79	12.30	12.96	3.04*	−7.18*
	(2.85)	(2.42)	(0.427)		
Work Status (1 = Full-Time)	0.646	0.351	0.758	10.54*	−3.92*
	(0.478)	(0.477)	(0.427)		
Income	6.56	4.69	7.73	7.48*	−4.68*
	(3.03)	(2.92)	(2.98)		
Occupational Prestige	33.58	38.85	40.70	−6.84*	−9.01*
	(12.34)	(13.31)	(14.07)		
Marital Status (1 = Married)	0.529	0.702	0.673	−5.76*	−4.80*
	(0.499)	(0.457)	(0.468)		
Personal and Financial Well-being					
General Happiness	1.88	2.24	2.18	−9.00*	−7.50*
	(0.674)	(0.624)	(0.614)		
Satisfied with Financial Situation	1.75	1.97	2.01	−0.52	−0.61
	(0.746)	(0.736)	(0.727)		
Racial Attitudes and Group Affect					
Blacks Shouldn't Push for Equal Rights?	—	—	2.93	—	—
			(1.04)		
Have Conditions for Blacks Improved?	—	—	—	—	—
How Close Do You Feel to Black People?	—	—	—	—	—
Groups Differences Due to Discrimination?	—	0.481	0.420	—	—
		(0.500)	(0.494)		

*$p \_ 0.01$ ($p < 0.05$ unless otherwise noted).

NOTE: Numbers in parentheses are standard deviations. N values for particular items vary because of nonresponses in particular years. Numbers in the columns are the results of tests of mean differences for Black males–Black females and Black males–White males, respectively.

in prestige than those held by young Black women (X_{male} = 33.58 compared to X_{female} = 38.85). Significant gender differences were also observed in the area of personal and financial well-being. As shown in table 2, young Black men reported mean general happiness scores noticeably lower than those of young Black women (X_{male} = 1.88 compared to X_{female} = 2.24).

Table 2 shows that with regard to comparisons by race, the gap between young Black men and White men in the 1970s was even greater than those involving young Black women. Compared to young White men, young Black men in the 1970s were poorly educated (X_{Black} = 11.79 compared to X_{White} = 12.96), more likely

TABLE 3. MEANS FOR KEY VARIABLES BY RACE AND GENDER: GENERAL SOCIAL SCIENCE SURVEY, 1980–1989

VARIABLES	BLACK MALES	BLACK FEMALES	WHITE MALES	T-TEST[1]	T-TEST[2]
Socioeconomic and Socio-demographic Status					
Educational Attainment	12.65	12.98	13.30	–3.00*	–6.25*
	(2.29)	(2.46)	(0.278)		
Work Status (1 = Full-Time)	0.669	0.489	0.774	7.50*	–1.33
	(0.470)	(0.499)	(0.418)		
Income	8.26	7.29	9.43	5.40*	–6.50*
	(3.35)	(3.44)	(3.01)		
Occupational Prestige	33.63	40.61	40.75	–11.08*	–10.95*
	(12.70)	(13.63)	(14.54)		
Marital Status (1 = Married)	0.339	0.538	0.574	–5.79*	–7.29*
	(0.490)	(0.498)	(0.494)		
Personal and Financial Well-being					
General Happiness	1.95	2.19	2.18	–8.00*	–7.70*
	(0.606)	(0.620)	(0.594)		
Satisfied with Financial Situation	1.65	1.87	1.95	–7.30*	–10.00*
	(0.688)	(0.728)	(0.728)		
Racial Attitudes and Group Affect					
Blacks Shouldn't Push for Equal Rights?	3.12	2.62	2.65	5.90*	5.22*
	(1.06)	(1.10)	(1.04)		
Have Conditions for Blacks Improved?	—	—	—	—	—
How Close Do You Feel to Black People?	—	—	—	—	—
Groups Differences Due to Discrimination?	0.812	0.486	0.392	0.90	1.16
	(0.392)	(0.499)	(0.488)		

*$p \_ 0.01$ ($p < 0.05$ unless otherwise noted).

NOTE: Numbers in parentheses are standard deviations. N values for particular items vary because of nonresponses in particular years. Numbers in the columns are the results of tests of mean differences for Black males–Black females and Black males–White males, respectively.

to be underemployed or not working at all (X_{Black} = .646 compared to X_{White} = .758), and when employed, received less income (X_{Black} = 6.56 compared to X_{White} = 7.73). Additionally, Black males, on average, were employed in less-prestigious occupations (X_{Black} = 33.58 compared to X_{White} = 40.70), were additionally less likely to be married (X_{Black} = .529 compared to X_{White} = .673), and were overall significantly less happy than their young White male counterparts (X_{Black} = 1.88 compared to X_{White} = 2.18).

Turning to table 3, one sees that although the social and economic situation for young Black males improved from 1972 to 1989, it failed to reach parity with young Black women and White men. If we look first at simple comparisons between young Black men and young Black women, these two groups appear to be very similar educationally, with Black men trailing slightly behind. With regard to work status, income, and occupational prestige, however, the data reveal a tremendous gap. Similar to results from the 1970s, young Black men in the 1980s reported significantly higher occurrences of full-time employment and larger incomes than their female counterparts. Nonetheless, young Black women were significantly more likely to report having been employed and to hold more prestigious jobs than young Black men ($X_{\text{Black men}}$ = 33.63 compared to $X_{\text{Black women}}$ = 40.61).

Significant mean differences between young Black men and women were also found for personal and financial well-being measures as well as for racial attitudes. As shown in table 3, young Black men did not appear to be as happy (X = 1.95) as their female counterparts (X = 2.19). Likewise, a small but significant difference emerged between how young Black men thought about their financial situations compared to the situations of young Black women. The former group was slightly more dissatisfied than the latter group.

Additionally, compared to young Black women, young Black men were much more likely to think that Black people should not push for equal rights ($X_{\text{Black men}}$ = 3.12 compared to $X_{\text{Black women}}$ = 2.62; see table 4). Echoing these findings, the data in table 4 show that young Black men, compared to young White men, did not fare very well between 1980 and 1989. Young White males' mean educational attainment score during that time period, for example, was 13.30 compared to 12.65 for their Black male counterparts, a difference that is significant at the .01 level. Additionally, the data highlight the serious challenges young Black males of that time span faced in the personal and economic spheres. Mean scores given for work status, income, occupational prestige, and marital status consistently placed those young Black males significantly behind their White male counterparts. Similar to their material disconnect, young Black males were emotionally disconnected as well; their general happiness score was significantly lower than that attained by young White males. Further, compared to White males, Black males were more likely to report having been dissatisfied with their financial situation and least likely to support Black people's push for equal rights.

The findings for young Black men surveyed during the 1990s tell a very similar story to that told in the 1970s and 1980s data. As shown in table 4, young Black men surveyed between 1990 and 1998 reported social and economic statistics superior to those for young Black males of the decades past, yet they fell behind similarly

TABLE 4. MEANS FOR KEY VARIABLES BY RACE AND GENDER:
GENERAL SOCIAL SCIENCE SURVEY, 1990–1998

VARIABLES	BLACK MALES	BLACK FEMALES	WHITE MALES	T-TEST[1]	T-TEST[2]
Socioeconomic and Socio-demographic Status					
Educational Attainment	12.93	13.48	13.77	−4.58*	−7.00*
	(2.13)	(2.52)	(2.56)		
Work Status (1 = Full-Time)	0.711	0.544	0.778	0.68	−2.58*
	(0.453)	(0.498)	(0.415)		
Income	9.85	8.78	10.28	5.94*	−2.53
	(2.81)	(3.36)	(2.70)		
Occupational Prestige	37.86	40.74	42.02	−0.96	−1.37
	(15.47)	(13.68)	(14.80)		
Marital Status (1 = Married)	0.342	0.491	0.497	−5.73*	−5.96*
	(0.475)	(0.499)	(0.500)		
Personal and Financial Well-Being					
General Happiness	2.00	2.18	2.19	−5.00*	−5.14*
	(0.636)	(0.620)	(0.584)		
Satisfied with Financial Situation	1.67	1.88	1.97	−5.68*	−7.69*
	(0.705)	(0.732)	(0.715)		
Racial Attitudes and Group Affect					
Blacks Shouldn't Push For Equal Rights?	3.08	3.04	2.20	0.42	8.80*
	(1.12)	(1.03)	(1.02)		
Have Conditions for Blacks Improved?	1.83	2.16	2.32	−4.46*	−6.48*
	(0.868)	(0.932)	(0.902)		
How Close Do You Feel to Black People?	1.63	5.78	5.16	−22.8*	−19.6*
	(3.21)	(2.07)	(1.85)		
Groups Differences Due to Discrimination?	0.737	0.447	0.302	9.60*	14.5*
	(0.441)	(0.497)	(0.459)		

*$p \_ 0.01$ ($p < 0.05$ unless otherwise noted).

NOTE: Numbers in parentheses are standard deviations. *N* values for particular items vary because of nonresponses in particular years. Numbers in the columns are the results of tests of mean differences for Black males–Black females and Black males–White males, respectively.

situated young Black women and White men. If we look first at educational attainment levels, young Black males completed, on average, a little less than one year of college ($X = 12.93$), whereas young Black women completed about a year-and-a-half of college ($X = 13.48$), and young White males completed close to two years of college ($X = 13.77$). With regard to work status and income, the data show that although young Black men did better in these areas than did their female counterparts, mean scores for young White men were significantly larger than those given for Black men. Mean differences associated with occupational prestige again reveal that compared to young Black women and White men, young Black men in the 1990s worked in the least prestigious jobs.

Despite young Black males' relatively poorer SES/SDS showing, they reported feelings of personal and financial contentment similar to those of the comparison groups. The mean general happiness scores for young Black men, Black women, and White men in the 1990s were 2.00, 2.18, and 2.19, respectively. These differences are significant but negligible. If we turn to the matter of whether young Black males of the 1990s were satisfied with their financial situation, the data show that young Black men reported feeling the least satisfied vis-à-vis the comparison groups ($X_{\text{Black men}} = 1.67$; $X_{\text{Black women}} = 1.88$; $X_{\text{White men}} = 1.97$); again, these differences, though significant, were not large.

Consistent with trends given for general happiness and financial satisfaction, young Black males between 1990 and 1998 reported more intense feelings of alienation and dissatisfaction with race relations than did either of the comparison groups. The data shows that despite their socioeconomic progress, young Black males of that era were less inclined to feel that conditions for Blacks had improved or that Blacks should push for equal rights. They were also less inclined, on average, to feel that social and economic differences between members of minority and majority groups were due to discrimination. By contrast, compared to young Black females and White males, young Black males reported feeling the least emotionally attached to other Black people.

Table 5 presents mean scores by race and gender for measures of SES/SDS, personal and financial well-being, and racial attitudes and group affect. The data presented in this table show that between 2000 and 2004 the effects of race and gender on young Black males' life chances had began to wane, as evidenced by the relatively small differences noted in mean scores. Looking first at educational attainment, one sees that although young Black males reported lower mean levels of schooling than their comparison groups, the differences between each of the three groups were negligible ($X_{\text{Black men}} = 13.09$, $X_{\text{Black women}} = 13.63$, and $X_{\text{White men}} = 13.80$). Likewise, all three groups surveyed between 2000 and 2004 indicated belonging to the same income group and were not very different occupationally. Similarly, minimal differences were reported between young Black men, Black women, and White men across levels of general happiness and financial satisfaction. Mean scores delineating how young Black males, Black females, and White males think about race differed much more widely than those for SES/SDS and personal and

TABLE 5. MEANS FOR KEY VARIABLES BY RACE AND GENDER:
GENERAL SOCIAL SCIENCE SURVEY, 2000–2004

VARIABLES	BLACK MALES	BLACK FEMALES	WHITE MALES	T-TEST[1]	T-TEST[2]
Socioeconomic and Socio-demographic Status					
Educational Attainment	13.09	13.63	13.80	−3.60*	−4.60*
	(2.32)	(2.44)	(2.63)		
Work Status (1 = Full-Time)	0.707	0.533	0.774	5.30*	−2.23
	(0.455)	(0.498)	(0.418)		
Income	10.19	9.34	10.61	3.90*	−2.00
	(2.93)	(3.44)	(2.67)		
Occupational Prestige	42.12	40.92	43.32		
	(15.52)	(13.72)	(14.92)		
Marital Status (1 = Married)	0.355	0.459	0.441	−3.47*	−2.69*
	(0.479)	(0.498)	(0.496)		
Personal and Financial Well-Being					
General Happiness	1.32	1.42	1.51	−1.39	−2.71*
	(1.11)	(1.16)	(1.14)		
Satisfied with Financial Situation	1.10	1.23	1.41	−1.94	−4.43*
	(0.986)	(1.08)	(1.13)		
Racial Attitudes and Group Affect					
Blacks Shouldn't Push for Equal Rights?	3.16	3.08	2.11	0.64	8.08*
	(1.10)	(1.03)	(1.04)		
Have Conditions for Blacks Improved?	2.21	2.18	2.35	0.33	−1.40
	(0.929)	(0.954)	(0.914)		
How Close Do You Feel to Black People?	3.43	5.91	5.40	−9.92*	−7.58*
	(4.06)	(2.12)	(1.84)		
Groups Differences Due to Discrimination?	0.633	0.400	0.255	4.96*	7.88*
	(0.484)	(0.490)	(0.436)		

*$p \leq 0.01$ ($p < 0.05$ unless otherwise noted).
NOTE: Numbers in parentheses are standard deviations. N values for particular items vary because of nonresponses in particular years. Numbers in the columns are the results of tests of mean differences for Black males–Black females and Black males–White males, respectively.

financial well-being. Although no significant difference was found between young Black men and women regarding their opinions about whether Blacks should push for equal rights, simple comparisons between young Black and White men reveal sharp and statistically significant differences. Dramatic differences were also found for the racial affinity measures. As shown by the data in table 5, young Black males were the least likely to feel close to other Black people, yet they were more likely to believe that social and economic differences between members of the minority and majority group were due to discrimination.

Taken together, these data empirically reveal just how disconnected young Black males are from mainstream society. Whether one focuses on young Black males in the 1970s or in the 1990s, one finds significantly lower social, economic, and personal well-being statistics for this group than for either their female counterparts or their White male counterparts. Indeed, with fewer years of schooling, young Black men worked in less prestigious jobs, earned less income, were less likely to be married, and in turn felt more unhappy and dissatisfied with life than either young Black women or White men. Further, young Black males reported being less likely to believe that conditions for Black people had improved and to feel close to other Black people, but they were more inclined to believe that differences in the material conditions of members of dominant and minority groups were due to discrimination than were either young Black women and White men. Given these findings, it is no wonder these young Black males consistently reported feeling the least happy or financially content.

Conclusion

Hip-hop began in the late 1970s and early 1980s as a critique of social and racial injustices, and government neglect as well as an attempt to negotiate the experiences of marginalization, brutally truncated opportunity, and oppression within the confines of postindustrial urban America (George, 1998; Rose, 1994). By the 1990s however, hip-hop had come under increased attack for what many saw as its complicity with commercialism, racism, and sexism (hooks, 2000; George, 1998). In this chapter, we sought to explore this tension emphasizing the changing influence of hip-hop on the attitudes, behaviors, and socioeconomic status of young Black males. Our discussion revealed a complex and nuanced picture of the predicament so many young Black males find themselves in and the culture they helped spawn to express their hurts and pains, joys and victories. Given this link between the state of young Black males and hip-hop culture, we believe that our discussion in this chapter is not just an intellectual exercise, but has real meaning for the way we understand and address some of the more intractable problems that young Black males face, such as long-term unemployment, social alienation, media misrepresentation, and differential judicial treatment, just to name a few.

By all accounts, young Black men faced tremendous social and economic challenges long before hip-hop appeared on the cultural landscape. Thus, we ask, what role, if any, has hip-hop culture played in exacerbating the other troubling statistics and, more directly, what is the hip-hop community's social responsibility, if any, to the plight of its young Black male members? By raising these questions, we are not suggesting that the U.S. government and other sectors of society have no role to play in improving these males' social and economic situations, because we believe they do. Indeed, we contend that it is imperative for the nation's political leadership to do more to create jobs that pay a livable wage; such action would go a long way toward eliminating the persistent income gaps noted for young Black males over time during the hip-hop era. It is also important for the nation's teachers and school administrators to exhibit just as much, if not more, concern and interest in young Black males' reading and writing abilities as they do in these young men's athletic prowess. With regard to the U.S. criminal justice system, we believe that a better job must be done of distributing justice more equitably, and a larger share of America's resources should be funneled into rehabilitation rather than punishment of the incarcerated, disproportionately large numbers of whom are young Black males. Finally, we challenge the Black middle class to lend more of its leadership, resources, and cultural capital to mentoring and ensuring the overall well-being of these young men. It is desperately needed.

Assistance from the broader society is believed to be secondary to the role young Black men must play in changing their social and economic status. Likewise, we believe that hip-hop artists and trendsetters can and must do more to change and offer alternative countervailing images and messages about what it means to be young, Black, and male. We further believe this can be done without compromising artistic expression or commercial appeal because hip-hop is such a powerful voice and effective educational tool. Social institutions are designed to maintain the status quo and thus cannot be expected to acquiesce to the needs and desires of young Black males. Hence, a large portion of the change we seek must come from within the hip-hop community. This has happened before, and it can happen again.

REFERENCES

Cruse, H. (1968). *Rebellion or Revolution?* New York: William Morrow and Company.

Davis, J. A. & Smith, T. W. (1972–2004). *General Social Surveys.* Chicago: National Opinion Research Center.

Delgado, R. (1989). Storytelling for oppositionists and others: A plea for narrative. *Michigan Law Review, 87,* 2411–41.

George, N. (1998). *Hip hop America.* New York: Viking.

Harris, C. (1993). Whiteness as property. *Harvard Law Review, 106*(8), 1707–91.

hooks, b. (2000). *Where we stand: Class matters.* New York: Routledge.

Lipsitz, G. (1998). *The possessive investment in whiteness: How White people profit from identity politics.* Philadelphia: Temple University Press.

Macedo, D. (1994). *Literacies of power.* Boulder, CO: Westview Press.

Miller, A. H., Gurin, P., Gurin, G., & Malanchuk, O. (1981). Group consciousness and political participation. *American Journal of Political Science, 25*(3), 494–511.

Omi, M. & Winant, H. (1994). *Racial formation in the United States* (2nd ed). New York: Routledge.

Putnam, R. D. (2000). *Bowling alone: The collapse and revival of American community.* New York: Simon & Schuster.

Rose, T. (1994). *Black noise: Rap music and Black culture in contemporary America.* Hanover, NH: Wesleyan University Press.

Steinhorn, L. & Diggs-Brown, B. (1999). *By the color of our skin: The illusion of integration and the reality of race.* New York: Plume Books.

West, C. & Hewlett, S. A. (1998). *The war against parents.* Boston: Houghton Mifflin.

PART 3

Access, Equity, and Postsecondary Education

Roots of the Black Male Challenge

A CALL FOR ACTION IN MICHIGAN

Gersham Nelson

After 140 years as citizens of the United States, many Black Americans face the compounding effects of disenfranchisement as well as new and more subtle forms of discrimination. Because of the patriarchal nature of U.S. society, Black males were specifically targeted by their White counterparts during the long struggle for human and civil rights. The nature of that struggle has changed, but Black males continue to be more conspicuously targeted and bruised, physically and psychologically. Thus, the specific issues surrounding affirmative action vis-à-vis Black men loom as vital in every state of the union, especially those like Michigan with large populations of Blacks. The abusive patterns of malfeasance perpetrated against Black males must be checked, and Black men's latent skills and talents must be rescued for the good of the community, the state, and the nation.

The literature on affirmative action is as substantial as it is controversial. Its most severe limitation is the paucity of historical context to heighten understanding and inform conclusions. Much attention, however, has been paid to issues of access related to higher education, jobs, health care, and legal representation. Stanford's work *Interracial America: Opposing Viewpoints* (2006) is perhaps the "point-counterpoint" tome on the affirmative action issue in the United States because it exposes the depth of thought that has been devoted to the issue as well as the shallowness, ignorance, and excessive self-indulgence it has evoked. Likewise, Lipson (2006) approaches the issue with sufficient insight to make a lasting contribution to the discussion. Others, however, like Bowen et al. (2005), ignore the history of legal barriers against Blacks as they seek to create a new classification of disadvantaged: poor Whites. This group, they argue, does not receive the extra consideration in terms of higher education selection awarded to athletes, alumni children, or racial minorities. Cursory examination of Bowen et al.'s work reveals that its approach, wittingly or unwittingly, obscures the issue of addressing the disadvantages that result from blatant discrimination. Among these, for example, is the cumulative effect of disenfranchisement, which has so profoundly limited educational opportunity for Blacks at every level that a disproportionately large number in Black students do not even receive a high school diploma. Yet these authors choose to ignore the larger reality to create an illusion of comparative disadvantage.

The most uncompromisingly pro–affirmative action is probably Katznelson's (2005) *When Affirmative Action Was White: An Untold History of Racial Inequality in Twentieth-Century America*. Katznelson's primary contention is anchored in history, thus the causes and effects of discrimination that he identifies in this book make a compelling argument. McWhorter's (2006) *Winning The Race: Beyond the Crisis in Black America* also strikes a necessary chord in the effort to seek solutions to the deep-seated historical dilemmas facing the Black male.

Much of the emerging body of work on the Black male today—including that of Hrabowski, Maton, and Grief (1998), Fashola (2005), Polite and Davis (1999), and Taylor (1997a, 1997b)—addresses education. These works further demonstrate intimate knowledge of the central issues confronting Black men and offer practical solutions. Most of these concerned scholars agree that the self-help approach, though essential, is insufficient to break the cycle of marginalization in the absence of government and community involvement.

Background

The debate over affirmative action is predictably contentious, partly because societies, like individuals, seldom acknowledge their wrongs or voluntarily offer to make amends to those they have wronged. Instead, they tend to engage in denial, conceal-ment, and rationalization of misdeeds. Abuses of Black Americans at the hands of fellow citizens, government culpability, and gross negligence are well documented, as cited and discussed below, but these injustices and their ramifications have yet to be fully acknowledged or addressed by our society. Although the enslavement of Africans in the United States was justified by law and practice, any attempt to advance redress or reparations for past exploitation or discrimination of Black people in the post-slavery United States invokes strenuous excuses and objections. Since the enslavement and extreme exploitation of Africans in the United States was a social or collective action, simple logic would suggest that settlement after the Civil War would need to have included acknowledgment of violations against the victims, and be accompanied by restorative measures including social and economic rehabilitation. Black Americans' successful transition from property status to full personhood and citizenship could have succeeded only with courage and due diligence on the part of a range of principals, especially state and federal governments.

Instead of restoration under the direction of the government after the Civil War, the Black American cause met with abandonment that allowed for extreme infringements upon the civil and human rights of Black people. The opponents of abolition and citizenship for Blacks triumphed. One hundred years would pass before most of the legal barriers erected against full participation by former slaves and their descendants in U.S. social and political life were removed. By then, however, the multigenerational cycles of deprivation among the Black masses had become deep and virtually intractable in the minds of the oppressed and among those who made and administered oppressive laws, or those who merely participated in prevailing discriminatory practices. Black people saw hope for social, political, educational, and economic advancement dashed. Like the system of slavery, these hopes were forcefully blocked by law in parts of the country, and attempts by Black males to assert their constitutional rights often resulted in conspicuous lynching.

The civil rights movement of the 1960s sought to engage U.S. society in a dialogue of sorts, reminding us of the preamble to our Constitution and the preeminence of individual rights. While no one should doubt the achievements of this movement, without an acknowledgment of wrongdoing, no commitment to supporting attempts at correction and wholeness can be deemed sincere under a system dominated by individualism. The victims of racial discrimination will remain forever trapped by the sociopsychological and economic impact of disenfranchisement by a majority committed to securing personal advantages. This predisposes the society to be forever haunted by visions of lynched Black men hanging from magnolia trees.

Significantly, as we move farther and farther away from the travails of the late nineteenth century, challenges to redress the wrongs perpetrated against Black Americans increase while the ramifications of the barriers erected in direct contravention of Black citizens' rights linger tenaciously. As a nation, some of the obstacles to redressing these wrongs include deficiencies in our knowledge of our history; our counterproductive focus upon and commitment to individualism; and our lack of political courage, which leads to political expedience. Understandably, the sheer difficulty of addressing centuries of human oppression makes our task seem monumental. Yet failure to accept and reconcile a history fraught with extreme violence against any people condemns us to indefinite cycles of misery and embarrassment.

This chapter asserts that because the Fourteenth Amendment was not enforced, the *Dred Scott v. Sandford* Supreme Court decision of 1857 maintained primacy as the law of the land. It further attests that this discriminatory status quo ruling was broadly codified in education, health care, transportation, and virtually every area of American life; and later confirmed in the 1896 *Plessy v. Ferguson* decision, which established the "separate but equal" doctrine that pervaded life in the American South for an additional 50 years. This chapter further argues that the Supreme Court, in its *Brown v. Board of Education of Topeka, Kansas* (1954) ruling, simply sidestepped the assumptions of *Plessy*, introducing a new doctrine of integration.

Addressing the Michigan context more specifically, this chapter argues that the University of Michigan's effort to pursue the doctrine of diversity under the banner of affirmative action is closely linked to the doctrine of integration. UM makes no pretence at seeking to address the larger historical issues of abuse and denial of Black civil rights. In light of the clear threat posed by recent Supreme Court rulings to apparent gains by Black Americans as a result of the civil rights movement, it is in the interest of every state in the union, including Michigan, to advance efforts aimed at ameliorating the worst effects of discrimination. Michigan, this chapter argues, can serve as a model for the nation if it undertakes a comprehensive approach to the Black male challenge. This effort would pursue initiatives to address such issues as k–12 education, employment, criminal justice, entrepreneurship, and health care in the Black community with special focus on

Black males, the most disadvantaged sector of its population. This approach goes beyond acknowledgment of the legacy of disenfranchisement and discrimination; it recognizes that the destiny of the state is inextricably tied to the well-being of its citizens. It demonstrates an understanding that Michigan's economic vulnerability in the wake of accelerated globalization creates an imperative for maximum human resource development. Michigan and the nation will need such to remain competitive and achieve a margin of success in the twenty-first century.

Slavery, Racism, and Citizenship

By the onset of the American Civil War, racism in the United States had evolved to the point where many southern Whites claimed that it was their natural and constitutional right to own Blacks as property. To them, no member of the Black race, identifiable by skin color and African features, was intended to serve any other function in society but that of a slave. Even though all American Whites did not share this view, free Blacks in northern states were generally disenfranchised, indicating that most White Americans objected to full citizenship rights for the people of African descent within their midst. Although Blacks had the right to vote by law in some regions of the North, in more cases than not that right was withheld from them. As the insightful French intellectual Alexis de Tocqueville, who toured the United States in 1831, wrote, "Race prejudice seems stronger in those states that have abolished slavery than in those where it still exists, and nowhere is it more intolerant than in those states where slavery was never known" (1966, 343).

During the 1860s, enslaved and free Blacks in the United States were caught in a political vortex out of which they were powerless to extricate themselves. As a result, they often found themselves tortured by the ebb and flow of the era's legislative and judicial tidal waves. The first of these waves was the Supreme Court's landmark ruling in the *Dred Scott v. Sandford* (1857) case. Held as a slave in Missouri, Dred Scott petitioned the Court for his freedom on the grounds that he had lived for seven years in both a free state and a free territory. The Court's response represents what is probably the clearest articulation of racism in America during that period. Chief Justice Roger Taney captured well the dominant societal sentiment regarding the status of Blacks, a belief that was to be enshrined in law and practice for decades thereafter and whose vestiges remain today. Of Blacks, the chief justice declared:

> They had for more than a century before been regarded as beings of an inferior order and altogether unfit to associate with the White race, either in social or political relations; and so far inferior, that they had no rights which the White man was bound to respect; and that the negro might justly and lawfully be reduced to slavery.... He was bought and sold, and treated as an ordinary article of merchandise and traffic, whenever a profit could be made by it. This opinion was at that time fixed and universal in the civilized portion of the White race. It was regarded as an axiom in morals as well as in politics, which no one thought of disputing, or supposed to be open to dispute; and men in every grade and position in society daily and habitually acted upon it in their private pursuits, as well as in matters of public concern, without doubting for a moment the correctness of this opinion.
>
> And in no nation was this opinion more firmly fixed or more uniformly acted upon than by the English Government and English people. They not only seized them on the coast of Africa, and sold them or held them in slavery for their own use; but they took them as ordinary articles of merchandise to every country where they could make a profit on them, and were far more extensively engaged in this commerce than any other nation in the world. (http://www. tourolaw.edu/patch/Scott/)

In essence, Taney concluded in no uncertain terms that no Black person, slave or free, could become a citizen of the United States. He further emphasized that "people of African descent were inferior beings not included in the phrase 'all men are created equal' in the Declaration of Independence nor were they afforded the blessings of citizenship" (http://www.tourolaw.edu/patch/Scott/).

Chief Justice Taney's declaration had resonance in mid-nineteenth-century U.S. society, particularly in the South where opportunities for the extreme exploitation of Black labor in the pursuit of wealth abounded. Given the pretensions that the United States was conceived of and established upon a foundation of freedom, dignity, and individual rights, the selective interpretation of such lofty ideals betrayed conspicuous fault lines in the bedrock of American justice—fissures that were destined to give way to national disaster.

In his dissenting opinion in the *Dred Scott* case, Justice Benjamin Curtis of Massachusetts observed that Chief Justice Taney was incorrect in suggesting that Blacks were never citizens of the United States. He cited examples of Blacks voting in Massachusetts at the time of the Declaration of Independence and in 1857 (Finkelman, 1985). Curtis also maintained that the chief justice's assertion that the English government had confirmed Blacks' status as merchandise also lacked currency. He notes that ambiguity on the subject existed in British law only through the first three decades of the nineteenth century. Indeed, in 1772, the chief justice of the British High Court, Lord Mansfield, had ruled (in the James Summerset case) that British law did not support the taking of deserted slaves by force to be sold to a Virginia planter (Brady & Jones, 1977). Lord Mansfield further observed that Summerset's capture, intended sale, and transport, required positive law, which, in his opinion, did not exist in Britain.

Even if one argues that Mansfield's ruling did not repudiate the slave system in the Americas, the British Parliament voted in 1833 to abolish slavery in all British territories. This was followed by action that dismantled the institution in areas under British rule. Thus, the ground on which Chief Justice Taney sought to anchor the majority decision in the *Dred Scott* case was as fragile as the political fault line he unwittingly aggravated.

Despite the widespread prejudice against Blacks throughout the United States at the time, Taney's unequivocal declaration was generally unpopular in the North. Many northerners viewed his opinion as clearly out of step with modernization. Legal scholars argue that if the Court had merely ruled against Scott on the narrow issue in question, the matter might have slowly disappeared from public debate (Davidson et al., 1990). However, the ruling did not merely have to do with one Black man's desire for freedom. It was not even just a case in the fight against slavery. It had more to do with the geographic expansion of the nation within the context of manifest destiny and the implications for White northerners' political and economic interests.

The budding modernization and industrialization of the nation's economy by 1860 briefly brought about a convergence of interest between Blacks and northern Whites and highlighted a contradiction between capitalism and slavery. The invasion and conquest of the Americas had given rise to chattel slavery to extract wealth from the vast amounts of available land, and some of that wealth had been invested in the development of machines. By the beginning of the nineteenth century, machines were proving to be more efficient, reliable, and faster than human labor. The principal strategy for wealth building in the United States had shifted from agriculture to manufacturing; and even agriculture would soon come to rely more heavily on machines, requiring fewer laborers but needing more consumers. The Court's ruling in *Dred Scott v. Sandford* would prove that efforts to preserve White privilege to own Blacks as property was incompatible with a new economy based on the industrialization northerners had embraced. By focusing on the specific White privilege of claiming Blacks as property, the U.S. Supreme Court inadvertently helped to lay the groundwork for the American Civil War.

By far the most problematic aspect of the *Dred Scott* ruling was the threat it posed to the political balance between the South, with its economy based on slavery, and the North, with its growing industrial base. The divergence of economic and political interests between the two regions had long been evident, but efforts had always been made to maintain a workable relationship through compromises. The acquisition of new territories challenged this balance, and the Court underscored the challenge by declaring that prohibiting slavery in a U.S. territory in the Missouri Compromise unconstitutionally deprived citizens of their property (Negro slaves). "It is the opinion of the court that the act of Congress which prohibited a citizen from holding and owning property of this kind in the territory of the United States north of the line therein mentioned, is not warranted by the Constitution, and is therefore void" (http://www.tourolaw.edu/patch/Scott/). As the prevailing political balance between northern and southern states gave way to increasing violence, Blacks had every reason to support the North to defeat the South, with hopes of reversing the Court's disposition to make slavery perpetual and irrevocable. Given the deepening roots of American racism, however, how could Black Americans truly secure their freedom and citizenship?

Black Citizenship: Between a Rock and a "Harder" Place

By the first half of the nineteenth century, it was becoming clear that in the wake of increased industrialization and modernization, when machines could do many routine tasks effectively and quickly, slavery could not persist. Britain and France had abolished slavery, and even the United States had abolished the trading of slaves early in the century. Thus, it seemed like a matter of when and not whether the Peculiar Institution would be abandoned in the United States altogether.

Notwithstanding these indicators, many southern Whites saw their interest in the issue as supported by the 1854 Kansas-Nebraska Act (which repealed the Missouri Compromise that had prohibited slaves in the territories) and in the Supreme Court's 1857 comprehensive ruling in the *Dred Scott* case. Fresh from these victories, southern politicians and planters hoped to increase their political influence in the 1860 presidential election, but this effort would prove disappointing.

The first sign of reversal for the South came imperceptibly from the famed debates between senatorial contenders Abraham Lincoln and Steven Douglas in 1858. Though the debates were part of the campaign for one of the two Illinois seats to the U.S. Senate, they attracted national attention. Pressed by Lincoln on the issue of how slavery could be legally excluded in territories that had not yet received statehood in view of the *Dred Scott* decision, Douglas responded that "slavery could exist only with the protection of positive law ... and whatever abstract rights slave owners possessed, they would not bring their slaves into an area that did not have a slave code" (Davidson et al., 1990, 550). Although Lincoln lost the election to Douglas, he was sufficiently impressive to be tapped later by his Republican Party to run as a presidential candidate in 1860.

Douglas's position, known as the Freeport Doctrine, was somewhat disconcerting to southerners, so a group of southern congressional representatives developed a new platform for the 1860 presidential campaign calling for a separate slave code for the territories. This would further heighten an already highly polarized presidential campaign. Lincoln won the presidential election with a mere 39.8% of the popular vote but 60% of the electoral vote in a four-way race. Douglas, his nearest rival, received 29.5% of the popular votes (Davidson et al., 1990, A.18). The win by the antislavery Lincoln was viewed by southerners as a serious threat to the *Dred Scott* ruling that had affirmed their right to own slaves in accordance with the Fifth Amendment. It subsequently contributed to their decision to secede from the union.

Secession would lead to civil war because of President Lincoln's commitment to preserving the union. Although Lincoln today receives much praise for abolishing slavery, he was more than willing to accommodate southern interests in that institution if it meant keeping the nation together. Not only was Lincoln slow to abolish slavery as a result, in the end he actually used abolition as a threat to bring the rebel southern states back into the union. In December 1862, he announced that all slaves within rebel lines would be freed unless the seceded states returned to their allegiance by January 1, 1863. When that day came, the Emancipation

Proclamation went formally into effect in slave states not already under Union Army control (Davidson et al., 1990).

Neither Lincoln's reluctance to abolish slavery outright nor his unwillingness to use Blacks as soldiers could contain the enslaved people's drive to be free. Even a small opening for resistance was enough for America's Blacks to make the traditional forms of enslavement impossible to sustain. Frederick Douglass, a strong advocate of arming Blacks to fight on behalf of the Union Army, understood well the opportunity the war presented: "Once let the Black man get upon his person the brass letter, U.S., let him get an eagle on his button, and a musket on his shoulder and bullets in his pocket, there is no power on earth that can deny that he has earned the right to citizenship" (National Archives, n.d.). Both sides gave thought to arming Blacks and were reluctant to do so, but Lincoln eventually relented and Blacks were recruited to fight for the Union Army. The results were impressive:

> By the end of the Civil War, roughly 179,000 Black men (10% of the Union Army) served as soldiers in the U.S. Army and another 19,000 served in the Navy. Nearly 40,000 Black soldiers died over the course of the war—30,000 of infection or disease. Black soldiers served in artillery and infantry and performed all noncombat support functions that sustain an army, as well. Black carpenters, chaplains, cooks, guards, laborers, nurses, scouts, spies, steamboat pilots, surgeons, and teamsters also contributed to the war cause. There were nearly 80 Black commissioned officers. Black women, who could not formally join the Army, nonetheless served as nurses, spies, and scouts, the most famous being Harriet Tubman, who scouted for the 2d South Carolina Volunteers. (National Archives, n.d.)

In Douglass's view, the involvement of Blacks in the Civil War spoke for itself. The question, for him and other antislavery activists, was whether Black people would be duly rewarded with citizenship, as they anticipated.

President Lincoln's postwar strategy was consistent with his stated goal to preserve the union. He subsequently made it easy for the former rebels to reestablish functional states within the Union; he was even amenable to providing compensation to former slave owners. One idea he did not entertain was that of providing back wages to former slaves, nor did he pursue social or political rights for Blacks. No evidence suggests that Lincoln ever envisioned that the government would provide assistance to help the former slaves become independent, contributing citizens, even though immigrants from Europe had routinely been provided land and other incentives to settle in the new territories before and well after the Civil War.

Abolitionists in the Congress argued that the former slaves should receive similar (if not equal) land privileges and protection. Moreover, a few legislators insisted that the federal government set the terms for the return of rebel states to the Union. Lincoln argued instead that these states had not left the union through illegalities; thus it was the federal government's responsibility to facilitate their restoration. Though this argument was seriously flawed, the president largely prevailed in his quest for leniency in dealing with the rebels. He also evidently had great difficulty supporting the interests of the newly freed and was sorely challenged in his efforts to get critical emancipation legislation passed. Having issued the Emancipation Proclamation, Lincoln was faced with the dilemma of permanently freeing all of the nation's slaves, including those held in Union states. Indeed, there were concerns that after the war this proclamation could be overridden, so an amendment was proposed to address this matter. Lincoln expended much of his political capital to get the abolition amendment passed. The bill passed the Senate in April 1864 by a vote of 38 to 6, but it failed to pass in the House of Representatives until January 1865 with a vote of 119 to 56 (*Great American History,* n.d.).

It is worth noting, however, that the Thirteenth Amendment of 1865 replaced an earlier amendment with the same number that was passed by both houses in 1861. That first amendment had called for slavery to be made legal in perpetuity. But for the secession of the southern states, that amendment might have been ratified. The second Thirteenth Amendment called for the very opposite of the first, declaring as follows:

SECTION 1: Neither slavery nor involuntary servitude, except as a punishment for crime whereof the party shall have been duly convicted, shall exist within the United States, or any place subject to their jurisdiction.

SECTION 2: Congress shall have power to enforce this article by appropriate legislation. (Davidson et al., 1990, A.13)

The challenges attending the abolition of slavery, notwithstanding a bloody Civil War that was won by the side generally thought of as being antislavery, was an ominous sign of the future for Black Americans. Some historians argue that although Lincoln vetoed Reconstruction-era terms that were intended to be more helpful to Blacks, he was a good politician and would likely have compromised with northern politicians to make Reconstruction more effective. His assassination in 1865, however, makes it impossible to tell if and how he would have modified a position that demonstrated little interest in the post–Civil War future of Black Americans, especially those who were only recently emancipated.

If President Lincoln proved to be uninterested in the welfare of Black Americans, his successor, Andrew Johnson, was an overt racist who openly supported efforts by southern politicians to establish virtual slavery with the imposition of the so-called Black Codes. Johnson assumed the presidency after Lincoln's assassination in 1865, but he was impeached in 1868 for his utter disregard for the legislative branch of the government. Not only did Johnson oppose efforts to help Blacks become participating citizens, he hastened to offer pardons to the leaders of rebel states and placed upon them few obligations to honor constitutional amendments intended to give freedoms and rights to former slaves. He also demonstrated a strong hostility to Blacks by his support and enforcement of the Black Codes and his efforts to dismantle the Freedmen's Bureau (formally, the Bureau of Refugees, Freedmen, and Abandoned Lands), which had undertaken significant rehabilitation work among Blacks in the aftermath of the war.

Between 1862 and 1866, southern Blacks saw their fortunes rise and fall like curtains on a stage. Between 1866 and 1877, the struggle for protection of their hard-fought rights became mired in debate, and those rights were eventually negotiated away by politicians. In many ways, the early postwar reconstruction efforts held promise for Black Americans. The so-called radical reconstruction advocates in Congress had called for military occupation of the South after General Robert E. Lee surrendered at Appomattox in April 1865. Such occupation, they argued, would ensure White southerners' compliance with federal antislavery and equal protection laws and requirements. Much too soon, however, such stringent approaches went awry for lack of support and commitment by the federal government. One of the best examples of this promise and loss was the establishment of the Freedmen's Bureau in 1865 and its subsequent dismantling in 1872. This agency provided food, medical care, and resettlement assistance for Blacks and supported the establishment of schools. It drew the ire of those who objected to freedom and opportunity for Blacks and was shut down before it could complete its work.

The Black Codes were put in place beginning in 1865 and they varied from one state to another, but they were all intended to "keep African-Americans as property-less agricultural laborers without political rights and with inferior legal rights" (Davidson et al., 1990, 608). The newly emancipated Blacks could not serve on juries, nor could they testify against Whites. Some states prohibited them from engaging in any occupation outside of agriculture without a special license; others prohibited Blacks from buying or renting farmland. President Andrew Johnson not only approved such provisions in state laws but also vetoed the 1866 Civil Rights Bill intended to protect Blacks' citizenship nationwide. Although Congress overrode this veto, the nightmare for Blacks in the South had already begun. Many Blacks of the era were understandably confused and angered to discover that notwithstanding the Emancipation Proclamation and the Thirteenth Amendment, they remained in a socioeconomic state only slightly better than slavery.

Dashed Promises and Hopes: Legal Reversals

In the aftermath of the Civil War, meaningful reconstruction was envisioned and even attempted, as noted above; yet these efforts fell victim to the politics and racism of the time. The vision of reconstruction articulated by such individuals as Thaddeus Stevens, Charles Summer, and Benjamin Wade would have protected the rights of Black citizens and effected fundamental changes in the South. It did not require radical thinking to understand, as Lyman Trumbull (considered a moderate) observed, that the freedmen would "be tyrannized over, abused, and virtually re-enslaved without some legislation by the nation for protection" (Davidson et al., 1990, 610). Indeed, the war seemed not to have ended in the South, as Whites frequently attacked Blacks lawlessly. Attacks against Black men were particularly brutal, establishing the foundation for a crisis that the nation has yet to reconcile.

The Freedmen's Bureau, though short lived, left rich and detailed records of the myriad atrocities committed against Blacks in the postbellum South. Its reports cover the states of Alabama, Georgia, Louisiana, Maryland, Mississippi, North Carolina, South Carolina, Tennessee, Texas, and Virginia, and the District of Columbia. The following introductory text preceded one set of reports:

> Records relating to murders and outrages and reports of murders, outrages, and riots were submitted by subordinate and field officers in either tabular or narrative form. Although the term "outrage" meant any criminal offense, it

usually referred to violent crimes by or against freedmen. The reports usually included the date of the incident and the county in which it took place; the names and race of the injured and accused parties; a brief description of the incident and the action taken, if any, by civil authorities and by the bureau; and the outcome. Most of the reports pertain to crimes committed by whites against freedmen, but crimes of whites against whites, freedmen against freedmen, and freedmen against whites were also reported. (Bureau of Refugees, Freedmen, and Abandoned Lands, 1865–69a)

This pattern of violence against Blacks, perpetrated with the goal of either intimidating or eliminating them, was allowed to continue at various levels for over 100 years; and it has not been fully confronted by U.S. society.

Given that southern legislators had passed into law several Black Codes denying freedmen the right to participate as citizens, Congress saw the need to pass the Fourteenth and Fifteenth amendments to the Constitution. Section 1 of the former declares the following:

All persons born or naturalized in the United States, and subject to the jurisdiction thereof, are citizens of the United States and of the State wherein they reside. No State shall make or enforce any law which shall abridge the privileges or immunities of citizens of the United States; nor shall any State deprive any person of life, liberty, or property, without due process of law; nor deny to any person within its jurisdiction the equal protection of the laws.

The Fifteenth Amendment contains the following provision:

The right of citizens of the United States to vote shall not be denied or abridged by the United States or by any State on account of race, color, or previous condition of servitude—The Congress shall have the power to enforce this article by appropriate legislation.

Constitutional amendments thus seemed appropriate and responsible approaches to protecting the welfare of the Black minority against the hostile White majority in the South. Yet even as the amendments were being passed, Blacks were being killed with impunity and their protections were being stripped away (Bureau of

Refugees, Freedmen and Abandoned Lands, 1865–69b). Such atrocities are widely believed to have increased after the Bureau was dismantled in 1872 and again after the Tilden-Hayes compromise of 1877 resulted in the removal of federal troops from the South.

The open and full abandonment of Reconstruction came in the wake of the 1876 presidential election, which was bitterly contested and yielded inconclusive results. In the absence of a clear winner in the race between northern Republican Rutherford B. Hayes and southern Democrat Samuel Tilden, a compromise was reached. This compromise called for the withdrawal of Union troops from the South and for the North to drop its objections to the unfettered power of southern state governments that were committed to excluding Blacks. As a result, the Republican candidate Hayes was allowed to assume the presidency. According to Davidson and his colleagues, however,

> Racism was why the White South so unrelentingly resisted Reconstruction; racism was why most Northern Whites had little interest in Black rights except as a means to and end, to preserve the Union or to safeguard the Republic; racism is why Northerners were willing to right off Reconstruction and with it the welfare of Black Americans. (1990, 638–39)

After the Tilden-Hayes compromise, the plight of Blacks in the South worsened considerably. Southern Blacks not only were more vulnerable to physical attacks, they had to endure a hostile Congress and Supreme Court as well as a federal executive who would repeatedly betray them. Worse still, local southern legislatures intensified their efforts to codify discrimination against Blacks with the passage of Jim Crow laws that overtly undermined the rights of Blacks. The North passed its share of racist laws as well, as Falck (n.d.) noted:

> More than 400 state laws, constitutional amendments, and city ordinances legalizing segregation and discrimination were passed in the United States between 1865 and 1967. These laws governed nearly every aspect of daily life, from education to public transportation, from health care and housing to the use of public facilities. African American children got their first taste of racial discrimination when they found themselves barred from attending school with White children, and being sent, instead, to inferior facilities. Growing up, these

children learned that their lives were equally restricted outside the classroom. They were forbidden from sharing a bus seat with a White passenger or to ride in the same compartment of a train. They were denied access to public parks and restaurants, and, in some states, were forced to enter public amusements like the circus through a separate entrance. Black movie theater patrons were seated in the balcony, separated from White customers in what was commonly referred to as "Nigger heaven." When they went to work, African Americans were forced to use separate entrances and bathrooms and to collect their paychecks at separate windows. Even in death, legislation ensured that the races would remain separate. Several states prohibited hearses from carrying both races, and cemeteries were required to maintain separate graveyards.

The challenge for Blacks, and especially for Black men, at this juncture of American history was obviously extraordinary. During an era of virtually unbridled economic revitalization and expansion, Blacks could not compete on equal terms for education or good jobs. Even more humiliating was the realization that Black men could not protect their families from intimidation or embarrassment of various sorts, and they often were afforded little or no protection against deadly violence. The contradictions were sufficiently consistent and conspicuous to foster a culture of fear, suspicion, and disrespect for the law among Black men in particular.

The Tilden-Hayes compromise created a political climate in which the reaffirmation of the *Dred Scott* decision, asserting the inferiority of Blacks in U.S. society, was all but inevitable. When this agreement was challenged as a violation of the Fourteenth Amendment, the Supreme Court upheld the status quo. Later, when the *Plessy* case was brought before the Court in 1896, the Court held that the doctrine of separate but equal was also consistent with the Thirteenth and Fourteenth amendments to the Constitution.

On the surface, Justice Ferguson's ruling in *Plessy* seems less problematic than the decision's larger contextual meaning. Writing for the majority, and seeming to contradict his own previous opinion, Ferguson ruled that the state of Louisiana did not contravene the rights of the Black citizen, Homer Plessy, who brought the suit before the nation's highest court. As surprising as his decision seems, however, it is perhaps even more surprising that the ruling was almost unanimous. Apparently, Justice Ferguson's assumptions were already widespread and served to strengthen the Jim Crow sentiment throughout the land.

Only one judge, Justice Harlan, dissented in the *Plessy* ruling, declaring that

> the present decision . . . will not only stimulate aggressions, more or less brutal
> and irritating, upon the admitted rights of colored citizens, but will encourage
> the belief that it is possible, by means of state enactments, to defeat the beneficent
> purposes which the people of the United States had in view when they adopted
> the recent [the Thirteenth and Fourteenth] amendments of the Constitution.
> (*Street Law and the Supreme Court Society*, n.p.)

Further testament that racism was on the rise nationwide is evident in the postbellum-era education laws. After the Civil War, legislators from states outside the South enacted 23% of the laws that authorized segregated schools. Likewise, 7 of the 12 laws that required race to be considered in adoption petitions were passed outside of the South (Falck, n.d.).

The writings of several Black intellectuals between 1865 and 1965, though sometimes expressing anger and frustration, consistently called upon public officials for justice while enjoining Blacks to resist injustice and discrimination with dignity. Frederick Douglass, who had worked diligently before and after emancipation to secure rights for Blacks, noted that the ebbs and flows of that struggle brought both hope and frustration. Though he celebrated the passage of the Thirteenth, Fourteenth, and Fifteenth Amendments, he despaired at their limited usefulness.

The poet Claude McKay felt obliged to call on his fellow Blacks to die nobly rather than endure the indignity of being hunted like wild prey. Richard Wright warned in his writings of the overflowing hostility and hatred that years of oppression had cultivated among Black people for Whites, while fellow writer Ralph Ellison wrote of the seemingly invisible status of the Black man in U.S. society. Other Black writers, scholars, and activists—like James Baldwin, Langston Hughes, Zora Neal Hurston, and Paul Robeson, to name but a few—analyzed the plight of Blacks, expressing both anger and optimism. W. E. B. DuBois, who worked with many of his contemporaries to exhume and record the enduring legacy of Black people's resistance to the dehumanization of slavery and second-class citizenship, early predicted that the race issue would persist well into the foreseeable future. He has been proven right. No amount of intellectual attainment, no amount of reason nor appeal to social justice or Christian virtue has seemed sufficient to bring U.S. society to respect the basic constitutional and human rights of its Black citizenry.

It would take 58 years after the *Plessy v. Ferguson* decision for Black Americans to receive a modicum of relief from the humiliating and fraudulent doctrine of separate but equal, partly because there were few national political risks to maintaining the status quo. Despite lofty declarations about human rights and dignity, the delay could be interpreted in ways that excluded minorities without political power. In the meantime, the plight of Blacks in the South remained stifling until the advent of the modern civil rights movement.

Separate Repudiated, Equality Ignored

Black Americans, sometimes in concert with their White allies, established numerous civil rights organizations during the first half of the twentieth century. These groups sought redress to racist oppression through an array of approaches but with only limited success. These organizations included the United Negro Improvement Association, the Urban League, the National Association for the Advancement of Colored People (NAACP), and a number of smaller and less well-known organizations.

As Blacks found more ways to participate in the life of the nation in the early twentieth century, contradictions sharpened between their worth and contributions and the legitimacy of the discriminatory practices employed to negate their value. These contradictions should have embarrassed the nation's leaders, especially after the involvement of thousands of Black soldiers in World War I, presumably to make the world "safe for democracy." The awkwardness of a segregated military was addressed in the aftermath of this war, but little else was done. The rest of U.S. society remained largely segregated, and so the incongruities increased at the national level, betraying to the wider world another serious fault line in our democracy. The disenfranchisement of Blacks undermined much of what politicians proclaimed to be the virtues of the "American experiment."

The case of opera singer Marian Anderson illustrates that challenge. In 1939, Sol Hurok, Anderson's manager, and officials from Howard University attempted to organize a performance for Anderson at Washington, D.C.'s Constitution Hall, which was owned by the Daughters of the American Revolution (DAR). Arguably the world's greatest contralto, Anderson had just returned from touring Europe and Australia, where her performances had been met with universal awe and adoration. The DAR denied Anderson use of its facility, however, and solely on the basis of her race. First Lady Eleanor Roosevelt intervened, arranging for Anderson to sing from the steps of the Lincoln Memorial to a crowd of about 75,000 enraptured listeners (Nelson, 1998). Nonetheless, the DAR's policy banning Blacks from performing in Constitution Hall was not lifted for several years after this incident.

In the aftermath of World War II, and with the United States assuming a larger role of global leadership, the fault line evident in the treatment of its racial minorities, especially Blacks, surfaced increasingly. In an era during which the battle over ideology was as important as the competition for dominance in military technology and space exploration, the United States carried at least as much ideological "baggage" as its chief rival, the Soviet Union. Moreover, there seemed no clear indication that the overtly hostile laws and practices, as well as the more subtle forms of racism that American society used to oppress and subjugate people of African descent would be addressed any time soon.

Fast-forward to 1954, when a successful challenge to *Plessy v. Ferguson* was launched, 58 years after separate but equal became the law of the land. In the Supreme Court's landmark ruling in *Brown v. Board of Education of Topeka, Kansas* (1954)—a decision that seemed to have come as a surprise to many politicians, particularly those from the South—the Court unanimously overturned *Plessy*. As Chief Justice Earl Warren declared:

> We conclude that in the field of public education the doctrine of "separate but equal" has no place. Separate educational facilities are inherently unequal." (http://brownvboard.org/research/opinions/347us483.htm).

Many southerners, however, still considered it their right to treat Blacks as inferior beings, and they were determined to defy the Court's decision. The fight to obtain and ensure Black equality was far from over.

Although the 1954 U.S. Supreme Court *Brown v. Board of Education* decision formally made segregation illegal, southern states continued to pass Jim Crow legislation well into the 1960s, particularly in the area of school segregation. Historian C. Vann Woodward estimated that 106 new segregation laws were passed between the *Brown* decision and the end of 1956. By May 1964, the South had enacted 450 laws and resolutions to frustrate the Supreme Court's decision. Many of these statutes were passed at the local level and were particularly dehumanizing (Falck, n.d.).

Unlike *Plessy*, the *Brown* case specifically addressed the question of education.

The 1954 ruling also maintained that the nation had been violating the rights of its Black citizens before and since they had gained citizenship. Celebration was warranted, and the NAACP, with its lead attorney Thurgood Marshall and the entire Supreme Court, led by Chief Justice Earl Warren, must forever be credited for breaking the back of entrenched injustice. Nevertheless, school integration alone could not be expected to address almost a hundred years of blatant civil rights violation, much less bring an end to it. It could not and has not. Several notable civil rights and voting rights laws had to be passed during the 1960s to supplement the Court's ruling, further underscoring the need for justice long denied. The nation clearly owed a large debt to Black Americans based on the centuries of injustice and abuse that had been measured out to them from the highest to the lowest levels of society. Ironically, however, Blacks would have to bear the biggest burden in the struggle to bring about segregation's antecedent: integration.

Post-*Brown*, Black Americans waged a continuous struggle for equal access to housing, job opportunities, transportation, and a wide range of other services before the government stepped in to provide support. In 1965 the Lyndon Johnson administration agreed that the government had long neglected the rights of its Black citizens and supported affirmative action policies in an attempt to create a level playing field for Blacks and Whites in America, particularly in the areas of job opportunities and education. Yet what constitutes this level playing field, and how long will it take to establish it? Unfortunately, that discussion has yet to be undertaken, though the policies implemented during the 1960s have been under attack ever since.

The *Bakke v. University of California at Davis* decision of 1978 limited the capacity of institutions to use quota systems to effect integration, and several subsequent rulings diminished the use of other remedies envisioned by civil rights and affirmative action advocates. The 1996 *Hopwood v. the University of Texas Law School,* and the 2003 *Grutter v. Bollinger* case emanating from the University of Michigan, indicate that effort to address the injustices that have been committed against Black Americans in general, and Black males in particular, will continue to be challenging in the foreseeable future.

Michigan's Call to Action

Slavery and racism in the United States have left deep and enduring scars in the Black community, particularly among males. The situation is sufficiently grave to require urgent, purposeful, and concerted action to arrest the disastrous spiraling of a frighteningly large number of Black males toward the margin of society. Michigan needs to take a comprehensive approach to addressing this situation. Community-based organizations, and faith-based initiatives, despite their indispensable contributions, are not adequate to the task. Purposefully directed efforts on the part of legislators and the governor are needed to address the Black male challenge. This is needed not only because of the history of abuse, civil/human rights violation, and neglect, but also because the state has a compelling interest in developing good and productive citizens.

Several civic leaders across the racial spectrum seem to have an appreciation for the impact that the nation's legacy of racial injustice has had on Black males. Political leaders in the states of Ohio and Indiana have acknowledged the dangers of ignoring the marginalization of this population in their state and have established commissions to explore ways of addressing this issue. From the early 1990s Ohio grappled with the issue of "Disadvantaged Black Males" and in 1999 created a freestanding agency called the Ohio Commission on African American Males. The agency focuses on unemployment, criminal justice, education, and health (http://www.aamec.us/). There is yet no evidence of substantial breakthroughs in the major challenges faced by Black males in Ohio, and the homicide rate in major cities with large Black populations in that state remains alarmingly high (http://www.aamec.us/Mission.html). Nevertheless, the issues are being discussed by politicians and other civic leaders. They have at least isolated some areas of significant need and are making attempts to better understand and address them.

Public officials in the neighboring state of Indiana have also demonstrated a level of awareness and concern enough to take some initial steps in examining some of the issues. The Indiana Commission on the Social Status of Black Males was established in 1993 and was charged with looking at criminal justice, education, employment, health, and social factors (http://www.in.gov/fssa/family/icssbm/pdf/2004-5annual.pdf). Indiana has hosted a number of conferences to focus attention on these issues, and has also established local commissions in an attempt to find local solutions.

While efforts by Michigan's neighbors, Ohio and Indiana, are commendable, neither of these two states has yet developed a comprehensive plan to address the plight of Black males. One institution that has embarked on a promising strategy is the University System of Georgia (USG). While not truly comprehensive, USG's strategy has the possibility of arresting the generational cycle of impoverishment and marginalization among Black males in the state and by extension have a positive impact on the entire Black family.

Responding to the increasing underrepresentation of Black males in higher education, the University System of Georgia launched a study in 2001 to identify causes and make recommendations to address this challenge. Although this study limited its scope to education, the resulting recommendations (http://www.usg.edu/aami/Summary_and_Final_Recommendations.pdf), could, in the long run, benefit the African American community and the society at large. It should be noted, however, that erasing the century-long impact of officially sanctioned and enforced barriers to education and to economic, social, and political opportunities will take extensive planning and effective implementation.

No one familiar with Michigan can doubt the urgency with which action is needed to address the Black male challenge. In 2004 Michigan, like the nation as a whole, had more Black men in jail than in college. There were 21,454 Black males enrolled in Michigan's universities and 24,300 in the state's prisons (Bureau of Justice Statistics, 2005). At the end of 2004 there were 3,218 Black male prison inmates per 100,000 Black males in the United States, compared to 1,220 Hispanic male inmates per 100,000 Hispanic males and 463 White male inmates per 100,000 White males (Bureau of Justice Statistics, 2005). It should be clear to all thinking individuals that this tragedy foreshadows greater economic and social turmoil for the state and especially its major Black communities.

Much like Ohio and Indiana, Michigan needs to create a commission to focus on the Black male challenge within the state. The Michigan commission, however, should be established in partnership with the state's higher education institutions, and major businesses operating in the state. The goal of this partnership will be to undertake a comprehensive study of the Black male challenge and identify potentially viable strategies to address issues such as: K–12 and postsecondary education, employment, criminal justice, entrepreneurship, and health care in the Black community with special focus on the Black male.

Few will any longer question the extreme dehumanization of slavery and U.S.

post emancipation laws directed against ex-slaves between 1865 and 1965. It is somewhat surprising then that there has been relatively little support for redress where evidence of violation is irrefutable. One could be sympathetic if the discussions in legislative chambers and the courts had to do with how to compensate those wronged by unconstitutional laws over a protracted period of time. In the absence of concerns about and actions in support of redress, Michigan and many other states face the larger and potentially far more expensive dilemma of the Black male exiting society to survive outside of the law. The imperative to arrest the marginalization of Black males transcends notions of affirmative action and of reparation, as worthy and just as these may be. Acknowledging past wrongs and compensating victims seems consistent with the rule of law. However, the history of affirmative action in the United States reveals that majority decision accompanied by individualism often delays justice, at best, and can represent the most formidable barrier to social justice. The call here, therefore, is neither for affirmative action nor reparation. This is a call for action in response to present reality that threatens all communities and, therefore, the well-being of the state. Time is simply not on Michigan's side, because the tide of globalism moves inexorably forward and will reward societies that are best positioned to compete. The social, political, and economic health of Michigan and many other states will depend on how quickly and effectively the challenge of the Black male is addressed.

REFERENCES

Baldwin, J. (1998). *Collected Essays.* New York: Library of America: Distributed to the trade in the U.S. by Penguin Putnam.

Bowen, W. G., Kurzweil, M. A., Tobin, E. M., & Pichler, S. C. (2005). *Equity and excellence in American higher education.* Charlottesville: University of Virginia Press.

Brady, T. & Jones, E. (1977). *The fight against slavery.* London: W. W. Norton.

Bureau of Justice Statistics. (2005). Retrieved May 10, 2006, from http://www. ojp.usdoj.gov/bjs/prisons.htm.

Bureau of Refugees, Freedmen, and Abandoned Lands. (n.d.). *Freedmen and abandoned lands.* Washington, DC: Library of Congress.

Bureau of Refugees, Freedmen, and Abandoned Lands. (1865–69a). *Freedmen and abandoned lands* (National Archives, Microfilm Publication M798 Roll 32).

Bureau of Refugees, Freedmen, and Abandoned Lands. (1865–69b). *Reports relating to murders and outrages* (1865–1868). (National Archives Microfilm Publication M1055 Roll 21).

Davidson, J. W., Geinapp, W. E., Heyrman, C. L., Lytle, M. H., & Stoff, M. B. (1990). *Nation of nations: A narrative history of the American republic.* New York: McGraw-Hill.

Dred Scott v. Sanford. 1857 Retrieved from http://www.tourolaw.edu/patch/ Scott/, Touro Law Center.

Du Bois, W. (1996). *The Oxford W.E.B. Du Bois reader.* Edited by E. Sundquist. New York: Oxford University Press.

Ellison, R. (1952). *Invisible man.* New York: Modern Library.

Falck, S. (n.d.). *Jim Crow legislation overview.* California State University, Northridge. Retrieved from http://www.jimcrowhistory.org/resources/ lessonplans/hs_es_jim_crow_laws.htm.

Fashola, O. S. (Ed.). (2005). *Educating African American males: Voices from the field.* Thousand Oaks, CA: Corwin Press.

Finkelman, P. (1985). *Slavery in the courtroom: An annotated bibliography of American cases.* Washington, DC: Library of Congress.

Hrabowski, F., Maton, K., & Grief, G. (1998). *Beating the odds: Raising academically successful African American males.* New York: Oxford University Press.

Great American History. (n.d.). Retrieved from http://members.tripod. com/~greatamericanhistory/gro2011.htm.

Hughes, L. & Meltzer, M. (1990). *African American history: Four centuries of Black life.* New York: N.Y. Scholastic.

Hurston, Z. (1995). *The complete stories.* New York: HarperCollins.

Katznelson, I. (2005). *When affirmative action was White: An untold history of racial inequality in twentieth-century America.* New York: W. W. Norton.

Lipson, H. D. (2006). *Talking affirmative action: Race, opportunity, and everyday ideology.* Lanham, MD: Rowman & Littlefield.

McKay, C. (2004). *Complete poems, 1890–1948.* Edited by William J. Maxwell. Urbana: University of Illinois Press.

McWhorter, J. (2006). *Winning the race: Beyond the crisis in Black America.* New York: Gotham Books.

Miller, T. (1988). *Frederick Douglass and the fight for freedom.* New York: Facts on File.

Miller, W. L. (1996). *Arguing about slavery: The great battle in the United States Congress.* New York: Alfred A. Knopf.

National Archives. (n.d.). Retrieved June 2, 2006, from http://www.archives.gov/education/lessons/blacks-civil-war/.

Nelson, G. (1998). *The life and works of Rudolph James: Founder of Black Adventism in Canada.* Langley Park, MD: Institute for Afro-American Scholarship.

Polite, V. C. & Davis, J. E. (Eds.). (1999). *African American males in school and society: Practices and policies for effective education.* New York: Teachers College Press.

Robeson, P. (1988). *Here I stand.* 1958; Boston: Beacon Press.

Stanford, E. (2006). *Interracial America: Opposing viewpoints.* Detroit: Greenhaven Press.

Street Law and the Supreme Court Society. (n.d.). Retrieved May 10, 2006, from http://www.landmarkcases.org/plessy/excerpts_min.html.

Taylor, G. (1997a). *Curriculum strategies: Social skills intervention for young African American males.* Westport, CT: Praeger.

Taylor, G. (1997b). *Practical application of social learning theories in educating young African-American males.* Lanham, MD: University Press of America.

Tocqueville, A. de. (1966). *Democracy in America.* (transl. George Lawrence). 1935. New York: Harper & Row.

United Stated District Court. (1953). *Brown et al. v. Board of Education of Topeka et al.* http://brownvboard.org/research/opinions/347us483.htm.

Wright, R. (1966). *Black boy: A record of childhood and youth.* New York: Harper & Row.

Wright, R. (1969). *12 million Black voices.* New York: Arno Press.

African American Male Collegians and the Sword of Damocles

UNDERSTANDING THE POSTSECONDARY
PENDULUM OF PROGRESS AND PERIL

M. Christopher Brown II *and* T. Elon Dancy II

The Roman politician and philosopher Cicero gives an account of a rich, young ruler named Dionysius and his courtier Damocles. The story goes that Damocles was verbally observant of the abundant wealth, blissful decadence, and ambrosial comestibles enjoyed by Dionysius. Dionysius asks Damocles if he wished to trade places with him to truly experience what Damocles believed to be a more fortunate way of life. Upon agreement, Dionysius provides Damocles with all the luxuries and indulgences the latter so coveted. While in repose, Damocles observes that a sharp and shining sword, fastened solely by a single horsehair, is swinging inches above his head. As explanation, Dionysius informs him that this is what the life of a king is really like—the weight of important decisions looming ominously overhead, an ever-present peril associated with every judgment and decision.

The decisions around how to improve the collegiate pipeline and enhance the chances for African American males across the nation to enter and successfully exit higher education is like that sword of Damocles. Higher education remains the most significant opportunity available to the majority of citizens of the United States for the improvement of their lives. The benefits of higher education have been

■ **249**

widely recognized and debated for decades. The demand for a collegiate education is as unrelenting and broad today as ever.

Just as postsecondary enrollments continue to increase at universities across the nation, so too do questions about for whom college-level instruction should be made available and through what means. What are the proper roles of race, merit, state residency, legacy status, athletic prowess, musical ability, or financial disadvantage in the American college admission process? What are the responsibilities of U.S. college graduates to their communities, the nation, their families, or themselves? These questions are exacerbated by the dilemmas and histories of racial politics in our schools and the nation.

Majority-minority contexts complicate the already challenging process of college-going and degree attainment. Early research on minorities in college investigated the nexus between cognitive gains and the retention of minorities who were integrating into majority-White settings (Allen, 1985, 1988; Cabrera et al., 1999; Donovan, 1984; Loo & Rolison, 1986; Nettles, Thoeny, & Gosman, 1986; Smedley, Myers, & Harrell, 1993). Additional research cites minority students' perceptions of unsupportive predominantly White academic communities, coupled with feelings of discomfort, social isolation, and stress, as causes for minority student attrition (Feagin, Vera, & Imani, 1996; Gossett, Cuyjet, & Cockriel, 1998; Lang & Ford 1992; Ponterotto, 1990; Sailes, 1993). The participation of African American males in higher education has been highlighted in the literature as glaringly disparate.

The research detailed in this article examines African American male college and university experiences to better inform a conversation about how Michigan's higher education institutions may buttress their African American male enroll-ment, academic engagement, and retention. The out-of-class experiences of African American men and the ways in which they are shaped by postsecondary social environments—as influenced by institutional norms, values, ideas, and attitudes—are evidenced in this literature. This research further notes that the in-class experiences of African American college and university men are shaped by the norms, values, ideas, and attitudes they confront within the classroom and academic settings. This work engages the contextual spectra of educational, psychological, sociological, and anthropological literature by centering African American males in the inquiry to inform the practices of Michigan institutions.

African American Males' Collegiate Participation

What do we know about African American male college/university students? To begin, we know that their enrollment at predominantly White institutions (PWIs) and historically Black colleges and universities (HBCUs) has increased significantly since the 1954 *Brown v. Board of Education* ruling, but it has become disproportionately gendered in the years following. In 1955, males comprised 55% of the African American undergraduate enrollment while women comprised 45% (Brown & Hurst, 2004). Between 1976 and 2000, however, African American men's college/university enrollment began to decline sharply. Presently, African American men account for only 37% of African American undergraduate participation in higher education, while African American women account for nearly 60% (Brown & Hurst, 2004).

Additional evidence suggests that different factors influence African American men's decision to pursue higher education post-high school than affect African American women. For example, in 1967, trends in college enrollment and completion for African Americans reflect 42% of black men and 33% of black women high school graduates were roughly one-third less likely than their white counterparts (60% and 46%) to have enrolled in or completed college (Cantave & Harrison, 2003). However, in 1976, young both black males and females (i.e., nearly half of each group) enrolled in college (Brown & Hurst, 2004), essentially closing the gap with white women (51%) while approaching the enrollment of white men (56%) which decreased from a high of 63% in 1969 (Cantave & Harrison, 2003). By 2000, African American male high school graduates were enrolling in college at nearly the same rate while the college enrollment rate for African American female high school graduates increased by 11 percentage points, to 43% (Brown & Hurst, 2004). Although the number of African American men awarded the bachelor's degree has increased by 52% since 1977, the number of African American women awarded bachelor's degrees has increased by 112% (Brown & Hurst, 2004). Discussions about this gender gap have recently occupied the agendas of many educational researchers, policy analysts, and media pundits, yet to understand the nature of the disparity, one must first acknowledge the gaps in enrollment between African American males and females at HBCUs compared to PWIs.

Without question, PWIs have received the greater flux of African American enrollment since *Brown.* The state of Michigan is no exception. In fall 2002, 90%

of students enrolled in a four-year college or university in Michigan were in-state residents. Completion rates among Michigan's institutions of higher education varied widely, however. For instance, the University of Michigan–Ann Arbor maintained the highest completion rate with 84% of its entering freshmen graduating within six years. Other Michigan institutions had lower graduation rates. Michigan State University's six-year graduation rate was 73%, while Western Michigan University was at 53%, Central Michigan University 47%, Eastern Michigan University 38%, and Wayne State University 34%. These Michigan enrollment statistics are illustrative of attrition rates shared across countless colleges and universities nationwide. Within each, almost without exception, African American males comprise a disparately enrolled populace.

College enrollment is predicted to increase through 2012 according to national demographic trends, but not so for the participation of African American males (Brown & Hurst, 2004; Dancy & Brown, 2008). Although the *New York Times,* among other popular periodicals, fervently publishes commentary after commentary on the perceived "crisis" of the Black male (Neal, 2005) these public conversations— and the very real and discouraging trends of reduced Black male enrollment and attrition in college—can and should not be ignored. However, ubiquitous inquiry by journalists and scholars into the experiences of African American men yields little understanding about their postsecondary participation trends. In the interim, these trends continue to be both disturbing and misunderstood in a broad range of literature on the topic that considers factors ranging from the economics of the African American community to the dynamics of the African American family. Most egregiously, that literature forgets to position African American males in the center of their inquiry.

African American Males in the K–12 Pipeline

The experiences of African American males in K–12 institutions inform their choices about college, yet as Polite and Davis note, "To be an African American male in school and society places one at risk for a variety of negative consequences" (1999, 1). Polite and Davis further assert that African American men learn early to exhibit behaviors that interfere with their institutional engagement and collegiate perceptions. These behaviors take shape early in African American males' schooling experiences and immediately begin to compromise their educational and social gains. Polite and Davis also maintain that young African American boys typically are taught to be independent and active. Those boys who display these behaviors often attain social rewards like popularity and attractiveness, they note, but the rewards often contribute to African American boys' academic difficulty and shirking from academic achievement.

Polite and Davis (1999) contend that the dilemma for boys heightens as they progress through school. More specifically, as school teachers disproportionately reward traditionally feminine behavior (e.g., conformity, quietness, and coopera-tion), they tend to punish traditionally masculine behavior (e.g., independence, adventurousness, and rebelliousness). Teachers' reports support ideas that boys' efforts to achieve an acceptable level of masculinity often go unrewarded and may disadvantage academic gains. Simultaneously, these reports describe teachers' concerns about gender differences in learning and the ways in which these dif-ferences may be linked to classroom behavior (Polite & Davis, 1999). These same reports also suggest that African American males learn early to equate the academic world to femininity and subsequently to reject that world. Subsequently, the collegiate experiences of African American men are influenced by these schooling constructions, placing men at risk for disparate academic outcomes in comparison to women (Davis, 1995). As Polite and Davis assert, along with Fleming (1984) before them, a number of well-rehearsed gender roles negatively correlate with African American men's collegiate perceptions by the time these men reach college age.

Other research corroborates Polite and Davis's (1999) assertion that teachers label African American males as unsalvageable in their early schooling experiences. This notion frames the gaze that Ferguson (2000) takes into the lives of young African American boys attending public school. In *Bad Boys: Public Schools in the Making of Black Masculinity*, Ferguson details ethnographic research she conducted at an urban elementary school over a three-and-a-half-year period from January 1990 to May 1993. She focused in her study on 20 fifth- and sixth-grade African American boys in an effort to increase awareness of the ways in which institutional practices and cultural representations of racial difference are covertly and informally reproduced to support the system of racial inequality in America. Ferguson labels 10 of her subjects *schoolboys* to describe those boys identified by the school as "doing well" (9). She labels 10 other boys as *troublemakers* given their reputations for "getting into trouble" (9). She asserts that this latter group created and experienced disciplinary problems in school in an effort to "recoup a sense of self as competent and worthy under discouraging work conditions" (22).

Ferguson's (2000) study highlights two main sources of inequality that disparately affect African American males' educational gains: (1) individual or institutional actions and the intersections of these two types of action, and (2) the ways in which stereotypes and racial myths shape and affect social understanding of cultural difference. She conducted a series of in-depth, unstructured interviews with the school's African American boys and their parents, classroom teachers, principals, and disciplinary staff as well as the district truant officer, school psychologists, social workers, and school janitors. Persistent observations buttressed this work. Ferguson found evidence that the school environment contributes to the marginalization of African American males. Specifically, labels such as *troublemakers*, placed upon African American boys by school authorities such as teachers, principals, and other school staff, predispose these boys to socially unaccepted and deviant life outcomes. Ferguson additionally contends that most African American males become less eager to persist in school during their fourth-grade year, opting to model themselves after future professional athletes or more infamous African American males in urban neighborhoods. Not surprisingly, she reported that higher education was not a dominantly perceived theme among the population of young, urban African American males in her study.

Scholars of note recognize the importance of cultural grounding to address the concerns posited in research that investigates the impact of systematic racial inequality on African American male outcomes in K–12 pipelines. For example, Alford's (2003) work qualitatively examines the Ohio-based Africentric Rites of Passage Program (AA-RITES) to understand how the cognitive development of adolescent African American males in urban areas is shaped. His findings, which reveal the strong, positive impact of the AA-RITES philosophy on urban Black male youths' cultural grounding, worldview, self-esteem, and ethnic identity enhancement, offer much in the way of substance to inform schooling practice.

Other research considers the influence of culture in the relationships between teachers and African American males in school. For example, Murrell (1999) conducted a synthesis of the results from a critical ethnography of classroom practices of mathematics instruction. His findings frame a need for K–12 educators to develop a pedagogical knowledge base that is informed by the discourse, dynamics, and behaviors African American males use to situate themselves in K–12 classrooms.

The 12 students who informed Murrell's study demonstrated similarities in behavior described in other research on young African American males (Polite & Davis, 1999). They also exhibited some differences. For example, Murrell's subjects were particularly forthcoming in articulating their points of view. A notable similarity, however, is that they also gave higher regard to the attention they received from others in the classroom and used that attention as a platform for expression while placing less emphasis on their knowledge of academic content. Additionally, the Murrell study's African American males used "cool pose" to cope with teacher probes during small-group interactions. As their teachers engaged new content in class, these students perceived the new instruction as a personal requirement of the teacher rather than accepting it for its curricular importance as a cornerstone for academic achievement. Murrell generalizes that African American male student behavior typically includes teacher-challenging approaches, an eagerness to display learned knowledge, a reluctance to admit ignorance, and a preference for verbosity and cool pose. Murrell asserts that teachers who wish to be responsive to the needs of their African American male students must understand that discourse routines and speech events promote interest, participation, self-efficacy, and purpose for these students and inform their relationships with their teachers.

Black Males in College

After the turbulent era of the civil rights movement, scholars directed increasing attention toward Black students and students of color on predominantly White college campuses. Researchers from psychological, anthropological, and educational disciplines have focused on the reasons why Blacks at all levels of education appear to have difficulty learning, adjusting, and staying in historically White institutions post-*Brown*. Several studies have provided data that reveal the extent to which Black and other racial/ethnic minority students have been successful in negotiating the college pipeline. Less research, however, addresses African American men's perceptions of college and the reasons why they do or do not persist to degree attainment. Although a significant number of African American men have attended and currently attend predominantly White institutions (PWIs) as athletes, research about them has been slow to emerge.

Fleming's (1984) study explores how African American students intellectually and psychosocially experience different college environments, and introduces a conversation about African American men's perceptions of college. Scholars of note still cite Fleming's analysis to inform their research about African American men's collegiate perceptions. Fleming posits that African American male PWI students are unable to maintain controlled feelings of detachment due to their subdominance and small numbers on campus. She uses the term *competitive rejection* to describe the ways in which African American men, upon entry to college or university settings, perceive themselves as least congruent with other students regardless of race and gender. She maintains that these African American collegiate men also perceive themselves as less significant in comparison to members of other racial/ethnic groups. Fleming's study also suggests that African American men's negotiation of competition in social and academic PWI contexts detrimentally affects their engagement, collegiate perceptions, and educational attainment. Therefore, an African American man who academically or socially competes at a PWI is at greater risk for attrition than White men and women or African American women. Fleming's findings further suggest that African American male PWI students risk truancy and attrition due to a loss of intellectual motivation and low self-image. Conversely, Fleming's research implies that African American men who attend historically Black colleges and universities (HBCUs) exhibit behavioral profiles indistinguishable from those of White males. She suggests that African American men's dominance tendencies gain prominence in the HBCU environment as they perceive these institutions as providing a more familiar and negotiable territory, in part because of the greater ease with which they can make informal attachments to faculty.

Davis focuses on the differences between African American men who attend HBCUs vis-à-vis those who attend PWIs and examines the relevant predictors for academic success for Black male students in both settings. Relevant findings from Nettles's (1988) survey of college students' academic and social experiences are congruent with Fleming's seminal research in the area. Those findings reveal that African American males at HBCUs were more socially integrated, got better grades, and perceived their schools as more institutionally supportive. Other research buttresses our understanding about the social gains African American male students accrue in HBCU environments. For example, Harper, Carini, Bridges, and Hayek (2004) used empirical evidence to show that African American male HBCU students neglect to make efficient use of their out-of-class time and are more likely to disappoint their instructors than are African American female students. Harper's investigation of the effects of out-of-class engagement on the experiences of 32 African American male student leaders in PWI settings illustrates that active engagement at the collegiate level enhances the undergraduate experience of African American males across collegiate contexts. The contributors to Cuyjet's (1997) work, *Helping African American Men in College,* proffer several theories, programs, and suggestions to assist African American men in their adjustment to collegiate communities as well as to inform the practice of institutional officials and the pedagogies of faculty. The presence of African American men in threatening and unfriendly collegiate environments is a largely cited theme in Cuyjet's work and other research.

Howard-Hamilton (1997) offers a lucid discussion about what postsecondary institutions must do to achieve a theory-to-practice approach that more thoughtfully considers the development of African American college men. She echoes a notion found repeatedly in the K–12 literature: that applying widely accepted, European-centered frameworks to African American men is counterproductive. She suggests alternately that the juxtaposition of racial/ethnic student development models like those proposed by McEwen, Roper, Bryant, and Langa (1990) with more traditional models can have a positive impact on African American male students' feelings of inclusion on the collegiate campus. She also describes four models purported to enhance African American men's development on college campuses, including (1) Cross's Nigrescence Theory; (2) Robinson and Howard-Hamilton's Africentric Resistance Model; (3) Erikson's Identity Development Model; and (4) Bandura's Social Learning Model. Proper implementation of these models, Howard-Hamilton maintains, requires mentoring by supportive individuals who are authentically committed to the overall goal of increasing African American males' sense of self-identity and collegiate engagement.

Dawson-Threat (1997) highlights the importance of faculty-to-student interaction for African American male college/university students in a broader conversation about institutional change. She also seeks to inform the pedagogical frame of reference for collegiate faculty who teach African American men, offering the following three recommendations:

- Provide African American male students with a safe space for expression of their personal experiences
- Facilitate and promote the understanding of difference and the negation of stereotypes

- Provide the opportunity for these students and others to explore Black manhood issues

Dawson-Threat contends that classrooms at PWIs can and should be constructed to foster an environment in which African American men can safely express their thoughts about experiences of salience to them. She further suggests that African American male college/university students' understandings of difference are informed by the stereotypes that others impose. The faculty/student interaction is paramount for creating communities in college, she points out, and for improving the collegiate perceptions of African American men.

Dancy and Brown (2008, retrieved on July 11, 2009 from http://www.jointcenter. org/DB/factsheet/college.htm) recently conducted a study whose purpose was to inform the research on African American college/university men by investigating the nexus between educational attainment and collegiate perceptions in the post-*Brown* era. Their study sought to expose the unique feelings of victimization by faculty, staff, and students that African American male students may feel on campus. It also sought to engender a greater understanding of how African American men negotiate their collegiate experiences in different contexts. Dancy and Brown use Terenzini and colleagues' (1992) *Transitions to College* interview protocol to assess African American male undergraduates' precollege, in-class, and out-of-class experiences. Among the themes that emerge from their study are that African American males' manhood and behavior are shaped differently in different collegiate contexts; additionally, both socially diverse experiences and faculty-to-student interaction matter for Black male college/university students.

Like Dawson-Threat (1997), Dancy and Brown (2008) offer several recommendations aimed at reshaping the epistemologies, axiologies, and pedagogies of both historically Black and White institutions of higher education. They assert that all colleges and universities can learn from the ways in which HBCUs have remained sensitive to the techniques that are effective in shaping affirmative and affirming African American male thinking and behavioral responses. They submit that faculty across all U.S. colleges and universities must abandon deficit model-based, prejudiced, naive, and Eurocentric ideals that disadvantage African American males. They additionally posit that all faculty, staff, and administrators in the higher education community should ground their pedagogies and practices in frameworks that are sensitive to African American men's unique raced and gendered experiences.

Conclusion

The state of Michigan finds itself positioned, like Dionysius, under a metaphorical Sword of Damocles. The issues surrounding how to recruit, retain, and graduate a diverse pool of Michigan collegians are indeed daunting ones. No standards are presently available by which to accurately assess what constitutes effective or sufficient integration or inclusion of the American "all" into the nation's or the state's ivy-lined halls and professional networks. In reacting to the problems and debating the solutions associated with and studying the outcomes desired for African American male collegians, Michigan, like every other state in the Union, encounters at every turn more questions and fewer answers. The complexity of the situation need not immobilize Michiganders, however. Those all-important first steps must be identified and taken post haste. The educational opportunities—and obligations—that must follow these initial steps will test Michigan's higher education commitment, energy, resources, and imagination in profound and enduring ways. The ongoing work of committed scholars and practitioners offers both hope and optimism for increased collegiate progress and educational attainment for African American males.

REFERENCES

Adler, P. A. & Adler, P. (1991). *Backboards and blackboards.* New York: Columbia University Press.

Alford, K. A. (2003). Cultural themes in rites of passage: Voices of African American males. *Journal of African American Studies, 7*(1), 3–26.

Allen, W. R. (1985). Black student, White campus: Structural, interpersonal, and psychological correlates of success. *Journal of Negro Education, 54*(2), 134–47.

Allen, W. R. (1988). The education of Black students on White college campuses: What quality the experiences? In M. Nettles (Ed.), *Toward Black undergraduate student equality in American higher education*, 57–86. Albany: State University of New York Press.

Astin, A. W. (1977). *Four critical years: Effects of college of beliefs, attitudes, and knowledge.* San Francisco: Jossey-Bass.

Astin, A. W. (1982). *Minorities in higher education: Recent trends, current prospects, and recommendations.* San Francisco: Jossey-Bass.

Astin, A. W. (1990). *The Black undergraduate: Current status and trends in the characteristics of freshmen.* Los Angeles: University of California, Graduate School of Education.

Astin, A. W. (1993). *What matters in college? Four critical years revisited.* San Francisco: Jossey-Bass.

Bandura, A. (1977). Self-efficacy: Toward a unifying theory of behavioral change. *Psychological Review, 84,* 191–215.

Brown, M. C., II & Hurst, T. (2004). *Educational attainment of African American males' post–Brown v. Board of Education:* Frederick D. Patterson Institute of the United Negro College Fund.

Cabrera, A. F., Nora, A., Terenzini, P. T., Pascarella, E., & Hagedome, L. S. (1999). Campus racial climate and the adjustment of students to college. *Journal of Higher Education, 70*(2), 134–60.

Cantave, C. & Harrison, R. (2003, Aug.). *College enrollment.* Joint Center for Political and Economic Studies. Retrieved on July 11, 2009 from http://www.jointcenter.org/DB/factsheet/college.htm.

Cope, R. & Hannah, W. (1975). *Revolving college doors: The causes and consequences of dropping out, stepping out, and transferring.* New York: Wiley.

Cross, W. E. (1991). *Shades of Black: Diversity in African-American identity.* Philadelphia: Temple University Press.

Cuyjet, M. (Ed.) (1997). *Helping African American men succeed in college.* San Francisco: Jossey-Bass.

Dancy, T. E., II & Brown, M. C., II (2008). Unintended consequences: African American male educational attainment and collegiate perceptions after *Brown v. Board of Education. American Behavioral Scientist, 5 1*(7), 984–1003.

Davis, J. E. (1994). College in Black and White: The academic experiences of African American males. *Journal of Negro Education, 63,* 570–87.

Davis, J. E. (1995). Campus climate, gender, and achievement of African American college males. Paper presented at the annual meeting of the Association for the Study of Higher Education.

Davis, R. D. (2004). *Black students' perceptions: The complexity of persistence to graduation at an American university.* New York: Peter Lang.

Dawson-Threat, J. (1997). Enhancing in-class academic experiences for African American men. In M. J. Cuyjet (Ed.), *Helping African American Men Succeed in College,* 31–42. San Francisco: Jossey-Bass.

Donovan, R. (1984). Path analysis of a theoretical model of persistence in higher education among low-income Black youth. *Research in Higher Education, 21,* 243–52.

Erikson, E. (1980). *Identity and the life cycle.* New York: W. W. Norton.

Feagin, J. R., Vera, H., & Imani, N. (1996). *The agony of education: Black students at white colleges and universities.* New York: Routledge.

Ferguson, A. A. (2000). *Bad boys: Public schools in the making of Black masculinity.* Ann Arbor: University of Michigan Press.

Fleming, J. (1984). *Blacks in college.* San Francisco: Jossey-Bass.

Fordham, S. & Ogbu, J. U. (1986). Black students' school success: Coping with the "burden of acting White." *Urban Review, 18*(3), 179–205.

Gossett, B. J., Cuyjet, M. J., & Cockriel, I. (1998). African Americans' perception of marginality in the campus culture. *College Student Journal, 32,* 22–32.

Harper, S. (2005). Leading the way: Inside the experiences of high-achieving African American male students. *About Campus, 10*(1), 8–15.

Harper, S. R., Carini, R. M., Bridges, B. K., & Hayek, J. C. (2004). Gender differences in student engagement among African American undergraduates at historically Black colleges and universities. *Journal of College Student Development, 45*(3), 271–84.

Hopkins, R. (1997). *Educating Black males: Critical lessons in schooling, community, and power.* Albany: State University of New York Press.

Howard-Hamilton, M. F. (1997). Theory to practice: Applying developmental theories relevant to African American men. In M. Cuyjet (Ed.), *Helping African American succeed in college,* 17–30. San Francisco: Jossey-Bass.

Irvine, J. J. (1991). *Black students and school failure: Policies, practices, and prescriptions.* New York: Praeger.

Lang, M. & Ford, C. A. (1992). *Strategies for retaining minority students in higher education.* Springfield, IL: Charles C. Thomas.

Loo, C. M. & Rolison, G. (1986). Alienation of ethnic minority students at predominately White institutions. *Journal of Higher Education, 57*(1), 58–77.

McEwen, M. L., Roper, L. D., Bryant, D. R., & Langa, M. J. (1990). Incorporating the development of African American students into psychosocial theories of student development. *Journal of College Student Development, 31*, 429–36.

Murrell, P. (1999). Responsive teaching for African American male adolescents. In V. C. Polite & J. E. Davis (Eds.), *African American males in schools and society: Policies and practices for effective education,* 82–96. New York: Teachers College Press.

Neal, M. A. (2005). *New Black man.* New York: Routledge.

Nettles, M. T. (1985). *The causes and consequences of college students' performance: A focus on Black and White students' attrition rates, progression rates and grade point averages.* Nashville: Tennessee Higher Education Commission.

Nettles, M. (1991). *Assessing progress in minority access and achievement in American higher education.* Denver, CO: Education Commission of the States.

Nettles, M. T., Thoeny, A. R., & Gosman, E. J. (1986). Comparative and predictive analyses of Black and White students' college achievement and experiences. *Journal of Higher Education, 57*(3), 289–318.

Pascarella, E. T. & Terenzini, P. T. (1991). *How college affects students.* San Francisco: Jossey-Bass.

Polite, V. C. & Davis, J. E. (Eds.). (1999). *African American males in school and society: Practices and policies for effective education.* New York: Teachers College Press.

Ponterotto, J. G. (1990). Racial/ethnic minority and women students in higher education: A status report. In J. D. Ponterotto, D. E. Lewis, & R. Bullington (Eds.), *Affirmative action on campus,* 45–59. San Francisco: Jossey-Bass.

Robinson, T. L. & Howard-Hamilton, M. F. (1994). An Africentric paradigm: Foundations for a healthy self-image and healthy interpersonal relationships. *Journal of Mental Health Counseling, 16,* 327–39.

Sailes, G. A. (1993). An investigation of Black student attrition at a large, predominantly White, midwestern university. *Western Journal of Black Studies, 17,* 179–82.

Smedley, B. D., Myers, H. F., & Harrell, S. P. (1993). Minority-status stresses and the college adjustment of ethnic minority freshmen. *Journal of Higher Education, 64*(4), 434–52.

Terenzini, P. T., Allison, K. W., Millar, S. B., Rendon, L. I., Upcraft, M. L., Gregg, P., et al. (1992). *The Transition to College Project: Final Report.* University Park: Pennsylvania State University, National Center on Postsecondary Teaching, Learning, and Assessment.

Tinto, V. (1994). *Leaving college: Rethinking the causes and cures of student attrition* (2nd. ed). Chicago: University of Chicago Press.

Willie, C. V. & McCord, A. (Eds.). (1972). *Black students at White colleges.* New York: Praeger.

Toward an Understanding of Misandric Microaggressions and Racial Battle Fatigue among African Americans in Historically White Institutions

WILLIAM A. SMITH

> We all say we hate [the University of] Michigan, but at the same time
> we know what a Michigan degree can do for us.
>
> » African American University of Michigan student

African American men live a life filled with racialized paradoxes. On the one hand, they are told that institutions of higher learning—particularly historically White institutions (HWIs)—are places where, through hard work, they can achieve the so-called American dream. Yet, for far too many young Black men HWIs represent a campus racial climate that is replete with gendered forms of racism and blocked opportunities not unlike the urban environments they navigated prior to their arrival to a postsecondary campus. Upon arrival to these campuses, they soon learn

---

The term *historically White institutions* is used in this chapter instead of "predominantly White institutions" to emphasize that the gross numbers or percentages of White American students have less to do with constituting the majority population on collegiate campuses than with the historical and contemporary racialized infrastructure that exist there; as witnessed in the current campus racial culture and ecology.

that racism, in its contemporary form, is pervasive; that Whites still benefit at the expense of Blacks and other groups of color; and that anti-Black male stereotyping and marginalization—or "Black misandric microaggressions"—causes them huge undue stress, what I term as *racial battle fatigue*. Racial battle fatigue is the psychological, physiological, emotional, and behavioral toll placed on People of Color who are responding to daily racial macro- and microaggressions.

On many HWI campuses today, Black males are still viewed as outsiders or illegitimate members of the academic community. As a result, it is common for Black male students to believe that their lives are constantly in danger from Black misandric agents, environments, and conditions (Pierce, 1995; Smith, Allen, & Danley, 2007). It is also common that these conditions produce emotional and physical distress, or racial battle fatigue, from frequently confronting racially based dilemmas as part of their postsecondary experiences.

Given the restrictions of time and space, this chapter will discuss only those racial dilemmas that are the most critical, mundane, and yet least often related to Black college men's psychological and physiological health. These include Black misandric microaggressions such as when Black male students are stereotyped as troublemakers, suspected of antisocial behaviors without requisite justification or evidence, and placed under increased surveillance by police and citizens as they move on- and off-campus (Smith, 2004; Smith, Allen, & Danley, 2007; Smith, Yosso, & Solórzano, 2006). This chapter specifically focuses on the Black male collegiate experience at HWIs in the state of Michigan by comparing it to that of Black college men at several peer institutions, including Harvard University, the University of California–Berkeley, and the University of Illinois. This comparison was conducted to determine whether the problems identified in Michigan are institutional (e.g., a "Michigan problem") or systemic (e.g., a universal problem with material, social, and ideological realities that are imbedded in all HWIs).

Understanding Racism, Black Misandric Microaggressions, and Racial Battle Fatigue

But as far as [racist] attitudes and stuff like that . . . stuff happens every year. I mean I don't see it changing much.

> » African American male, University of Michigan student

One of the most comprehensive definitions of White racism, in the U.S. context, is that of a "socially organized set of practices, attitudes, and ideas that deny African Americans and other people of color the privileges, dignity, opportunities, freedoms, and rewards that this nation offers White Americans" (Feagin, Vera, & Batur, 2001, 17). Bonilla-Silva (2001) adds to this understanding by suggesting that the foundation of racism is not solely based on the ideas that individuals may have about others, but the social edifice erected over racial inequality. He adds, perhaps optimistically, however, that if racial inequality and the practices that maintain it are eliminated, "Racism and even the division of people into racial categories will disappear" (22).

Pierce (1970, 1975, 1995) characterizes racism as a public and mental disorder based on the false belief, despite evidence to the contrary, that innate inferiority correlates with dark skin color. When examining "the substance of today's racism," Pierce (1974) contends, "one must not look for the gross and obvious"; rather, one must identify and measure the impact of what he calls the "subtle, cumulative miniassault" of racial microaggressions (516). In adapting Pierce's work, Smith, Yosso, and Solórzano (2006) define racial microaggressions as (*a*) subtle verbal and nonverbal insults directed at people of color, often automatically or unconsciously; (*b*) layered insults based on one's race, race-gender, class, sexuality, language, immigration status, phenotype, accent, or surname; and (*c*) cumulative insults that cause unnecessary stress to people of color while privileging Whites.

Given the ubiquitousness of racism, racial microaggressions are not unique to Black men or to African Americans. Their withering effects are felt by all nondominant racial and ethnic groups in the United States, individually, collectively, and cumulatively. Distinctive types of microaggressions, however, can target one group while avoiding another. Black misandric microaggressions are those racial microaggressions that specifically target and affect Black males.

Black misandry is an exaggerated pathological aversion toward Black males that is created and reinforced in societal, institutional, and individual ideologies, practices, and behaviors including scholarly ontologies (or understandings of how things exist), axiologies (or values such as ethics, aesthetics, religion, and spirituality), and epistemologies (or ways of knowing). Like Black misogyny, or aversion toward Black women, Black misandry exists to justify and reproduce the subordination and oppression of Black males while concomitantly erecting edifices of racial and gender inequality. As a result, Black males on HWI campuses tend to be marginalized, hated, rendered invisible, held under suspicion, put under increased surveillance, or assigned to one or more socially acceptable stereotypical categories (e.g., lazy, unintelligent, violent, hypersexual, athletic, etc.) without regard for their individual character or status.

Racial Battle Fatigue: The Slow (but Silent) Killer

Black male HWI students are routinely confronted with forms of racial discrimination for which many have only limited energy, resources, or counterstrategies to cope and resist (Smith, Allen, & Danley, 2007; Smith, Yosso, & Solórzano, 2006). These additional experiences are unnecessary burdens that further complicate the competitive process of completing a postsecondary degree. According to Steele (1997), Black college men, like those at the University of Michigan, reported being perplexed, aggravated, stunned, and irritated by the lack of protection their academic achievements provide them, especially from racist stereotypes. When these young men, who have survived earlier structural obstacles and achieved identification with the educational domain, are faced with the burden of having to endure racist stereotypes even while on campus, the emotional impact is enough to threaten their future achievement. Some even totally "disidentify" with the academic domain, Steele asserts. According to Smith (2004), the diagnosis is racial battle fatigue. The symptoms: increased levels of stress, resulting in both psychological symptoms (e.g., frustration, shock, anger, disappointment, resentment, anxiety, helplessness, hopelessness, fear) and physiological symptoms (e.g., headaches, teeth grinding, chest pain, shortness of breath, high blood pressure, muscle aches, indigestion, constipation, diarrhea, increased perspiration, fatigue, insomnia, frequent illness).

The notion of racial battle fatigue synthesizes and builds onto the traditionally discipline-specific research literature and studies of the stresses associated with, the responses to, and the coping strategies for racism (Pierce, 1974, 1975, 1995; Smith, 2004; Willie & Sanford, 1995). It further draws upon the literature on combat stress syndrome (also known as combat stress fatigue, combat trauma, combat injury, or post-traumatic stress disorder) to conceptualize the debilitating effects of living and working in a hostile environment (Shay, 2002; Shay & Munroe, 1999; U.S. Department of the Army, 1994). Racial battle fatigue is manifested when the physiological, psychological, and emotional strain imposed upon persons belonging to racially marginalized, oppressed, and stigmatized groups becomes too much to bear. A certain amount of these individuals' emotional and physical energies that could otherwise be used for productive and creative intellectual ideas and professional development goals are dedicated instead to fighting against or warding off the daily doses of racism, or macroagressions and microaggressions, they encounter.

The most horrific and extreme consequences of racial battle fatigue is that it kills people. Of the slightly more than 1 million people of color among the nearly 9 million Michigan residents recorded by the 1970 Census, 95% were Black. Of these, 75% lived within the city limits of Detroit, compared to 10% of the state's White residents. Within a 10-year period (from 1959–61 to 1969–71), the life expectancy at birth for Black and White females increased by about one year. For White males, life expectancy essentially remained unchanged. For Black males, however, life expectancy decreased by more than three years during this same decennial period. In 1969–71, life expectancy for Black males was 61 years. For White males it was 68 years; for Black females, 69 years; and for White females, 75 years. Between birth and death, these data suggest that there were major differences in the quality of life for each of these groups.

By the 2000 Census, the life expectancy and the quality of life for Michigan residents had improved for each group, but more so for some than for others. Seventy-five percent of Michigan's residents of color were Black, representing a 20% decrease between 1970 and 2000. The majority of the state's Black residents still lived in Detroit, which was 83% African American (McKinnon, 2001). According to the *State of Men's Health: Michigan 2004* report, women had a longer life expectancy than men (79.3 compared to 74.3 years). White females (at 80.1 years) and White males (at 75.3 years) had a longer life expectancy than Black females (at 75.0 years) and males (at 67.8 years). Although life expectancy increased over time for all groups, the disparities by race and gender remained. The overall life expectancy age for Black males in 2003 was comparable to that of 30 years ago for White males and Black females. Viewed another way, these data reveal that about 40% of Michigan's Black males never saw the age of 65.

The quality of life for Blacks and other nondominant racial groups was such a major concern that the U.S. Secretary for the Department of Health and Human Services (USDHHS) convened a task force in 1985 to report on Black and other minority groups' health issues (USDHHS, 1985). This report raised national attention by noting that 60,000 excess deaths were occurring annually because of gender-based health disparities, primarily among African American males. In a 2005 report that focused specifically on African American men in Michigan, the first state-level appointed surgeon general in the country, Dr. Kimberly Dawn Wisdom, presented a list of facts that African American men should know about their health and well-being. This report identified the leading causes of death for Black men in Michigan—heart disease, cancer, diabetes-related diseases, and unintentional injuries—and indicated that the death rates for Black men was almost one-and-a-half times more than that for White men. It further indicated that Black men in Michigan were 17 times more likely to die from homicide than were White men, and they were 30 times more likely than White females and 26 times more likely than women of color to have their life end because of foul play. Moreover, Michigan Black males' probability of dying in early adulthood (ages 30 to 34) surpassed their probability of dying in infancy, an earlier age than that at which the probability of White males, White females, and Black females dying exceeded their rate of infant mortality. For every 100,000 Black males born to mothers in Michigan's metropolitan areas, 2,680 died in infancy. This risk of death was not met or exceeded again until Black men reached the ages of 30 to 34 years, whereas 3,358 of every 100,000 Black Michigan males who turned 30 years old in 2005 could expect to die before turning 35 years old.

As these reports and studies reveal, Michigan's Black males are dying in infancy, early adulthood, and pre-retirement age before other racial or gender groups. Not surprisingly, most research studies on health and mortality rates for these and other African American males concentrate on how these men themselves contribute to the inequities (e.g., poor diet, infrequent doctor visits, lack of exercise, or engagement in risky behaviors). Although this focus is important, the influence of stress from racial microaggressions on poor health outcomes also merits serious research focus. Additional attention must be paid to the environmental contexts that produce racial battle fatigue. For example, what effect does growing up in an environment where the life expectancy and the control of the Black male body is constantly under threat play in determining Black men's health outcomes? Researchers must begin to examine the conditions that lead Black men to heightened exposure to societal risk and racist treatment, and identify the available resources to prevent them (Williams & Braboy, 2005).

The Hidden Cost of Education in Socially Controlled "White Spaces"

The cherished and highly sought after bachelor's degree oftentimes is cited as a proxy for increased economic returns or socioeconomic status or SES (Cheeseman Day & Newburger, 2002). This measure is also used to explain the presence or absence of various quality-of-life indicators for its possessors. However, recent studies of predominantly Black populations have found an inverse relationship for health outcomes (e.g., rates of hypertension, depression, anxiety, life satisfaction, mortality indicators) between Black male college and high school graduates (Diez-Roux et al., 1999). Although the college graduates had higher incomes, and in all probability better diets and generally improved lifestyles including lower levels of cigarette smoking, physical inactivity, and being overweight; the chronic race-related stressors associated with historically White spaces are suggested as the cause for the rise in poor health outcomes among these men.

According to James (1994), for Black women, moving up the SES ladder was inversely related to their self-reported stress, but it was positively related to stress for Black men. Another study found that suburban residence was associated with lower mortality risk for Whites but predicted elevated mortality risks for Black men (House et al., 2000). Williams (2003) suggests that the stressors faced by middle-class Black men may also account for their elevated patterns of suicide risk, which previously had not been very common among this group. Over the past two decades, Williams notes, the suicide rate has remained the same for White men but has expanded markedly for young Black men. These findings suggest the importance of research aimed at determining whether Black men who seek or who are trying to maintain middle-class standing through higher education are being exposed to racism and Black misandric microaggressions that are adversely affecting their physical and mental health.

Black misandric environments, like other "White spaces" in which submission-dominance relationships are present, are characterized by a controlling of the space, time, energy, and mobility of Black males. Such environments typically lead Black males to become increasingly defensive in their thoughts and actions (Feagin, Vera, & Imani, 1996; Pierce, 1995; Smith, Allen, & Danley, 2007; Smith, Yosso, & Solórzano, 2006). As Pierce asserts:

Defensive thinking then becomes increasingly necessary as the victim must anticipate assaults and offensive strategies from the dominator. These assaults may come from any direction, at any time or place. Any person required to manage more uncertainty and unpredictability becomes increasingly wary and hyper vigilant. In essence, the victim's thinking becomes more focused on general monitoring and surveillance tasks needed to thwart expected and unexpected offenses. (1995, 281)

Black males attending Harvard University, the University of California–Berkeley, and the University of Illinois reported experiencing negative or hostile racial climates and Black misandric microaggressions similar to those experienced by their counterparts at the University of Michigan and Michigan State University (Smith, Allen, & Danley, 2007). In common, these respondents maintained that the HWI climate created and reinforced at least four common Black misandric stereotypes: (1) of Black men as criminals and predators; (2) of Black men as possessors of inner-city, ghetto-specific knowledge and behaviors, (3) of Black men as student-athletes, and (4) of Black men as anti-intellectuals.

For many African American male college students at HWIs, the experience of being perceived by Whites as potential criminals (e.g., shoplifters, rapists, purse snatchers, or carjackers) has become so commonplace that they typically expect, accept or dismiss such perceptions without much direct response (Prillerman, Myers, & Smedley, 1989; Steele, 1997; Swim et al., 2003). However, because Whites on HWI campuses often respond to Black men's physical presence with a heightened state of fear, Black male HWI students sometimes perceive this false perception as an insult and experience elevated emotional distress as a result. This misperception is nonetheless a reprehensible Black misandric microaggression and a personal and group-level insult to Black males who consider themselves intelligent, peaceful and law-abiding citizens.

The criminalization of African American males was among the most frequent and offensive microaggressions reported by the respondents. It was also the most pervasive and caustic, required the most assertive use of adaptive coping strategies, and had the most lasting effects, encroaching upon all aspects of these students' lives. Several recalled taking casual strolls on their campuses only to be greeted with fear and contempt by their White counterparts. They related numerous incidents of campus and local police deployment to suppress and control their presence and to keep them in "their place."

The second form of Black misandric stereotyping experienced by these Black college men was that of their being treated universally as possessors of ghetto-specific knowledge and behaviors, irrespective of the locales in which they were raised. The most egregious shortcoming of this form of stereotyping is its failure to consider the diversity of community and economic backgrounds, tastes, desires, and behaviors that are Black Americans' life experiences. That is, the Whites at these HWIs tended to consider all their Black male counterparts as the embodiments of the worst of urban Black inner-city culture—in other words, as possessing a weak work ethic, along with a proclivity for "gangsta" lifestyles and rap music, violence, sexually promiscuous behaviors, and dysfunctional family values. Across each campus the Black male respondents in both studies indicated that they were frequently asked to demonstrate ghetto-specific behaviors and viewed as having more "street smarts" than "book smarts." Not surprisingly, many reported feeling physically and emotionally drained by their efforts to repudiate these stereotypes.

Equally common for these Black male HWI students was being stereotyped as student athletes rather than simply as students attending college on their academic merit alone. This stereotype, according to Stone, Perry, and Darley (1997), presents Black males with a "backhanded" compliment: whether athletes or not, Black men are viewed as having superior natural athletic ability but inferior intellectual ability to Whites and students of other racial/ethnic groups.

The view of Black male students as anti-intellectual, a view the respondents deemed commonplace on HWI campuses, reinforces the notion of Black men as not belonging to the academic community in any important or legitimate way. It also validates the misperception of Black men as intruders, troublemakers, and outsiders on campus until they can prove beyond a reasonable doubt that they belong in college, a stereotype that supports Blumer's (1958) "sense of group position" proposal. Blumer suggests that racially prejudiced individuals see their group as the basis of comparison for other groups. Hence, viewing Blacks, and Black males in particular, as less intelligent—indeed, as anti-intellectual—supports the White racist view that Whites are more intelligent or superior.

In response to each of these perceived racial microaggressions, African American male students reported feelings of frustration, shock, avoidance, withdrawal, disbelief, anger, aggressiveness, uncertainty, confusion, resentment, anxiety, helplessness, hopelessness, and fear. To be sure, they reported variations in the intensity or severity of the microaggressions experienced. For some, the symptoms were acute, while for others they were chronic; for some, they were simple and singular, while for others they were multiple and complex. However, there was unanimous agreement among the Black male HWI students across campuses that the college environment was much more hostile and unwelcoming for African American males than for students of other racial and gender groups.

Conclusion

Far too many African American male students on HWI campuses are overburdened with racial "stuff." The dream of eliminating racism and Black misandry from historically White campuses seems a distant one, however. The discriminatory and stereotypical microaggressions Black men too often face in these historically White spaces place additional stressors upon them that interfere with, if not compromise, their mental, emotional, and physical health as well as their educational achievement. Every aggressive effort possible must be engaged to destroy these social diseases, both vestige and root.

This chapter presented two important theoretical frameworks for understanding the unique experiences of Black males on HWI campuses: Black misandric microaggressions and racial battle fatigue. In doing so, it was intentionally theoretical and discursive, highlighting both the general kinds of environments that cause the physiological and psychological stress-responses of racial battle fatigue in Black males and exposing Michigan's HWIs as similar to other postsecondary institutions nationwide in their treatment of Black males. Indeed, U.S. higher education is part of a historic and systemic pattern of discrimination—ideological and behavioral—that needs further and continued exorcism. The academic universe is but a mirror image of the larger society. Hence, academia must come to grips with its racist past and take the moral high road to help itself and the larger society develop more healthy social relationships between racial and ethnic groups nationwide.

In Michigan's historically White institutions of higher learning, as in similar institutions elsewhere across the nation, the academic community has had a long and difficult struggle with its racist past of exclusion and intolerance. Today, Michigan institutions, particularly the University of Michigan, are viewed as leaders in recognizing the benefits from a racially/ethnically diverse campus. Michigan institutions have had to learn how to overcome their painful past in order to create a better future. This community has pursued, with some success, answers to racial problems, and there is an atmosphere of positive change on campus concerning race questions. This is realized in the representation of racially and ethnically diverse faculty; the opening up of the curriculum to reflect diverse viewpoints; first-class research centers that focus on racial diversity issues in varying social domains; and many top-notch administrators who appear committed to creating a positive campus racial climate. Yet there is still much more work to do in Michigan and elsewhere. In the words of James D. Anderson, "Various solutions to these challenges have been half-heartedly attempted—many of the 'Band-Aid' variety. Very few have introduced lasting changes in approaches to educating African American and other underrepresented students. If we expect to successfully educate our college-age students from undergraduate through graduate or professional school, we must support them and find ways of ensuring that success" (2002, 38).

REFERENCES

Anderson, J. D. (2002). Race in American higher education: Historical perspective on current conditions. In W. A. Smith, P. G. Altbach, & K. Lomotey (Eds.), *The racial crisis in American higher education: Continuing challenges to the twenty-first century*, 3–22. Albany: SUNY Press.

Blumer, H. (1958). Race prejudice as a sense of group position. *Pacific Sociological Review, 1*(1), 3–7.

Bonilla-Silva, E. (2001). *White supremacy and racism in the post-civil rights era.* Boulder, CO: Lynne Rienner Publishers.

Cheeseman Day, J. & Newburger, E. C. (2002, July). The big payoff: Educational attainment and synthetic estimates of work-life earnings. *Current Populations Reports,* P23-210. Washington, DC: U.S. Bureau of the Census.

Diez-Roux, A. V., Northridge, M. E., Morabia, A., Bassett, M. T., & Shea, S. (1999). Prevalence and social correlates of cardiovascular disease risk factors in Harlem. *American Journal of Public Health, 89,* 302–7.

Feagin, J. R., Vera, H., & Batur, P. (2001). *White racism* (2nd ed.). New York: Routledge.

Feagin, J. R., Vera, H., & Imani, N. (1996). *The agony of education: Black students at White colleges and universities* (2nd ed.). New York: Routledge.

House, J. S., Lepkowski, J. M., Williams, D. R., Mero, R. P., Lantz, P. M., Robert, S. A., & Chen, J. (2000). Excess mortality among urban residents: How much, for whom, and why? *American Journal of Public Health, 90,* 1898–1904.

James, S. A. (1994). John Henryism and the health of African-Americans. *Culture, Medicine, and Psychiatry, 18,* 163–82.

McKinnon, J. (2001). "The Black population: 2000." August. Washington, DC: U.S. Bureau of the Census. Available at http://www.census.gov/prod/2001pubs/c2kbr01-5.pdf.

Pierce, C. M. (1970). Offensive mechanisms. In F. B. Barbour (Ed.), *The Black seventies,* 265–82. Boston: Porter Sargent.

Pierce, C. M. (1974). Psychiatric problems of the Black minority. In S. Arieti (Ed.), *American handbook of psychiatry,* 512–23. New York: Basic Books.

Pierce, C. M. (1975). The mundane extreme environment and its effect on learning. In S. G. Brainard (Ed.), *Learning disabilities: Issues and recommendations for research,* 111–19. Washington, DC: National Institute of Education, Department of Health, Education, and Welfare.

Pierce, C. M. (1995). Stress analogs of racism and sexism: Terrorism, torture, and disaster. In C. Willie, P. Rieker, B. Kramer, & B. Brown (Eds.), *Mental health, racism, and sexism,* 277–93. Pittsburgh: University of Pittsburgh Press.

Prillerman, S. L., Myers, H. F., & Smedley, B. D. (1989). Stress, well-being, and academic achievement in college. In G. L. Berry & J. K. Asamen (Eds.), *Black students: Psychological issues and academic achievement,* 198–217. Newbury Park, CA: Sage.

Shay, J. (2002). *Odysseus in America: Combat trauma and the trials of homecoming.* New York: Scribner.

Shay, J. & Munroe, J. (1999). Group and milieu therapy for veterans with complex post traumatic stress disorder. In P. A. Saigh & J. D. Bremner (Eds.), *Posttraumatic stress disorder: A comprehensive text,* 391–413. Needham Heights, MA: Allyn & Bacon.

Smith, W. A. (2004). Black faculty coping with racial battle fatigue: The campus racial climate in a post-civil rights era. In D. Cleveland (Ed.), *A long way to go: Conversations about race by African American faculty and graduate students at predominately White institutions,* 171–90. New York: Peter Lang.

Smith, W. A., Allen, W. R., & Danley, L. (2007). Assume the position . . . You fit the description: Psychological experiences and racial battle fatigue among African American male college students. *American Behavioral Scientist,* 5 1(4), 551–78.

Smith, W. A., Yosso, T. J., & Solórzano, D. G. (2006). Challenging racial battle fatigue on historically White campuses: A critical race examination of race-related stress. In C. A. Stanley (Ed.), *Faculty of color: Teaching in predominantly White colleges and universities,* 299–327. Bolton: Anker Publishing.

State of men's health: Michigan (2004). Washington, DC: Men's Health Network.

Steele, C. M. (1997). A threat in the air: How stereotypes shape intellectual identity and performance. *American Psychologist,* 52(6), 613–29.

Stone, J. J., Perry, Z. W., & Darley, J. M. (1997). White men can't jump: Evidence for the perceptual confirmation of racial stereotypes following a basketball game. *Basic and Applied Social Psychology, 19,* 291–306.

Swim, J. K., Hyers, L. L., Cohen, L. L., Fitzgerald, D. C., & Bylsma, W. H. (2003). African American college students' experiences with everyday racism: Characteristics of and responses to these incidents. *Journal of Black Psychology, 29,* 38–67.

U.S. Department of the Army. (1994). *Battle fatigue GTA 21-3-5 warning signs: Leader actions.* June. Washington, DC: U.S. Department of the Army.

U.S. Department of Health and Human Services (USDHHS). (1985). *Report of the secretary's taskforce on Black and minority health.* Vol. 2: *Crosscutting issues in minority health.* Washington, DC: Government Printing Office.

Williams, D. R. (2003). The health of men: Structured inequalities and opportunities. *American Journal of Public Health, 93*(5), 724–31.

Williams, D. R. & Braboy Jackson, P. (2005). Social sources of racial disparities in health, *Health Affairs, 24*(2), 325–34.

Willie, C. V. & Sanford, J. S. (1995). Turbulence on the college campus and the frustration-aggression hypothesis. In C. V. Willie, P. P. Rieker, B. M. Kramer, & B. S. Brown (Eds.), *Mental health, racism, and sexism,* 253–75. Pittsburgh: University of Pittsburgh Press.

It'll Be Me

EMPOWERING AFRICAN AMERICAN MALE STUDENTS

WALLACE BRIDGES

You put me in Macbeth *and* Carmen Jones
And all kinds of Swing Mikados
And in everything, but what's about me?
But, someday somebody'll
Stand up and talk about me
And write about me
Black and beautiful
And sing about me
And put on plays about me!
I reckon it'll be me myself
Yes, it'll be me.

» Langston Hughes, "A Note on Commercial Theatre," 1949

These lines from Langston Hughes's 1940s poem "A Note on Commercial Theatre" echo my convictions about education and theatre. I am convinced that it must be me who educates the public on the value of an African American theatre presence. More importantly, I am convinced that in large part it must be me, a professional African American male, who takes action to help solve the educational crisis facing young African American males. As I humbly take personal responsibility to contribute constructively to the advancement of a solution to this alarming trial, I invite everyone else to take action as well. When I say take action, I do not simply refer to an appearance at a conference or an anonymous cash donation to an important cause. I speak of considered, consistent, and collaborative active involvement in the education of young African American males.

When I was invited to write a chapter examining solutions to this challenge, I used that invitation as an opportunity to review how I may have influenced the advancement of African American males within my personal spheres of influence: in the family, in education, and in the theatre arts. I reflected on my efforts to lead by example at home, in the classroom, on the stage, and in the community. I questioned whether I had identified enough meaningful ways to incorporate my love of education and theatre into projects and programs that positively influence African American males. I recalled having many opportunities to influence my now 25-year-old son's development so that he could achieve personal success and contribute constructively to society, and wondered whether I had taken full advantage of those opportunities. Reflecting upon the African American males who have taken my college classes, I asked myself if I had been a positive role model who not only espouses positive values and standards but also lives what he teaches. I also thought about my impact as a director on African American male actors. Had my directing style encouraged any of them to pursue careers in the theatre? According to the research, my presence—as an African American professor, actor, and director—should have had a profound impact on the African American males who pass through my classrooms and theatres. The sources I reviewed to prepare this chapter, ranging from online sources, periodicals, and books to my networking experiences and humble perspectives, confirmed this to be the case.

Consider, for example, the dire statistics regarding African American male failures in the academic community that Worley (2006) describes in the *Journal News* of Westchester County, New York:

A 2004 report by The Civil Rights Project at Harvard University and The Urban Institute noted that 43 percent of Black males graduated from high school in 2001, compared with 56 percent for Black females and 71 percent for White males.

Worley reports that African American males' academic achievement not only falls behind that of their White peers but also behind that of African American females. He further adds that "the gender gap in college is widest among Blacks, with Black women accounting for 63 percent of enrollees compared to 37 percent for Black men." Although the article goes on to list what others may view as an overwhelming litany of failure, I contend that there is another way to look at the challenges facing African American males, and that is to realize that having knowledge about these challenges is the first key to finding solutions to them.

The presence of three specific challenges facing African American male youth—lack of positive role models, peer pressure against academic achievement, and low expectations by teachers and communities—clearly tells me that we educators must do more to develop programs that effectively combat these pressures. Those of us who are African American and male must provide consistent, positive role models for these youth and work to instill within them the value of academic achievement. We need to program our schools and communities to enforce high standards of academic excellence for African American male students. We know what *needs* to be done. What we need now is to implement the strategies necessary to accomplish these goals. And who will take the lead on this? Again echoing Langston Hughes, I say, "Yes! It'll be me."

This chapter will examine some of the key obstacles that prevent African American males from participating equally in American society and education, both in the state of Michigan and in the United States. It will also share insights on some programs that have successfully overcome those obstacles as well as suggest other innovative and creative options.

The Challenges before Us

Most of the successful educational programs for African American males involve one or more of the following factors: community collaboration, mentoring programs, African American male role models, and ultimately empowering young African American males to succeed. Regarding the first of these factors, research has clearly shown that broad-based community collaboration is essential. According to Jackson (2005), however, the problem of African American male educational underachievement "is not even on the radar of many Black churches, businesses, elected officials, media outlets, civil rights, and social service organizations." Although this may be so in some communities, it is clearly not the case in Michigan. We of Michigan's African American communities are attending summits and conferences focusing on this issue around the country. We are reading about and reviewing what successful programs are doing to change the dynamic of educational failure for Black male youth. We are taking our own steps to solve this problem. Like me, many of us are working within our own spheres, but we may need to do more. We may need to reach out to other groups for help.

I recently attended a community meeting on how to advance tourism in Lake County, Michigan. During this meeting, David Lorenz, vice president of Travel Michigan, led a session that included members of the state Chamber of Commerce and local citizens and business owners from Baldwin and Idlewild, Michigan. The flyer distributed during that session highlighted two key concepts: "What can I do now?" and "Network! Network! Network!" The speakers emphasized throughout their presentations that despite any single individual or community's good intentions, one cannot nor should not operate in a vacuum. We can only achieve success if we collaborate for the good of African American males, for the good of family, and for the good of society as a whole.

Mentoring and role modeling are additional critical components of successful educational programs for African American males. Clearly, the presence and involvement of successful African American role models is important in influencing young African American males; however, that is not always possible. In integrated learning environments, young African American males may not always have handy access to role models from common backgrounds. In 2002, only 7% of K–12 teachers nationally were African American compared to 17% of the collective K–12 student body (Denn, 2002). For that reason, since 1992 Washington State University has implemented the Future Teachers of Color program, which shepherds minority teacher-candidates through the financial aid, mentorship, outreach, and job search processes.

Oftentimes, educators and community leaders who are not African American males wish to contribute meaningfully to the advancement of African American males' academic achievement but perceive a challenge in that they do not directly identify with these youth. They may even suffer some apprehension in their attempt to relate to and to serve African American students. They can still contribute, however, by networking with African American male role modes and inviting them to their classrooms as guest speakers, or by taking these students on field trips to institutions where they can interface with African American role models on the job.

Lastly, young African American males need to be empowered from an African American male perspective. John (2000) in his poem "Father to Son" stresses that young African American men need adults—be they the biological parents, foster parents, or extended family members—who care enough to be there for them and who can teach them basic values. Young Black men need to be praised when they do well and challenged when they do not, John continues. He contends that they need role models who can "teach [them] that [their] people need [them] / to become [teachers] in life / and that to do that [they need] / to become [students] of life." The enlistment of mentors and role models to support such efforts, especially those who share heritage and gender in common with these youth, has been shown time and again to result in classroom and life successes for African American males.

Sometimes, however, African American male professors experience a dilemma when encountering African American male students with poor study skills. I recall the case of an African American male student who came to speak to me about his failing grade. When he claimed he did not understand why he had received such marks, I pointed out to him that he had not turned in some assignments and done poorly on others, and that he had a pattern of tardiness, having missed five days of class. He asked if I could "work with him" to get a D in the course. I assured him that this was not possible without violating university rules or lowering academic standards, and suggested that his challenge was due to his limited study skills. The student, however, was in denial about this critical fact. After our discussion, I felt a deep sadness that was assuaged only by my belief that I did "the right thing" by holding him to the same standards of excellence I hold for all my students.

I once directed a production of LeRoi Jones's play *Dutchman* for the Frank L. Ross Laboratory Theatre. This play was not a part of my regular directing load, but I could not bypass the opportunity. One of my favorite student actors at the time played the role of Clay, and he presented me with quite a few challenges relating to his lack of punctuality and failure to work up to my established standards of excellence. We had many conflicts about these issues, and I spent quite a bit of time and energy trying to make my student see the error of his ways. More than five years later, I received a phone call from this young man that assured me that the values I had enforced and the time I had spent had not been completely lost on him. After years of working in New York City to become a professional actor and with so many other actors out of work, he had learned that producers do not have time for actors who are late or lazy. He thanked me for pushing him to adhere to a strong work ethic.

Alternately, some African American fathers and father-figures go about correcting their sons in ways that do not elicit the desired response or behavior. They know only the yelling and the hitting—hurtful lessons learned from their own fathers or other adult caretakers. They often mean well but may not have the tools necessary to raise an African American boy properly. Sometimes, simple quiet symbolic actions can do the job. For example, my son is an alumnus of Eastern Michigan University, where I teach, and I am proud to say that he is doing well in his career, but that was not always the case. He had a few tough times during high school, and you can bet I was there for him then, whether he wanted me to be or not!

I recall a period when my son simply was not applying himself in some of his high school classes. Fortunately, the university term ends before the public school term ends, and this provided me with the opportunity to visit his classes—all six of them—for two consecutive days. It was amazing how this action got his attention and encouraged him to shape up in class. In another instance, he decided that he wanted to quit the high school baseball team after playing for just a week or two. Of course, I explained to him that quitting was not an option; he would have to finish the season he started, but he did not have to rejoin the next year. Naively, I assumed that that, as they say, was that. A few days later, however, I decided to drop by my son's school to check on his baseball practice. When I walked onto the field I did not see him anywhere. I asked the coach if he had seen him, and he said that he had not been to practice for several days. I checked in the team's locker room; no son. I went to the school office to ask if anyone had seen my son, and no one there could provide me with any information about him. Then I noticed three young men hanging out in the hallway and heard one of them says, "Isn't that your father?" Calmly, I confronted my son, walked him back to the locker room, made him change into his uniform, and walked him back out onto the baseball field. He finished playing ball that season, not because I forced my will upon him, but because he learned the value of living up to one's commitments by my demonstrating my own commitment to keeping up with him and his whereabouts.

In his 1986 play *Fences*, two-time Pulitzer Prize–winner August Wilson tells the story of Troy Maxson, an African American father in 1950s Pittsburgh who does not have the emotional tools needed to properly raise his son Cory, a high school senior who has been offered a football scholarship at a nearby college. Given Troy's own earlier disappointments and rejections by the professional baseball leagues of his day, he believes Cory will suffer the same rejection and should instead stay home and continue working at the local grocery. He forbids Cory from taking the scholarship and thus keeps him from achieving his goals. When Cory responds angrily, Troy takes umbrage, echoing the harshness of his own upbringing in telling his son:

> You grown.... We done established that. You a man. Now, let's see you act like one. Turn your behind around and walk out this yard. And, when you get out there in the alley ... you can forget about this house. See? 'Cause this is *my* house. You go on and be a man and get your own house. You can forget about this 'cause this is mine. (Wilson, 2000, 966)

Wilson thus questions, through theatre, the effectiveness of generations-old approaches to childrearing, and specifically fathering, that may not have provided African American men with the best examples for raising sons in the contemporary period. They contrast significantly with the approach John (2000) recommends in his contemporary poem "Father to Son":

> *cry with your son, laugh with your son,*
> *never ever fear your son,*
> *no matter*
> *what ugliness he passes through*
> *stay there with him*
> *don't back off he needs you to be the one to make him hurt a little*
> *so he won't wind up hurting a lot*
> *each him that a man demands respect*
> *by demanding of himself that he*
> *give respect*
> *to all that cross his path*
> *that if a man challenges him to be a man*
> *and fight*

*that he can only be a man if he does not depend
on violence to gain his sense of manliness.*

Too many African American parents today are overwhelmed, overworked, and not necessarily trained in the best ways to ensure the successful academic development of their children. In many cases, they are in single-parent situations with limited resources; when they are part of a nuclear, middle-class, or affluent family, they often suffer the same parenting struggles as their White counterparts. Many need the help of African American educators, professionals, and community leaders to identify, find, and use the tools they need to better prepare their sons. Others simply need to step up and be proactive regarding their children's education by becoming active members of the Parent-Teacher Association and participating in school-sponsored activities, reviewing their children's homework periodically, attending parent-teacher conferences regularly, and following up with teachers regarding their children's progress and problems in school.

Programmatic Issues and Exemplars

More formal programs designed to uplift African American males in education and in society generally are needed, but a number of programs are already in place throughout Michigan and the rest of the nation. These programs can provide valuable guidance for informing the development of other programs. For example, the University System of Georgia funds its African American Male Initiative program at six colleges and universities that are striving to help African American male students succeed academically. Their efforts include a summer bridge program, a precollegiate summer residential institute, a K–12 Saturday Academy/Postsecondary Readiness Enrichment Program, and a Minority Outreach Program that targets rising seventh-grade African American males for mentoring and tutoring aimed at enhancing their college preparation and reducing their high school dropout rate (Board of Regents of the University System of Georgia, 2003; "Georgia Regents Continue to Tackle Black Male College Enrollment, Retention," 2004). Particularly noteworthy is the University of Georgia's Gentlemen on the Move program, a mentoring and academic support program whose goals are to develop and nurture academic and social excellence in African American male youth.

Some communities may wish to consider providing an all-male academic environment for African American male students like that of the Eagle Academy for Young Men in the Bronx, New York City. This school's development was supported by the organization One Hundred Black Men, whose ranks include former New York City mayor David Dinkins, actor Danny Glover, the late attorney Johnny Cochran, and entertainer Bill Cosby. Its mentoring program connects each student with a mentor from One Hundred Black Men during his entire high school experience. The school's principal, David Banks, maintains that "the Eagle Academy is an idea whose time has come and [that it fills] a great need in the community" (Wayans, 2004). He adds,

> Hearing statistics stating that 50 percent of African American men are unemployed or unemployable is unconceivable. We felt we needed to take a chance. Teachers have to create a curriculum based on how boys learn and they provide hands-on experiences to address boys' natural competitive nature.... Far too many young men are not making it. Single-sex education may not be the answer but it is worth the try. (Wayans, 2004)

Eagle Academy students attend school on weekdays until 5:30 P.M., working in study scenarios after regular class. Dinner is also provided because of the length of the school day. Students also attend school on Saturdays until noon, focusing on intramural activities and classes that involve collaborative planning and leadership activities.

Businesses have also gotten involved to support initiatives that address African American male academic and social achievement. In 2006 in Westchester County, New York, the New York Power Authority (NYPA) sponsored a seminar on role models and leadership for 20 African American students from Ossining High School.

Another NYPA initiative, Project Earthquake, demonstrates how businesses can actively support the education of young African American men in a way that benefits not only African American men but also the community at large. Project Earthquake exposes young African American males to different types of professions, and according to program coordinator Martin McDonald, its participants are at-risk students who can "greatly benefit from career events like this one where they receive tangible advice from African American men with established careers.... It adds a sense of attainability and promise to their future" ("NYPA to Sponsor Career Day for Students at Ossining High School," 2006). The NYPA's efforts in Westchester are supported by other local initiatives that encourage African American male students to complete their education and focus on a career. Since 1990 the African American Men of Westchester organization has sponsored several programs that have positively influenced over 600 African American male youths. These include its annual Youth Network Day for young men from ages 13 to 21, which engages local African American men as role models to deliver workshops on a variety of topics such as education, family values, and community commitment.

Clearly, these Georgia and New York examples represent proactive ways to address the academic challenges facing African American males, but there are other programs and activities of note. Within my personal sphere of influence, theatre and education, I know of a number of institutions of higher learning and professional groups that encourage African American male youths to participate in theatre. By doing so, they are encouraging these young men to participate in a field that is usually overlooked by the African American community because of something I call the "Tennis-Hockey-Golf Syndrome"—that is, the historic tendency for African Americans not to participate in large numbers in certain fields. We know, of course, that Tiger Woods and the Williams sisters have done a lot to change that perspective, but organizations like the Black Theatre Network and the National Black Theatre Festival are changing these perceptions.

The Black Theatre Network's (n.d.) stated goals are "to expose the beauty and complexity of Black life, in America and throughout the African Diaspora . . . [to] celebrate and perpetuate the theatrical vision and expertise of our ancestors and share it with the world . . . to both broaden and strengthen our work and help to support Black Theatre locally and globally." The organization, whose web site address is www.Blacktheatrenetwork.org, conducts annual conferences and programs that encourage young African American theatre artists and educators, and it is grounded in a strong educational foundation. The National Black Theatre Festival (www.nbtf.org) holds activities in Winston-Salem, North Carolina, every odd-numbered year that involve theatre professionals and educators. The festival is supported in part by the North Carolina Black Repertory Company and by the National Endowment for the Arts. It features major stage, television, and film stars (National Black Theatre Festival, n.d.). Both these initiatives have made a profound impression on young African American theatre artists.

Michigan has had some success in its efforts to elevate African American males' academic achievement. The Michigan Department of Education's (2006) Michigan Blue Ribbon Exemplary Schools program serves three purposes: (1) it identifies and recognizes outstanding schools across the state; (2) it makes research-based effectiveness criteria available to schools so they can assess themselves and plan improvements; and (3) it encourages schools to share with other schools their best practices for educational success. To be recognized as exemplary, a school must demonstrate a strong commitment to educational excellence for all students. The criteria also require that winning schools must have made Adequate Yearly Progress (AYP) according to the federal No Child Left Behind law. Schools who have applied must engage in peer reviews, site visits, and extended research and data collection. Although it is important to note that the eight Michigan Blue Ribbon schools do not serve a majority of African American students, particularly males, educators in schools that do can be encouraged by the successes of these schools, and use their programs as models to improve their own.

Within my sway, I am currently working to develop a program to encourage African Americans to strive for careers in education and theatre. To that end I have collaborated with the Idlewild (Michigan) Merry Makers and Eastern Michigan University Theatre to teach theatre workshops and produce Afrocentric theatre productions in Idlewild, a small resort community in the western part of the state. In 2004, this group produced Samm Art Williams's play *Home*; and this year we produced *Ain't Misbehavin': The Fats Waller Musical Show*. Each year we accept two or three interns from Baldwin High School to work backstage on the production and to participate in other activities with the company. Interest in this project is growing, and long-term goals include an education outreach program that reaches from Eastern Michigan University to Baldwin High School to Baldwin Elementary School. Plans involve incorporating students and local community members into full seasons of plays that reflect the African American experience.

In my African American Theatre courses, I teach students about an Afrocentric perspective and about dispelling stereotypes. I believe these two concepts are invaluable to helping empower African American males. African American males need to experience educational models that relate to their own first-person perspectives—namely, the discourse of the African American male. They should be exposed to subject matter and curricular materials that represent their own demographic. They need to be constantly reminded of their history, of their ancestors' successes in overcoming harrowing obstacles, and of their forebears' resilience, so they can too aspire to succeed.

My classes also stress dispelling negative stereotypes. The media has convinced too many young African American males that their image is wrapped in music videos and the gangster mentality. Sadly, many have bought into it. As educators, we Black men consistently need to teach our young boys why and how these images and mentalities are destructive, and model positive behaviors in their stead. We can stress constructive values to them with regard to education, home, community, and work. We can emphasize the importance of honest effort, hard work, reliability, punctuality, efficiency, and effective communication. We can help them to understand that all actions have consequences and that ignorance of those consequences will hold them back.

In 1986 the playwright George C. Wolfe wrote a scathing satire on African American identity titled *The Colored Museum,* which I teach in my classes. The play includes a scene, "Symbiosis," in which a successful African American businessman is in the process of throwing away items from his cultural past. The Man says, "My first pair of Converse All-Stars: Gone! My first Afro comb: Gone! My autographed pictures of Stokely Carmichael, Jomo Kenyatta, and Donna Summer: Gone!" (Wolfe, 1996, 465–66). The Kid, the Man as a teenager, soon appears and challenges the Man to hang on to his cultural past, but the Man eventually throws the Kid into the trash as well. The message of this scene for African American men is that we should neither forget our history nor forget that we each have a personal stake in the academic and professional futures of our Black male youth. Instead, we should encourage Black male youth to seek out and take advantage of opportunities to be "in the know." We should help them to make the best choices for their futures, not the easy choices or the fast ones. We should also help them to set goals, plan strategies, and commit to accomplishing their objectives.

Young African American men need help to counter a destructive mind-set—the perspective that studying efficiently and advancing academically is equivalent to "acting White"—and we adult males must help them to dispel this notion. I have heard many African American male students complain that their friends and peers make fun of them or treat them like outsiders because they strive to excel academically. Ultimately, high-performing African American males should be encouraged to find their own song, secure in the knowledge that they are highly regarded and valued within their own communities as well as in the mainstream of society.

I remember as a high school sophomore in 1970s Oklahoma, I always wanted to be an actor. I did not know why, but it was apparently a natural impulse. I recall not receiving much encouragement from friends and adults, who said things like, "Why do you want to do that theatre stuff? You know those White folks don't want you there." Once, while I was walking home from school, the football coach sidled up to me in his car and asked me if I was a prospective football player. When I responded that I was in theatre, you should have seen his car burn rubber speeding away! Though I did not get a lot of encouragement from those sources, my high school speech and drama teachers were supportive. That is why I am so adamant about the importance of encouraging young African American males to follow their own song and impulses rather than discouraging them from pursuing their natural interests. We African American men especially must appreciate and encourage the songs of our youthful counterparts. As Jaiya John relates in his poem, "Father to Son," we must "encourage [them] to tell [their] story / in as many ways as possible / in [their] clothing / in [their] walk / in [their] speech / the people [they keep] in [their lives]."

Conclusion

Now the training of men is a difficult and intricate task. Its technique is a matter for educational experts, but its object is for the vision of seers. If we make money the object of man-training, we shall develop money-makers but not necessarily men; if we make technical skill the object of education, we may possess artisans but not, in nature, men. Men we shall have only as we make manhood the object of the work of the schools—intelligence, broad sympathy, knowledge of the world that was and is, and of the relation of men to it—this is the curriculum of that Higher Education which must underlie true life. On this foundation we may build bread winning, skill of hand and quickness of brain, with never a fear lest the child and man mistake the means of living for the object of life. (Du Bois, 1903)

A number of successful models are already in operation and several innovative practices are being advanced to achieve DuBois's objectives today. It is clear, however, that African American men must take the lead in this. We must take action now to ensure the advancement of future generations of African American males and the advancement of our society. We must take the initiative to collaborate and work to guide these youth to success. We cannot wait for others to do it; we have to approach this challenge with the mind-set that "It'll be me."

REFERENCES

Black Theatre Network. (n.d.). Retrieved May 17, 2006, from http://www. Blacktheatrenetwork.org.

Board of Regents of the University System of Georgia. (2003). *Summary and final recommendation of the Board of Regents of the University System of Georgia's African American Male Initiative.* Atlanta: Board of Regents of the University System of Georgia.

Denn, R. (2002, March 15). Black teachers are hard to find. *Seattle Post-Intelligencer.* Retrieved April 17, 2006, from http://seattlepi.nwsource. com/disciplinegap/61967_staff13.shtml.

Du Bois, W. E. B. (1903). *The talented tenth.* Retrieved May 21, 2006, from http:// teachingamericanhistory.org/library/index.asp?document=174.

Georgia Regents continue to tackle Black male college enrollment, retention. (2004). *Black Issues in Higher Education,* July 15. Retrieved April 13, 2006, from http://www.findarticles.com/p/articles/mi_moDXK/is_11_21/ ai_n6145437.

Hughes, L. (1989). Note on commercial theatre. In A. Woll, *Black musical theatre: From* Coontown *to* Dreamgirls (p. 231). 1949; Baton Rouge: Louisiana State University Press.

Jackson, P. (2005). The massive failure of Black males in the American education system. *Baltimore Chronicle and Sentinel,* February 23. Retrieved April 13, 2006, from http://www.bridges4kids.org/articles/3-05/Balt2-23-05.html.

John, J. (2000). Father to son. Retrieved May 17, 2006, from www.jaiyajohn.com.

Michigan Department of Education. (2006). *State Board of Education announces 8 blue ribbon schools for 2005–06.* Lansing, MI: Martin Ackley.

National Black Theatre Festival. (n.d.). Retrieved May 17, 2006, from http:// www.nbtf.org.

NYPA to sponsor career day for students at Ossining High School (2006, March 16). *New York Power Authority News*. Retrieved April 13, 2006, from http://www.midwestleague.com/indivpitching.html.

Wayans, J. (2004). *Eagle Academy for African American Males*. Retrieved May 12, 2006, from http://www.insideschools.org/fs/school_profile.php?id=1295.

Wilson, A. (2000). *Fences*. In S. Barnett, W. E. Burto, L. Ferris, & G. Rabkin (Eds.), *Types of Drama: Plays and Context* (7th ed.), vol. 2, 942–73. 1986; New York: Longman.

Wolfe, G. C. (1996). The colored museum. In J. Hatch & T. Shine (Eds.), *Black theatre U.S.A.: Plays by African Americans (The recent period, 1935–Today)* (Revised and expanded ed.), vol. 2, 451–72. New York: Free Press.

Worley, D. (2006). Forum focuses on aid to Black male students. *Journal News*, March 31. Retrieved April 13, 2006, from http://www.thejournalnews.com/apps/pbcs.dll/article?AID=/20060331/NEWS02/603310330/1024/NEWS08.

About the Contributors

Anthony Troy Adams is professor and chair of the Department of Criminology, Sociology, and Geography at Arkansas State University, Jonesboro. He earned his Ph.D. in Sociology from the University of Michigan, Ann Arbor (1990). His research addresses school violence and discipline, inequalities in education, scholarship of teaching and learning, service learning, and a new research exploration on the geographical-spatial distribution of nutrition and its correlates, race and class. Aside from his administrative responsibilities, Dr. Adams has regularly taught courses in introductory sociology, statistics, research methodology, and sociology of education.

Derrick L. Anderson lived with HIV for thirteen years until he died of non-HIV-related complications in December 2006. Originally, from Detroit, Anderson served on the state of Michigan's Persons Living with AIDS Task Force, which advises the state health department on HIV and AIDS policy. He attended the XIII International AIDS Conference in Durban, South Africa. Anderson always stressed the importance of having gay men involved in their communities. He argued that Black gay men must be brave enough to engage the larger Black community, so that everyone can fight the AIDS epidemic together.

Wallace Bridges is professor of theatre and mainstage director at Eastern Michigan University Theatre. Bridges has been teaching at Eastern since 1992. He earned a bachelor of arts degree in speech and drama at Cameron University in Lawton, Oklahoma, and a master of fine arts degree in Theatre (Directing) at Western Illinois University in Macomb. He teaches acting, play direction, introduction to theatre, and African American theatre to undergraduate students, as well as designing and teaching two of these courses online. Bridges is a member of Actors Equity Association and Screen Actors Guild. He acts professionally onstage, in commercials, television, and film. He appears in the feature films, *Betty Anne Waters*, *High School*, and *Flipped*, and also appears in the HBO television series, *Hung*.

M. Christopher Brown II is executive vice president and provost at Fisk University. He previously served as professor and dean of the College of Education at the University of Nevada, Las Vegas, vice president for programs and administration at the American Association of Colleges for Teacher Education (AACTE), director of social justice and professional development for the American Educational Research Association (AERA), as well as executive director and chief research scientist of the Frederick D. Patterson Research Institute of the United Negro College Fund. Dr. Brown has held faculty appointments at Penn State University, the University of Illinois at Urbana-Champaign, and the University of Missouri–Kansas City.

Yvonne Callaway is professor in college counseling in the Department of Leadership and Counseling at Eastern Michigan University. Her doctoral studies were pursued at Wayne State University in Detroit, where she earned a Ph.D. in Counselor Education and Supervision. Dr. Callaway's teaching and research expertise include group counseling, multicultural counseling, counselor assessment, and campus communities.

Nancy Copeland is an associate professor of Educational Media and Technology at Eastern Michigan University. She received her doctorate from Wayne State University in instructional technology and specializes in effective integration of educational technology for teaching and learning. Her current scholarly activities focus on effective distance learning environments emerging technologies for K–16 education, and preservice and new teacher technology integration capacity. She has more than 15 years experience in higher education in areas of teacher training, instructional design, and multimedia development. As senior personnel on National Science Foundation and PT3 (Preparing Tomorrow's Teachers to Use Technology) grants, she has directed the development of online resources for preservice and practicing teachers. Dr. Copeland also serves as technology consultant for the Office of Urban Education and Educational Equity.

T. Elon Dancy II is assistant professor of Educational Leadership and Policy Studies at the University of Oklahoma. His Ph.D. was conferred at Louisiana State University. Dr. Dancy's research and scholarly writing focus on the intersection of race and gender in colleges and universities. More specifically, this agenda focuses on identifying the strategies for improving African American men's social and academic experiences in different college contexts, as well as understanding African American male constructions of manhood and sense-making. Additionally, careful attention is paid to assessing African American male persistence and outcomes. His research and commentary have been published in *American Behavioral Scientist,* other academic periodicals, and volumes. He has presented original data collection and other scholarly work at several national conferences. His scholarship carefully considers topics of curricular change, the sociohistorical nature of schooling, and culturally relevant pedagogies in college.

Scott Jackson Dantley is an associate vice president of institutional effectiveness and planning and professor of Chemistry at Coppin State University. Dr. Dantley has four degrees in Chemistry and Science Education, receiving his Ph.D. in science education at the University of Maryland. His research interests include understanding minority students (i.e., male) science content knowledge development, comparing international science performance, and exploring science policy issues. His work has appeared in numerous journals and books as well as been presented in several countries. Journals include *The Electronic Journal of Science Education* and *The National Journal of Urban Education and Practice.* Recent international presentations include Bogotá, Colombia; Shanghai, China; and Istanbul, Turkey.

James Earl Davis is a professor in the Department of Educational Leadership and Policy Studies at Temple University and has affiliate appointments in African American Studies and Women Studies. James has a B.A. in Sociology from Morehouse College and a Ph.D. from Cornell University. His research focuses on educational policy, urban school reform, and issues of race, class and gender. Specifically, his scholarship has engaged questions about the academic and social experiences of African American boys and young men placed at risk for underachievement and school disengagement. His work has appeared in numerous journals, including *Gender & Society, Urban Education, American Journal of Evaluation,* and *Educational Researcher.* He is coauthor of *African American Males in School and Society: Policies and Practices for Effective Education* (with Vernon Polite) and *Black Sons to Mothers: Compliments, Critiques, and Challenges for Cultural Workers in Education* (with M. Christopher Brown II). He has taught at the University of Delaware and Cornell University. His research has been funded by the Spencer Foundation, the National Science Foundation, Marcus Foundation, and the U.S. Center for Substance Abuse Prevention.

Donna Y. Ford is a professor in the Department of Special Education at Vanderbilt University. She has been a professor of Special Education at The Ohio State University, an associate professor of Educational Psychology at the University of Virginia, and a researcher with the National Research Center on the Gifted and Talented. She also taught at the University of Kentucky. She earned her doctor of philosophy degree in Urban Education from Cleveland State University. Her research primarily examines gifted education and multicultural/urban education. Specifically, her work focuses on recruiting and retaining culturally diverse students in gifted education, multicultural and urban education, minority student achievement and underachievement, and family involvement. She consults with school districts and educational organizations in the areas of gifted education and multicultural/urban education.

Deborah A. Harmon is an associate professor in Curriculum and Instruction in the Department of Teacher Education and the director of the Office of Urban Education and Educational Equity at Eastern Michigan University. Her doctoral studies were pursued at Colorado State University, where she earned a Ph.D. in Education

Leadership and Teacher Education with cognates in multicultural education, urban education, and gifted education. Her research areas include cultural competence, recruitment, and retention of minority students and teachers, creating culturally responsive classrooms, and mentoring students of color. Dr. Harmon developed the MARS Program: Minority Achievement Retention and Success, which has enjoyed success for six years. Dr. Harmon consults with school districts across the country on gifted education, creating culturally responsive classrooms, and strategies that address the achievement gap.

Toni Stokes Jones is a professor in the Educational Media and Technology program area of the Department of Teacher Education at Eastern Michigan University. She is also a member of the Board of Examiners for the National Council for Accreditation of Teacher Education, and the Teacher Education Department Graduate Coordinator. Dr. Jones received her Ph.D. in Instructional Technology from Wayne State University, and has an M.Ed in Instructional Technology and a B.S. in business education–secondary. Dr. Jones's research and writings examine preservice teachers technology integration capabilities, integration of the SmartBoard in the elementary classroom, technology access and capabilities of college students especially females, the use of telecollaborative projects in the elementary classroom to teach students about multicultural relationships and the injustices associated with segregation and desegregation, multicultural webquests for gifted students, and academic service learning effectiveness by preservice teachers.

Roderic R. Land is an assistant professor in the Department of Education, Culture, & Society and Department of Ethnic Studies at the University of Utah. His teaching and research specializations include sociology of education; critical race theory; critical pedagogy cultural/ethnic studies in education; and social foundations of education. He is the coeditor of *The Politics of Curricular Change: Essays on Hegemony and Power in Education* with M. Christopher Brown II (2005). His writings have addressed how color-blind ideologies have served to legitimize black subordination in education and examined African American student perspectives on race, reform, and redistributive justice. Dr. Land is very active on campus and within the community, often engaged with advising honors students and in youth mentoring, in addition to service in a number of national professional associations.

Jacqueline Leonard is an associate professor of Mathematics Education at Temple University. She teaches in the Department of Curriculum, Instruction and Technology in Education. Dr. Leonard earned her Ph.D. at the University of Maryland at College Park. Her areas of professional interests include mathematics education, teacher education, cultural pedagogy, and technology. She is primarily interested in applying and extending the work of Drs. William F. Tate and Gloria Ladson-Billings in critical race theory by addressing issues of equity and access in mathematics education. Currently, her work focuses on the use of culturally relevant teaching as a means to enhance the learning of African American students and other students of color in urban classrooms.

Kristy Lisle is an education solutions specialist with TaskStream in New York. She previously was assistant dean at the Graduate School of Education and Allied Professions at Fairfield University, Fairfield, CT. Dr. Lisle has become a national leader in program assessment, accreditation, and professional dispositions. She most recently served as department chair and assessment coordinator of the Department of Education at Blackburn College. Her research focuses on creating caring school communities for at-risk students.

Gersham Nelson is dean of the College of Arts, Humanities, and Social Sciences at the University of Central Missouri. He previously was the executive associate to the provost and vice president for Academic Affairs at Eastern Michigan University. Dr. Nelson formerly held the position of the head of the Department of History and Philosophy. Dr. Nelson earned his Ph.D. in Latin American History at the University of Illinois. His academic interests include Latin America and Africa, south of the Sahara.

Vernon C. Polite is currently professor and dean of the College of Education at Eastern Michigan University. Dean Polite not only founded the School of Education at Bowie State University but also served as the Dean of the College of Education at Bowie State University prior to his appointment at EMU in May 2005. Prior to his time at Bowie State, Polite was the Dr. Euphemia Lofton Haynes Professor of Education at the Catholic University of America from 1996 to 2001. In that position, he coordinated all graduate educational administration programs. He was an assistant professor at the Catholic University of America from 1991 to 1995 and an associate professor there from 1995 to 1996. He also has taught in Oak Park Public Schools in Michigan and Boston Public Schools and worked in the U.S. Virgin Islands for the Department of Education. Polite received his doctorate in K–12 Educational Leadership/Sociology from Michigan State University; his master's degree in Secondary Education/Social Studies from Boston State College, and his bachelor's degree in Sociology from Boston University.

Cheryl Price is a doctoral fellow in the Office of Urban Education and Educational Equity at Eastern Michigan University. She earned her B.S. in Special Education, and a M.A. in Educational Leadership at EMU. She is the assistant coordinator for the Minority Achievement Retention and Success Program (MARS), a professional development program designed to serve minority students enrolled in teacher preparation programs in the College of Education at EMU.

Robert W. Simmons III is director of the Center for Innovation in Urban Education and assistant professor of Science Education in the School of Education at Loyola University, Baltimore. Prior to his current post, he held a faculty appointment at Eastern Michigan University. His current research agenda focuses on the experiences of African American teachers and students, issues in urban education, and service learning. Dr. Simmons has explored international education issues through work/research in the Dominican Republic, Japan, and Costa Rica. Dr. Simmons is a contributing author to the highly acclaimed book *White Teachers in Diverse Classrooms: Creating Community, Combating Racism* (2006) and his work on service learning and urban education has been featured in leading publications.

William A. Smith is an associate dean in the College of Education at the University of Utah and an associate professor in the Department of Education, Culture, and Society and the Ethnic Studies Program. Smith also serves as a special assistant to the President and faculty athletics representative. He received his Ph.D. from the Educational Policy Studies Department at the University of Illinois at Urbana-Champaign. Dr. Smith joined the African American Studies program and the Department of Sociology at Western Illinois University as an assistant professor. In 1997, Smith was awarded a two-year postdoctoral research fellow at the Center for Urban Educational Research and Development (CUERD) on the campus of the University of Illinois at Chicago. His research efforts at CUERD have cumulated in numerous presentations, papers, and a coedited book, *The Racial Crisis in American Higher Education: Continuing Challenges to the 21st Century* (2nd edition, SUNY Press, 2002), which has been overwhelmingly received since its publication.

Marwin J. Spiller is an assistant professor of Sociology at the University of Maine. Spiller is a native of Chicago and received his Ph.D. from the University of Illinois at Urbana-Champaign. His research and teaching interests are in the areas of race and ethnic relations, as well as social, economic, and political inequality. More specifically, Spiller authored "Race, Class, and the Political Behavior of African-American Young Adults, 1960–1998" in *The Expanding Boundaries of Black Politics*, edited by Georgia A. Persons (2007). This work examines the influences of social and economic change on levels of political participation among African-American young adults in the civil rights and post–civil rights generations.

Gilman W. Whiting is assistant professor and director of undergraduate studies at Vanderbilt University. He earned his doctorate from Purdue University. At present he teaches on the African American diaspora, black masculinity, race, sport, and American culture and qualitative research methods. He also teaches for the Peabody College of Education in the Department of Human Organizational Development. His research includes work with young black fathers, low-income minorities, welfare reform and fatherhood initiatives, special needs populations (gifted, at-risk learners, young black men and scholarly identities), and health in the black community. He is currently working on a book project entitled *All Eyes on Me: Young African American Fathers, the Welfare State, and Outlaw Culture.* He has articles forthcoming in *Gifted Child Quarterly* and *Gifted Education.* He is editor of *On Manliness: Black American Masculinities* (2008).

Eboni M. Zamani-Gallaher is an associate professor and coordinator of the Graduate Certificate Program in Community College Leadership in the Department of Leadership and Counseling at Eastern Michigan University. She holds a Ph.D. in Higher Education Administration with a specialization in community college leadership and educational evaluation from the University of Illinois at Urbana-Champaign. Prior to joining the College of Education at EMU, she previously held an appointment as a faculty member at West Virginia University and was a Fellow of ACT, Inc. and Mathematical Policy Research Institute in Washington,

DC. Her teaching, research, and consulting activities include psychosocial adjustment and transition of marginalized collegians, transfer, access policies, women in leadership, and institutional practices affecting work and family balance. Her most recent scholarship includes coauthorship of *The Case for Affirmative Action on Campus: Concepts of Equity, Considerations for Practice* (Stylus Publishing) and co-editing *Organization and Governance in Higher Education: An ASHE Reader*, 6th edition (Pearson Publications).